Professional Work

Professional Work

A Sociological Approach

Kevin T. Leicht and Mary L. Fennell

First published 2001

2 4 6 8 10 9 7 5 3 1

Blackwell Publishers Inc.
350 Main Street
Malden, Massachusetts 02148
USA

Blackwell Publishers Ltd
108 Cowley Road
Oxford OX4 1JF
UK

Library of Congress Cataloging-in-Publication Data
Leicht, Kevin T.
Professional work : a sociological approach / Kevin T. Leicht and Mary L. Fennell.
p. cm.
Includes bibliographical references and index.
ISBN 0-631-20724-4 (alk. paper) — ISBN 0-631-20725-2 (pb. : alk. paper)
1. Professional employees. 2. Executives. I. Fennell, Mary L. II. Title.

HD8038.A1 L45 2001
305.5′53—dc21 2001018475

British Library Cataloguing in Publication Data
A CIP catalogue record for this book is available from the British Library.

Typeset in 10/12pt Bembo
by Graphicraft Limited, Hong Kong
Printed in Great Britain by TJ International, Padstow, Cornwall

This book is printed on acid-free paper.

Contents

Figures

Tables

Acknowledgments

Mary and I owe a debt to numerous people for contributing to the research that is part of this book. Our research was supported by grants from the National Institute on Aging (AG#13987), the National Science Foundation (SES-9310557), and a grant from the College of Liberal Arts at The Pennsylvania State University. We also received support (in money and in kind) from the Sociology Departments of Brown University and The University of Iowa, the Center for Gerontology and Health Care Research at Brown University, the Population Studies and Training Center at Brown University, and the Population Research Institute at the Pennsylvania State University. Leicht spent two years at the Obermann Center for Advanced Study at The University of Iowa, a fantastic research environment whose director, Jay Semel, provides a very stimulating place for research and writing that is separated from the daily grind of academic life. We thank each of these institutions and owe them a tremendous debt of gratitude.

We also have numerous research assistants that contributed to this research in different ways and at different times. Without their help, we doubt that this project would have gotten off the ground. These include Joyce McKenney, Leslie Kilgore, Bethany Maher, Gina Ruggieri, Julie Meyer, Thomas Stuckey, Heather Wendt, and our collaborators on portions of the work reported here, Kristine Witkowski and Bruce Skaggs.

We also would like to thank Susan Rabinowitz at Blackwell Publishers for her consistent and steady support of our project. Her general patience with our bumbling starts at assembling this book was truly remarkable, and we missed several deadlines for producing our manuscript we "easily" thought we would meet. We also thank Ken Provincher for helping in the later stages of the production process and Anthony Grahame for his careful copyediting of our (initially ungainly) text.

Finally, we would like to thank our spouses, Dennis Hogan and Brenda Leicht, for their consistent patience and support. We have spent numerous days over the past few years conversing about our project in each other's living rooms, on trips that probably should have been devoted to leisure activities rather than academic pursuits, and at moments when we've brought our children together for family activities. Their patience with, and sharing of, the passions that drive us has made this project much easier than it otherwise would have been. They are living proof that, whatever perils Mary and I have faced as professionals, we each made one good decision. God bless you both.

1

Professional and Managerial Work in the Twenty-first Century

Most Americans who go to college eventually want a managerial or professional job. Managerial and professional jobs have been the heart and soul of middle-class advancement in the United States since World War II, especially for students who are the first generation of their families to attend college. However, many observers now say that the prerogatives and prestige that used to follow automatically with managerial and professional jobs are no longer assured. High salaries, interesting work, high levels of job autonomy, and job security were once taken for granted upon making it to an elite white-collar job, but no longer. We seek to provide a partial explanation of how these changes have occurred and what they mean.

This book examines current work arrangements of managers and professionals. Sociologists and other students of the workplace have focused on different segments of the workforce, such as blue-collar workers (Burawoy 1979; 1985), women in the workforce (Reskin and Roos 1990), or union-management relations (Cornfield 1986). We have chosen to focus on a narrower range of occupations traditionally located at the upper end of most prestige rankings. We think that this focus is a useful complement to the more traditional focus of occupational sociology on blue-collar workers, technological change, and workplace deskilling. Part of our interest is driven by the widely-held observation that relatively elite managerial and professional positions face an uneven present and an uncertain future. Traditional professional work arrangements are being abandoned and new arrangements for the delivery of managerial advice and professional service are being attempted. But part of our interest stems from our belief that managerial and professional work can be profitably studied as a subset of relatively elite jobs in the US economy. We hope that examining both types of work comparatively will produce new insights about each one.

We think that professional and managerial jobs are worthy of examination in their own right for three important reasons: (1) professional and managerial jobs are the focus of the aspirations of most college-educated young people, (2) professional and managerial jobs represent that segment of the labor market that is usually defined as desirable by large segments of American society (your parents and friends would be proud of you for accepting one of these positions), and (3) professional and managerial jobs have experienced changes that are both similar to and different from changes experienced by other occupational groups as a result of the globalization of the US economy.

Our main goals for this book are (1) to discuss some of the basic issues surrounding managerial and professional work over the past 20 years while (2) providing a tentative explanation for recent changes in managerial and professional work that incorporates insights into the role that each group plays in a globalized and debureaucratized economy.

The major underlying theme we will explore as a tentative explanation for changes in managerial and professional work is that *managers and professionals are changing places in an increasingly unified elite division of labor.* Professionals and managers once occupied distinctive niches in the labor market characterized by different organizing principles, goals, and aspirations. The changes in professional work since the 1970s, combined with changes that have accompanied corporate restructuring, have produced a melding of professional and managerial work worlds. The result of this combination is not merely an exchange of roles. Instead, managers and professionals are defining (and have defined for them) a new set of roles that partially reflect old, established roles played by their counterparts and also reflect new activities that are not straightforward combinations of managerial and professional work. In the process, elite managers are becoming the "new professionals" while professionals are being captured by organized stakeholders that consume and pay for professional services.

AN OVERVIEW OF RECENT ORGANIZATIONAL CHANGES IN THE WORKPLACE

Most popular and academic discussions of the workplace in the 1990s emphasize a series of changes that have made working life uncertain and difficult. Many of these changes directly affect managerial and professional jobs. The workplace of the 1990s is characterized by:

1 *flatter organizational hierarchies*, as new information technologies eliminate the need for middle layers of management;
2 the growing use of *temporary workers* employed on an as-needed basis to perform specific jobs for the duration of single projects;
3 the extensive use of *subcontracting and outsourcing* to external firms and/or suppliers to produce products and services that were once provided by permanent, in-house employees;
4 *massive downsizing of the permanent workforce* as organizations need fewer management and support people and replace skilled workers with either computer-skilled operators or unskilled machine tenders;
5 a *postunionized bargaining environment* where unions have either no place or reduced power, and have no structural ability to gain a foothold to bargain with employers; and
6 *virtual organizations* that exist as a web of technologically driven interactions rather than as a distinctive, physical work-site that can be concretely located in geographic space.

To illustrate the workings of these trends as they affect professionals and managers, let us look at some typical accounts of workplace change as they affect individual working lives.

John is a bank manager for the trust department of a local branch bank in Grand Rapids, Michigan. John's job requires him to manage the trust accounts of clients in a variety of circumstances. He knows his clients' needs well and pays close attention to how he can manage his clients' money better. John has an MBA from a local, state-supported university and has worked for the local bank for around 20 years, rising up the managerial ranks.

In 1994 John's bank is purchased by a multistate banking conglomerate. As part of the leveraged buyout, the banking conglomerate consolidates departments across the banks it owns, leaving only a skeleton staff representing each banking service at each branch bank. In this process most of John's friends in the trust department are laid off. John is left as the only trust officer in his branch bank, and he communicates via electronic mail with the management of the trust department for the entire multistate banking system. Since most of the vice presidents and the president of the bank were also laid off, John has no avenues of advancement left at his bank. He can remain as a trust officer or get a different job elsewhere.

Julie received a Ph.D. in English in 1988. She makes a living teaching courses at several small colleges in the suburban Boston area. Her schedule requires that she visit three different campuses during a typical week, and she teaches between three and five English courses every semester. While her teaching evaluations are consistently good, Julie has given up on the major career aspiration that used to be the bread-and-butter of the job market for humanities Ph.D.s: the relatively permanent, tenure-track position at a university.

Julie's friends and fellow workers in the colleges where she teaches are a broad mixture of permanent employees (professors with tenure) and temporary instructors like her. Julie's contract is usually renewed every year but is subject to the uncertainties of university funding and changes in course demand. Julie has noticed that fewer and fewer of her associates actually have regular, permanent positions with the universities they work for. Most are temporary instructors like her who sign contracts to teach specific courses on a year-by-year basis. Julie sees no prospects for improving her situation and is thinking about leaving the academic labor market entirely.

Mary is an MD who has recently graduated from the local medical school near her hometown of Denver, Colorado. After completing her residency she returns to Denver to look for a position in a local pediatrics practice. Mary expects to have little trouble securing a position in a practice setting that is to her liking.

For some years before the 1990s a position like this would be easy to find. In fact, during the 1960s Mary could have reasonably considered starting her career as a solo practitioner or could have joined with several of her recently-graduated friends to form a small private practice of their own. The expense of medical school and the expenses associated with setting up a state-of-the-art private practice render this all but impossible in the 1990s. Mary also underestimated the effects that Health Maintenance Organizations (HMOs) and Preferred Provider Plans (PPOs) would have on the labor market for new physicians. Both new organizational arrangements cluster large numbers of doctors into group practices and pay each practice a fixed rate for treating patients insured by the HMO or PPO. These arrangements increase the incentives to work physicians harder, leading each to see more patients during a typical day and spending less time with each patient. The "system" no longer renders payment for individual services performed by physicians in each practice and discourages the employment of new physicians.

After several months of searching for a good work arrangement, Mary accepts a job with a local outpatient surgical care center. In this job (often referred to as a "doc-in-the-box") Mary sees patients on a walk-in basis that have a series of problems that require immediate attention or emergency care. The surgical care center charges low, discounted fees for minor medical services and pays the physicians it employs far less than those who work in other group practice arrangements. Mary, and the other physicians at the surgical care center, view these positions as temporary places to park themselves and make payments on their student loans until better employment opportunities open up.

Mark is a lawyer who works as an insurance agent in Des Moines, Iowa. Mark has had a law degree for ten years and passed the Iowa bar exam on his second attempt. After graduating from a local law school Mark took a position as an associate in the same firm he worked in as a legal intern after his second summer in law school. The firm, one of the most prestigious in Des Moines, represents several large corporate clients who have funneled hundreds of thousands of dollars in legal work through the firm over the past 20 years.

After being on the job for around a year Mark begins to notice that his firm is not as financially stable as he thought it was. He and the other associates in the firm are expected to produce around 2,000 billable hours worth of work each year, and the partners in the firm routinely meet and discuss other ways of generating revenue for the firm. The large corporate clients who are the staple of the law firm's financial base begin to do much of their routine legal work in-house, hiring salaried attorneys of their own to do work that used to produce revenue for Mark's firm. The strategies Mark resorts to in his search for new clients yields little in the way of steady, revenue-generating work for his law firm (a few wills, some estate planning, occasional litigation work, etc.). Further, most of the other local companies that are capable of generating sustained billable hours of legal work have also hired in-house attorneys. Under the circumstances, Mark has little chance of being promoted to partner and (in any case) there won't be much in terms of profits from the firm's activities to increase his income. After six years with his law firm, Mark quits his job and becomes an insurance agent, writing occasional wills and estate plans for a small number of private clients.

Each of these examples highlights the types of changes in professional and managerial jobs that are occurring and have been occurring since the early 1980s. You might be tempted to view the changes that occurred to Mark, Mary, Julie, and John as "one shot" experiences of bad luck, not unlike being struck by lightning or being a crime victim in a major city. But these experiences are far from unique, and these changes in job opportunities in law, medicine, higher education, and management affect not only professionals and managers but also their clients, consumers, and co-workers.

The most obvious place where changes in professional and managerial jobs have affected the rest of us is as consumers of health care. Group practice arrangements and other changes in the delivery of health services have changed our ability to gain access to certain types of health care and have put greater emphasis on preventative and primary care at the expense of expensive, specialized interventions (surgery, cancer treatments, etc.). Physicians now face clinical practice norms and care delivery targets that define what they can do and that subject deviant or "overly intensive" treatment regimens to utilization review committees who oversee physician activities. All of this limits the discretion that individual physicians have to diagnose and treat disease.

As employees in, for instance, a bank of the kind where John works, more decisions are made away from the local branch bank. People like John are increasingly responsible for carrying out the mandates and desires of the multistate bank to raise revenues and minimize the delivery of services that do not contribute to the bottom line. The other employees in John's division must put up with managerial control that is not sensitive to local conditions, and John is required to prove that he has attempted to carry out corporate mandates that he (often) doesn't approve of or thinks are ridiculous.

Are Changes in Professional and Managerial Work Linked Together?

We believe that professional and managerial work is being transformed by dynamics that are linking them in a complex web of connections that transform the functions of each. The workplace that results from this transformation is more collaborative, debureaucratized, and electronically networked. The downsizing, outsourcing, flattened organizational hierarchies, and networks of relationships that business firms are moving toward (at different speeds) look a lot like collaborative professional practice settings. The corporate, for-profit, group medical practice with multiple locations, utilization managers, corporate executives focusing on profits, and hundreds of salaried or contracted physicians looks a lot like the multidivisional corporation of the late 1970s.

Ironically, few people who have studied the history of business management would deny that managers (and their academic representatives in business schools) have engaged in attempts to become more like a classic profession. Following Abbott (1988) we refer to activities that attempt to further the professional aspirations of occupational groups as *professional projects*. Professional projects are sets of activities that are oriented around the goal of making managerial jobs more professional in appearance and orientation. The activities of most professional projects are directed toward enhancing the legitimate domain of the occupation and defining their interests relative to potential competitors and overseers (see also Larsen 1977; Abbott 1988).

At first glance you would think that there would be a precise definition of professional work. We all seem to "know" that doctors and lawyers are professionals and we expect them to engage in certain types of behaviors as their clients or patients. The qualities that Americans expect most of professionals include some evidence of *certification*, *objectivity*, *disinterestedness*, adherence to a set of *professional ethics*, and a *service orientation* (see Friedson 1986). In short, we expect professionals to put our interests first, to engage in maximum efforts on our behalf, and to be competent in carrying out their tasks. In exchange for these expectations, we customarily grant professionals wide leeway to do their work. We don't tell brain surgeons how to do surgery and we don't determine whether we need it or not. We don't tell lawyers how to pursue our personal injury case or whether we even have a case or not. In exchange for our deference to their expertise, we expect them to use their professional authority in our best interests.

Basic Definitions

Our discussion of the professions uses a number of terms that may be unfamiliar to you. To help streamline our discussion, we provide a set of definitions in the box. We have done this so that you can refer to these definitions as you read the rest of the book.

Professionalism is a powerful cultural metaphor in most western cultures. But this set of expectations about interactions with professionals only defines the relationship between the professional and the client. They don't say anything about the relationship of professionals to each other or the relationship between professions and other occupational groups. The use of the term professional project is designed to focus our attention on those sets of interactions in addition to the interactions we may have with professionals as clients and patients.

For our discussion we adopt a definition of the professional project that combines the work of Friedson (1986) and Abbott (1988). Specifically, most professional projects attempt to (1) enhance the *autonomy and*

Profession/professional: (1) used as a folk concept to signify (a) prestige, respect; (b) full-time work for pay; (c) to perform some task with great skill or proficiency; (2) used as a sociological concept to study: (a) elite classes of occupations with a focus on the characteristics or attributes of such occupations as a taxonomy (the attribute model of professions; see A. M. Carr-Saunders and P. A. Wilson 1933); or more recently, as (b) a process model, to study the processes through which certain occupations come to acquire power, develop monopolies, and/or lay claim to the status of a profession (see J. Roth 1974).

Professional associations: Formal groups of professionals, usually organized by discipline or certification, with various functions and forms. Professional associations can operate as simple membership or affiliate groups, lobbying groups, informational groups, or they can wield peer review and/or practitioner control over the profession.

Professional projects: Based on the work of Friedson (1986) and Abbott (1988), professional projects are attempts to (1) enhance the autonomy and freedom of action for occupational incumbents under a set of well-defined professional norms; and (2) defend a specific task domain from encroachment by competing occupational groups or stakeholders.

Professionalization: The result of a successful professional project; an occupation is professionalized to the extent that it successfully defines a set of work tasks as their exclusive domain, and successfully defends that domain against competing claims.

Deprofessionalization: The process by which professional prerogatives become eroded.

Proletarianization: The loss of earnings power and prestige that often accompanies the loss of professional prerogatives. Proletarianized professionals work in contexts where none of their prerogatives remain, and the content, control, and location of the work are managed by outsiders.

Autonomy: The ability of a work group or individual to control one's own work behavior and work conditions.

Multidivisional form: A form of organizational structure associated with large, diversified corporations, in which departments are structured as divisions within the firm, and these divisions are organized along product lines, rather than functional lines.

freedom of action for occupational incumbents under a set of well-defined professional prerogatives (see Friedson 1986); and (2) defend a specific *task domain* from encroachment by competing occupational groups and stakeholders. For example, during the 1980s a number of nursing associations in various states sought to change state legislation on the definition of clinical nurse practice. These lobbying attempts focused on changing the legal definitions of what nurses were and were not allowed to do, with and without physician supervision. Most proposed legislation sought to broaden the decision-making autonomy of nurses in the clinical setting (for example, to prescribe as well as administer medications), and to defend these work-setting rights from competing claims from physician-assistants.

The problem with studying professional projects is that they usually are a product of *collective volition*. Professional groups (like the American Medical Association, American Bar Association, or American Nursing Association) know that they are defining, defending, and broadening their work domains. Each individual member may have a slightly different reason for participating and slightly different goals that they hope will come from these actions, but the organizations exist to protect and expand the interests of professional occupations. Professionals who join these groups know this.

The problem with studying managerial work in this way hinges on whether managers collectively organize and participate in professional projects. Clearly there are management associations (like the American Management Association, The Academy of Management, and the National Association of Personnel Administrators). But do these organizations engage in self-conscious activities to protect and broaden the domain of managerial work?

We think that it is possible to consider managerial work as a professional project if we take into account a broader set of mechanisms that help managers (as individuals and as a defined occupational group) to pursue similar aims. The central mechanism that allows managers to pursue their version of a professional project is the widespread cultural acceptance of *managerial prerogatives*. Managerial prerogatives are sets of activities that others believe are protected from interference by outside constituents. In the case of managers, managerial prerogatives are an extension of the widely-held cultural norm in market economies that the owners of capital have the right to invest, sell, and dispose of financial assets as they see fit, without interference from those who might be affected by those decisions. Entrepreneurial prerogatives and property rights become managerial prerogatives when managers are hired as representatives for investors (see chapter 3). Appeals to managerial prerogatives and the elaborate legal and corporate edifus that exists to defend freedom of contract and private property rights give managers a ready-made set of cultural and economic appeals for defending their decisions and freedom of action.

Most discussions of professional projects have focused on the histories of well-established professions (physicians and lawyers) or occupational groups with professional aspirations that are never quite realized (for example, pharmacists, accountants, and engineers; see Tang and Smith 1996; Leicht and Fennell 1997). But what would a professional project entail for managers in general and personnel managers attempting to control the terms of employment relations in particular? We argue in this book that the development of different ways of managing the employment relationship are part of a larger historical trend that involves (1) the growing definition of a distinctive domain of action that is the exclusive prerogative of business managers, (2) the defense and furtherance of freedom of action (autonomy) in that domain, and (3) a defense of that domain against encroachment by competing occupational groups and stakeholders. Because the mechanisms used to defend the autonomy of managers differs from those used by established professional groups, we refer to this cluster of activities as the *managerial project.*

An inquiry into the managerial project

The managerial project first involves the development of a managerial occupational group with a set of interests that are distinct from those of investors and capitalists (see Bendix 1956). The specific tasks that managers historically have sought to define as theirs were managing capital and human resources in ways that maximize investor profits. These tasks were carried out in an increasingly complex and sophisticated business environment. Managers became more autonomous as investors faced greater problems in determining how well their agents were truly representing their interests (this is referred to as the "agency problem" in management research, see Daft 1995). Freedom of action and a distinctive occupational niche can be defended by defining managers as "professional trustees" who represent the financial interests of investors in business firms. Managers have tried to portray themselves as having the distinctive expertise necessary to produce the appropriate mix of capital and human resources that will maximize profits for the business firm.

The managerial project also involves defining the domain of managerial tasks against employees and other nonsupervisory workers, including engineers, computer consultants, accountants, and others who have professional aspirations of their own. Historically, we argue that threats to the autonomy of managers lead to defenses of the managerial project through the creation of new rationales for the expansion of professional autonomy. This defense occurs at the same time as the defense of managerial autonomy from investors because (collectively) managers don't want to gain control over investment decisions only to watch them flounder as they lose control over the workforce.

While we don't think that managerial and professional projects are identical, there have been a related set of changes in professional work that have changed the autonomy and task domain of many professional and semi-professional groups. We argue that these changes are making professional work look more like conventional white-collar work in a corporate environment controlled by managers. Below we outline the major dimensions of this shift. These changes are contributing to the creation of an integrated model governing relatively elite positions in the US economy.

The increasing diversity of professional work settings

Most research on the relationship between professional employees assumes that professionals were controlling other professionals (see Friedson 1986, 1994). Some have argued that control relationships have changed from informal and collegial relationships to formalized relationships that look like conventional managerial hierarchies.

Now the range of organizational settings where professionals work has moved away from models of the solo practice, the partnership, group practice, large law firm, or the modern, bureaucratized hospital. Professionals are found as salaried employees of for-profit and not-for-profit organizations, in government units of all sorts, in non-governmental organizations (NGOs), endowed research organizations, universities, foundations, and corporations (Abbott 1988, 1991; Derber and Schwartz 1991). In many of these work settings the control of professional work no longer rests with peers or even the administrative elite of the profession. Instead, control over professional work is vested in managers of the employing organization. Some argue that the control of professional work by nonprofessionals extends to decisions concerning compensation (as in corporate law firms, see Tolbert and Stern 1991) and to the evaluation of professional performance. The use of practice protocols by insurance companies to evaluate physician's performance is the most obvious example of the evaluation of professional work by outsiders (see Hafferty and Light 1995).

In some cases, professional accountability has shifted as professional practice takes on a new organizational form. For example, one of the fastest growing segments of the legal labor market is the market for in-house counsel for legal departments of large corporations. We know very little about the structure of in-house legal departments. We know that women who have graduated from law schools in recent years have been attracted to these positions (Roach 1990) and that different employment patterns and advancement opportunities exist for men and women in corporate legal departments. In medicine, a similar change is underway in the rise of managed care organizations (MCOs) that link physicians and third-party payers as either employees (as in HMOs) or contracted providers (as in preferred provider organizations). In both types of managed care settings, medical work and clinical decision-making are directly subject to the control of the managed care organization. Both law and medicine exhibit trends toward incorporation of the worksite into large, multi-organizational firms that are widely dispersed.

Given the expansion of types of work settings where professional work is done, there are a series of unanswered questions concerning the movements of professionals within and between them. Traditional ideas about which professional work settings are most valued, prestigious, and well-compensated are no longer reliable. The hallowed settings of the university-based teaching hospital, the private law firm, or the tenured faculty position have slipped on dimensions of stability, security, and autonomy. Within different professions we have no firm handle on the extent to which the relative prestige ranking of various settings has changed or is changing (Halliday 1987; Fligstein 1990; Hagan 1990), or how newly-developed practice settings fit into those rankings (Leicht et al. 1995). Although physicians at first resisted participating in managed care organizations, it would appear that now even the most esoteric specialists have decided to join the trend. Most physicians now assume that the age of managed care is inescapable. Since public policy and private insurers are placing greater emphasis on primary care physicians as gatekeepers in the managed care system, will this change the rankings of specialties within medicine because of the referral power granted to primary care physicians? Recent data suggest an increase in the number of medical students preferring primary care over specialization

(Kassenbaum et al. 1995), which might lead to long-term changes in the specialty balance in medicine.

In corporate law, the traditional long-standing relationship between the corporate customer and the law firm is being jettisoned in favor of "spot contracting" with multiple firms or the development of in-house legal departments (Tolbert and Stern 1991). We don't know if these changes have affected the status rankings of specialties within the legal profession. We don't know whether significant mobility occurs across diverse work settings. We also don't know if it is better for one's career to work in a broad diversity of work settings or to focus on advancement in a particular type of professional practice.

The convergence of control structures for professionals

Ironically, the increasingly diverse settings where professional work takes place is not translating into equally diverse mechanisms for controlling professionals on the job. Instead, these mechanisms seem to be converging around a common model. This result is predicted by institutional theories of organizations. *Institutional isomorphism* is a process of social change that moves groups of organizations toward similar practices and structures over time as they compete for political power and legitimacy. DiMaggio and Powell (1983) outline three mechanisms that produce isomorphism: *coercive pressure* from governing bodies or the state; *mimetic pressure* to copy existing practices that other organizations have used successfully; and *normative pressure* from powerful professional groups within organizations.

One can see the power of normative pressure in the traditional organization of the medical profession. The power of the profession to negotiate the terms and conditions of employment for doctors once assured that; (1) medical procedures would be paid for on a fee-for-service basis, (2) doctors would have the ultimate authority over patient care and act in the patient's best interests, and (3) doctors would be part of collegial practices and work settings where they interacted as a "community of equals," each acting as an autonomous professional but also seeking advice and productive professional interactions from other doctors.

The normative pressures from the profession to organize medical practice in this way put the burden of proof on those who wished to organize medical practice in some other way. Even though many practice settings deviated significantly from this organizational ideal, the institutionalized ideal was a yardstick that was used to assess the quality of the practice setting for doctors.

During the 1980s the practice of medicine was attacked from forces outside the profession who demanded more accountability and cost containment. These groups, led by insurance companies and large employers, began to question the efficiency and overall quality of medical care delivered under the predominant institutional model. Employers and large insurance companies were powerful stakeholders in the medical care delivery system. When the norms governing professional work are in flux, and the power of the profession becomes unstable, the balance of power may shift toward outside stakeholders such as large insurance companies and big employers. Coercive pressures for accountability and efficiency lead other professional practice organizations to "mimic" or copy successful ways of accommodating (and lessening) these pressures.

Friedson (1994) suggests that this questioning of professional practices will open up avenues for a "new professionalism," one that blends control through expertise with an openness to inspection and evaluation by peers and the public at large. We suspect such a model will be possible in the future, but right now there is plenty of evidence that control over professional work is moving firmly in the direction of corporate and bureaucratic control. Professional practice in many sectors of the economy is driven by pressure for revenue generation, accountability to the state, and actions to avoid lawsuits.

We see examples of this shift in almost every professional practice setting. In medicine, the primary emphasis has shifted from access and quality issues to issues of cost containment and service reduction (Alexander and D'Aunno 1990; Flood and Fennell 1995; Prechel and Gupman 1995). Clinical practice guidelines have been developed and used across medical specialties to standardize clinical practice. These guidelines also have been used by managed care plans to deny reimbursement and shape cost-effective service delivery (Hafferty and Light 1995). Lawyers are pressured to build up stables of clients and maximize billable hours (Nelson 1988; Wallace 1995) while the decisions of judges are shaped by sentencing guidelines and tort law (Tonry 1993; Stolzenberg and D'Alessio 1994; Kramer and Ulmer 1996). Engineers are increasingly pressured to demonstrate the cost effectiveness of their designs (R. Perrucci 1971; Whalley 1991). Scientists in the private sector and in universities are expected to generate research grants and to follow guidelines on the use of human subjects, data security, and reporting procedures (Gieryn 1983; Long 1992; Long et al. 1993). Since the mid-1980s, university curricula have been modeled on guidelines issued by the

American Association of Colleges, and quality assessment in higher education emerged from the curriculum reform movement (Banta and Associates 1993; Ratcliff 1996). In all these examples, practice guidelines have reshaped both the content and structure of professional decision-making and provided a vehicle for measuring accountability among professionals. Measures of compliance with practice guidelines are used as increasingly important indicators of appropriate or high quality work.

In many ways, these changes in control structures reflect changes in the impact of external threats to professional autonomy (Friedson 1984; Hafferty and McKinlay 1993). For example, in medicine the intrusion of managed care has inserted an additional layer of authority between doctor and patient. This layer of authority often constrains referrals to specialists since the choice of specialist and the treatment the specialist provides is constrained by contract relationships and reimbursement policies. The content of medical work is constrained by the use of clinical practice guidelines by HMOs and managed care organizations to structure clinical decision-making. Guidelines have been adopted as part of "total" or continuous quality improvement (CQI) methods to assess quality and control costs (Burns et al. 1992; AHCPR 1995). Practice profiles are routinely constructed through chart audits and compared to guidelines for recommended practice patterns. Physicians who have deviant profiles are then encouraged to adjust their practice behaviors to better comply with the organization's preferred profile. This process reduces physician control over medicine's core technology (Hafferty and Light 1995).

The popularity of the CQI movement in health care is an interesting organizational phenomena itself which suggests the importance of mimetic isomorphism as a process of change. Very little evidence is available to justify the claims of effectiveness of CQI in medical settings. Nonetheless, the Joint Commission on Accreditation of Healthcare Organizations (JCAHO) has rewritten its accreditation procedures to promote the use of CQI in hospitals (JCAHO 1992). Hospitals and clinics have rushed to train their members in the language and methods of CQI in order to benchmark their organization's performance against the rest of the industry (Flood and Fennell 1995).

Medicine is not alone in its acquiescence to external pressures for accountability and cost containment. Universities are subject to severe financial pressures, as federal support for tuition grants and research funding has steadily declined. Rewards within the university are increasingly distributed on the basis of revenue generation. Promotions, prestigious chairs, and salary increases are given on the basis of a mix of criteria where innovative scientific research is still valued but is increasingly displaced by an emphasis on research that is funded or that generates patents (Long 1992; Bok 1993; Long et al. 1993). At the same time, many academic disciplines in both the sciences and the liberal arts are subject to increasingly difficult pressures to retain talented faculty in the face of limited and dwindling rewards. The private sector has expanded its search for top quality professionals and represents an increasingly valued alternative career track for people who would have become academics (Abbott 1991).

The diversification of interests among professionals

Changes in professional practice settings almost naturally lead to questions about maintaining the unity of interests among professionals themselves. If organizational arrangements are splintering, one could reasonably expect the interests of professionals in widely differing work settings to diverge as well. The debates about these changes are often couched in terms of professionalization, deprofessionalization, and (in some cases) proletarianization (see Derber and Schwartz 1991). *Professionalization* is the byproduct of a successful professional project. An occupation is professionalized to the extent that it succeeds in defining a set of work tasks as their exclusive domain and successfully defends that domain against competing occupations and oversight by clients and outside interests. *Deprofessionalization* is a process whereby the professional prerogatives of an occupation are eroded. A profession starts to lose control over its task domain and professional work begins to look like conventional white-collar work with a complex hierarchical structure and elaborate systems of accountability. *Proletarianization* refers to the loss of earnings power and prestige that accompany the loss of professional prerogatives. Instead of a reorganized profession with a reduced set of professional prerogatives, proletarianized professionals work in contexts where none of these prerogatives remain and the content, control, and location of the work is done by outsiders. The proletarianization analogy comes from descriptions of nineteenth-century factory work, where artisans and craftsmen were herded into large factories and subjected to managerial discipline tied to a single, large work process (see Thompson 1963; Gordon, Edwards, and Reich 1982).

Debates about professionalization and deprofessionalization often fail to separate the content of professional work from the context where the work is performed (see Abbott 1991). These concepts could give you the false impression that professions revert to organizational forms found at earlier times in history. But social change rarely runs in reverse like a cassette tape. Instead, professional work is moving in new directions that are distinctive departures from traditional professional life or the pre-professional history of most occupations.

Further, the relationship between diversification of professional interests and deprofessionalization is not well specified. Why would we expect diversification of professional interests to harm professional projects? What evidence is there that professional interests have diversified in response to recent changes in professional practice settings?

Evidence for the diversification of professional interests is fragmentary at best. Researchers usually point to the growing racial, ethnic, and gender diversity of recent cohorts as a sign of the diversification of professional interests (see Menkel-Meadow 1989 and Epstein 1993 for law; Zuckerman et al. 1991 for science, Chamberlain 1988 for academia; Morrison and Von Glinow 1990 for management; and Bonner 1992 for medicine). Other research points to well-publicized disputes within professional associations or challenges to their governance of the professions (Halliday 1987; Hafferty and Light 1995). Relatively little research asks professionals from different backgrounds working in different organizational contexts what they view as the nature of their professional role or how they view their professional roles (but see Hoff 1997). Evidence regarding the effects of cost containment on professional divisiveness is relatively fragmentary as well, with most of the evidence confined to medicine (see Hafferty and McKinlay 1993; Leicht et al. 1995). In theory, uniform pressures for cost containment should produce relatively uniform responses that mitigate the effects of diversified professional interests on professional practice. However, there is relatively little research on the effects of cost containment on the content and context of professional work (but see Feder et al. 1987; Clark and Estes 1992; Flood et al. 1994; Prechel and Gupman 1995).

A MODEL OF THE CHANGING ELITE DIVISION OF LABOR

The combined set of changes in professional and managerial work lead us to offer a tentative model of the new elite division of labor. To help visualize the changes we will discuss throughout the book we provide figures 1.1 and 1.2 as stylized (and simplified) descriptions of our argument.

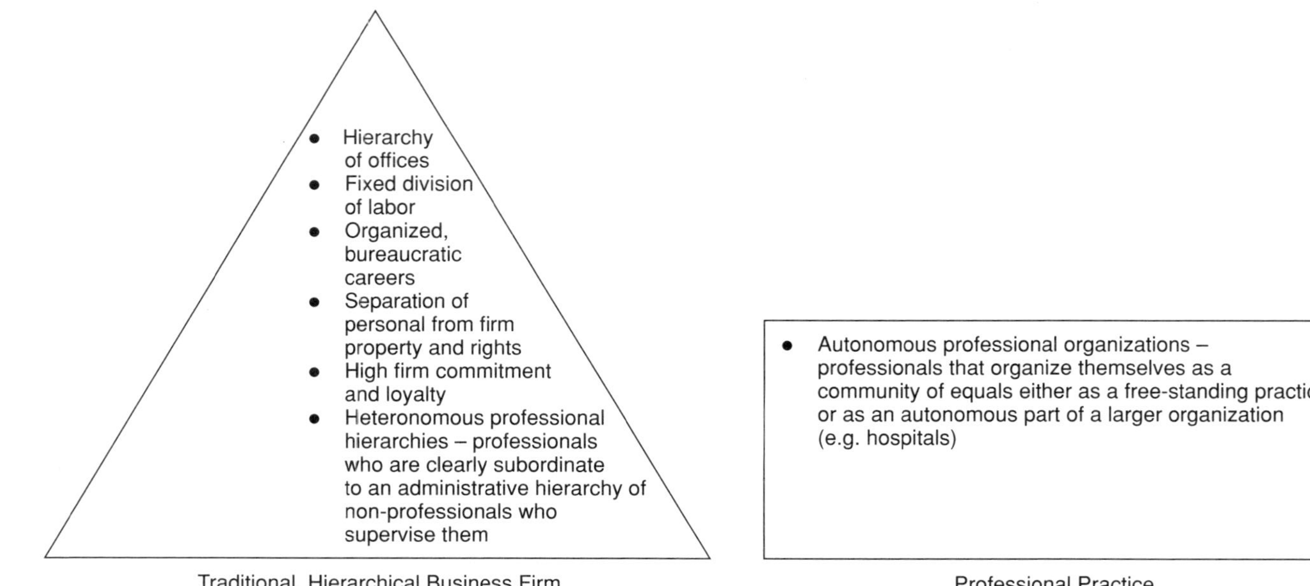

• Hierarchy of offices
• Fixed division of labor
• Organized, bureaucratic careers
• Separation of personal from firm property and rights
• High firm commitment and loyalty
• Heteronomous professional hierarchies – professionals who are clearly subordinate to an administrative hierarchy of non-professionals who supervise them
Traditional, Hierarchical Business Firm
• Autonomous professional organizations – professionals that organize themselves as a community of equals either as a free-standing practice or as an autonomous part of a larger organization (e.g. hospitals)
Professional Practice

Figure 1.1 The traditional organization of professional work

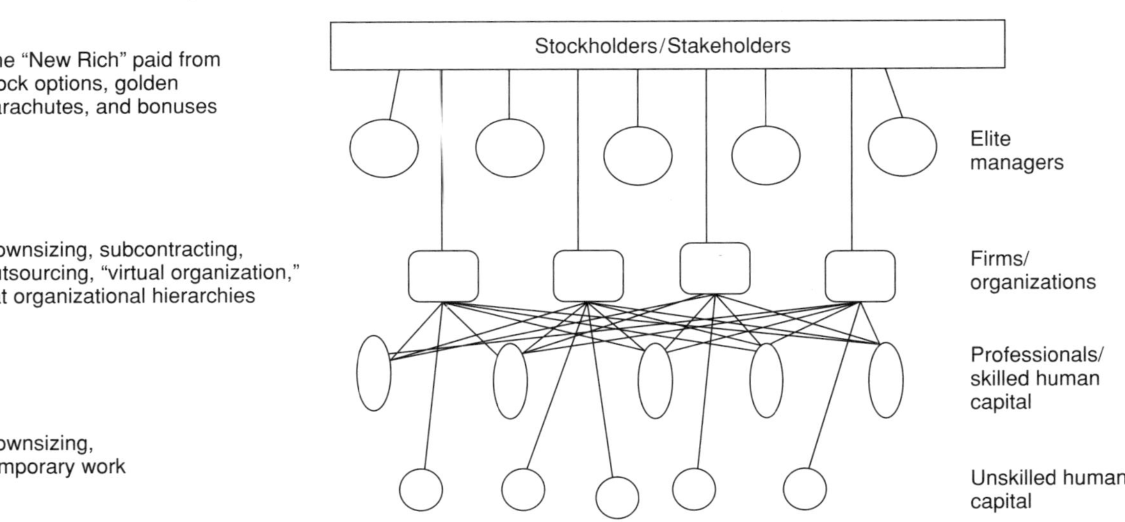

Figure 1.2 A model of the neoentrepreneurial organization of managerial and professional work

The traditional elite division of labor is represented in figure 1.1. Prior to the 1980s, managers and professionals occupied distinctive labor market niches with different institutional arrangements. Most professionals aspired to work in what W. Richard Scott (1992) terms an *autonomous professional organization*. These were organizations created by professionals for the delivery of professional services. Decision-making was usually informal and collaborative, and the professional members of the organization were responsible for hiring, staffing, and compensation decisions for each other and for subordinate employees. The idealized autonomous professional organizations were physicians' practices (under fee-for-service reimbursement) and private law firms, but similar organizational arrangements could be found among engineers, architects, accountants, and financial consultants. The key to these organizations was their relatively simple, informal organizational structure and the autonomy they provided for professionals.

The typical picture of managerial work prior to 1980 is a virtual antithesis of the autonomous professional organization. The typical managerial hierarchy was organized as a bureaucracy, with a fixed hierarchy of offices and an organized career progression that was deeply ingrained in the organizational structure and the minds of participants. The purpose of this extensive hierarchy was to produce a system of organizational accountability that would keep managers set on the task of managing in the firm's interest. The hierarchy also served as an information gathering and disseminating device, allowing top managers to assemble information on far-flung, complex operations while giving them an organized way of communicating with hundreds or thousands of subordinates without personally engaging each one.

In addition to a hierarchy of detailed organizational ranks leading from the bottom of the organization to the top, traditional management hierarchies tended to produce detailed and relatively fixed job titles and divisions of labor. There is a permanence to the positions that people occupy and a defined organizational chart that describes the patterns of communication and accountability.

Motivating managers working in complex bureaucracies has always presented a challenge, one that was never satisfactorily solved in most cases (see Jackall 1988). Ideally, managerial workers are provided with a structure of incentives that foster long-term commitment and loyalty. Promises of regular promotions, pay increases, and good benefit packages combine with the development of firm-specific skills to make long and stable tenure with the same firm an attractive option for most people. Even in situations where managerial careers "stall out" (most managers never make it anywhere near the top of the hierarchy) the traditional manager was taken care of in ways that made lateral moves to other firms unattractive.

These pictures are stylized presentations that suggest that there was almost no overlap between the worlds of managerial and professional work. This was (and is) only partially true. There were professional groups that worked in traditional, hierarchical organizations at least some of the time. In many cases (hospitals are the most prominent example), professionals worked in autonomous units within larger organizations, providing professional services in departments they organized and staffed. In other cases, professionals were part of *heteronomous professional hierarchies*, situations where professionals are supervised by an administrative hierarchy of nonprofessionals. In both cases, the qualities of managerial hierarchies are left intact. In one case, the autonomous professional staff is "grafted" onto a functioning hierarchy of nonprofessional employees. In the other, professional workers are absorbed into the hierarchical organization and dominated by it.

This traditional picture of managerial and professional work contrasts sharply with our more recent model (figure 1.2). This model we label "neoentrepreneurialism" and it is discussed more extensively in chapter 4 (see also Skaggs and Leicht 1997). The key to understanding this model is to realize that managerial and professional work are now caught in a complex web of exchanges. Only some of these exchanges go on within a single organization or firm. In place of CEOs and senior professionals who lead organizations through direct command and control, there are large groups of stockholders and stakeholders who put direct pressure on strategic groups in the system. Their major interests are increasing profits, decreasing costs, and increasing accountability.

The elaborate chain of command that exists to gather information and disseminate commands has been replaced by an electronic communications network that provides (more-or-less) instant communications ability and unprecedented monitoring capacity. This increases the ability of the labor market to attribute specific action and outcomes to specific people who can be instantly rewarded. This communication network also eliminates the need for most middle managers, the group deriving the greatest employment opportunities from the traditional hierarchical organization of work.

The disappearance of middle management is accompanied by other changes that profoundly affect the working lives of other strategic groups in the labor market:

1 *Elite manager's compensation and reputations increasingly are divorced from the performance of specific firms.* The rise of financial capital (Fligstein 1990) combined with the increased use (and size of) stock options, bonuses, and "golden parachutes" has left the connection between corporate performance and elite managerial compensation indirect at best. Stockholders increasingly demand short-term profits, leading managers to engage in drastic measures to increase shareholder value. These demands, and tying elite managers' compensation to stock prices, reduces the connections between elite managers and specific firms.

2 *Professionals face an increasingly organized set of stakeholders and customers who are interested in cost containment and accountability.* Stakeholders increasingly organize themselves into consumer groups that mandate the costs for professional services and the protocols that professionals will follow in delivering those services. Many professionals end up "captured" by groups of organized stakeholders who then exclusively employ a specific group of professionals as subcontractors. These professionals don't provide services on a fee-for-service basis. Instead, organized groups of consumers and stakeholders contract with professionals for services provided to large numbers of individual clients. Cost containment and oversight is enhanced by the external communications network that allows for the gradual breakup of bureaucratic work organizations. But this elimination of hierarchy is accompanied by stakeholder organization outside of specific firms, allowing organized groups to "capture" autonomous professional organizations.

3 *Firms increasingly are corporate entities that exist to bring together specific people for specific tasks.* Rather than representing hundreds or thousands of employees with fixed assets and a quasi-permanent organizational structure, firms represent elite managers and financial stakeholders looking for quick profits from short-term investments. They hire managers and technical professionals on an "as needed" basis, subcontracting and outsourcing as much of the routine work as possible.

4 *Unskilled workers live a precarious existence as steady jobs with good wages are replaced by temporary jobs that are poorly paid and provide few (if any) benefits.* The ability to move financial assets to different parts of the world, and the increasingly modular nature of most production activity, makes firm investments in specific locations as tenuous as they have ever been.

Ultimately, the changing organization of professional work is complicated by other features of contemporary work organizations. Managers have distinctive interests of their own (Marglin 1974; Barley and Kunda 1992). These interests involve the creation of workplace norms concerning autonomy and accountability that are similar to those allegedly enjoyed by professionals. The relationship between professionals and employing organizations is complicated by the decline of bureaucracy as an organizing principle of work organizations (see Boyett and Conn 1992). It is no longer true (if it ever was) that managers are oriented toward control of their employees. Instead, we argue that managers are oriented toward maximizing their autonomy and that this explains their behavior more readily than control orientations, especially with regard to professional employees. At a minimum we need to be sensitive to broader changes in workplace organization that go beyond the traditional emphasis on professionals in bureaucracies, and that is what our book attempts to do.

In sum, managers and professionals are moving in different but overlapping directions. Each group aspires to gain control over their work tasks and relative freedom from accountability to outside constituents. Professionals once had this level of autonomy and are in the process of losing some of it. Elite managers have used various cultural arguments and legal mechanisms to assert this control and recent changes in the organization of work have given them the unprecedented opportunity to advance their interests and claims. We believe that great insights can be gained by comparing these two groups within the elite division of labor.

THE PLAN OF THIS BOOK

We hope that the rest of our presentation will serve as a useful introduction to and analysis of the changing world of work for managers and professionals. We have organized our beginning chapters to review twentieth century history of professional work (chapter 2) and managerial work (chapter 3). Chapter 4 examines the new entrepreneurial workplace, and chapter 5 reviews three classes of contemporary theory that can help frame our questions about professional and managerial work, from the micro to the meso and macro levels. Here we focus on theories of professional careers, theories about change in organizations, and theories about the professions as institutions. Then we look specifically at contemporary changes in professional and managerial organizations and work settings (chapter 6). Changes in the professions themselves are examined, with particular emphasis on demographic and interest diversity within professions (chapter 7). In chapter 8 we switch to a focus on social stratification among professionals and consider what the analysis of larger institutional contexts can tell us about the organization of work. Finally, chapter 9 discusses the labor market implications of the neoentrepreneurial workplace and the future of managerial and professional work.

2

Conceptual Background: The Expert Division of Labor and Professional Work

As Freidson reminds us, knowledge is power. The notion that specialized bodies of knowledge can be used as a basis for distinguishing between groups of actors, and as a basis for distributing power across groups, dates back to Durkheim (1933). Formal knowledge was linked to the concepts of rationalization and rational action by Weber, and the rational-legal bureaucracy is the cornerstone of modern theories of management and administrative methods. In our focus on professions, the status of the expert is based on the professional's control over formal knowledge systems, which then confers social power to those who produce knowledge (especially science) and use it (in technology) over those who have no such knowledge and perhaps both need and/or fear it. Formal knowledge (and the expert division of labor to which it gives rise) is by definition nondemocratic, sometimes elitist, and often manipulative (Foucault 1977; Brint 1994). Given the historical association between professional status, prestige, and power, it is no wonder sociologists have spent decades trying to define the characteristics of professions, and more recently, the processes through which professions acquire, maintain, or lose power.

Defining a Profession: Trait Models of the Professions

The classic early literature on the professions developed a taxonomy of characteristics so we could recognize which occupations were professions and which were not. These characteristics varied from author to author, but the list usually focused on eight key dimensions, summarized in table 2.1. This set of characteristics gave rise to a school of

Table 2.1 Defining characteristics of professions

1. Knowledge based on theory; complex intellectual techniques;
2. Mastery of knowledge base requires long period of training, usually university based, which is technically specialized and designed to socialize trainees into the culture and symbols of the profession;
3. Tasks are inherently valuable to society, relevant to key social values (health, technological progress, legal rights, etc.);
4. Practitioners are motivated by service to the client's welfare and to the profession;
5. Performance of tasks characterized by high degree of autonomy;
6. Practitioners exhibit long-term commitment to their profession;
7. Practitioners enjoy a well-developed sense of community within the profession; and
8. The profession has a well-developed code of ethics that guides professional behavior and defines the profession's values.

theories known as "trait" or attribute theories of professions. Occupations were evaluated based on their conformity or deviance from these traits. Trait models were popular in the 1950s and 1960s (Carr-Saunders and Wilson 1933; Parsons 1937; Goode 1957; Hughes 1958; Wilensky 1964).

Later researchers grew dissatisfied with trait models for a variety of reasons (summarized in Roth 1974 and Abbott 1988). The number and listing of traits seemed arbitrary and there was little agreement regarding which traits were critical and which traits were superfluous for professional development. Until recently, trait theories were silent regarding the manipulative aspects of development undertaken by the professions themselves. Some observers rightly questioned whether the ability or inability to conform to a list of professional traits was influenced by forces outside of the functional value of the knowledge the profession controlled. Further, questions of the relevance of traits led to questions of whether different traits were substitutable; would strict licensing compensate for lack of control over credentials? Could strong professional associations "bid up" the rewards and prestige of an occupation without control of education and licensing? Does it matter whether professionals actually adhere to a professional code of ethics or does the mere existence of the code itself constitute sufficient justification in the eyes of consumers?

In spite of the criticisms of trait theories as explanations for and definitions of professions, they do provide us with a set of places to look for changes in professional life. For example, if there was a rash of closings of law or medical schools, we would suspect that this was not merely due to the sagging financial conditions of specific universities. Financial instability would do little to explain why specific programs were eliminated and why some universities decided to eliminate their law or medical schools all at the same time. Instead, we would suspect that these decisions were reflections of larger upheavals in law and medicine and we would begin to look for the sources of this upheaval.

As another example, suppose that a specific profession abandoned its licensing procedure or decertified the accrediting body that labeled educational institutions as fit to train new professionals. We would view these as signals of change and seek to understand the sources and determinants of that change.

In short, trait explanations may not explain the development of professions very well, or processes of change within or across professions. The claims that all professions must have a specific set of traits to justify their status may be arbitrary. But trait theories have pointed us toward a set of well-established institutional markers whose disappearance may be indicative of greater change than their initial creation signaled. At a minimum, trait theories point us to a set of specific actions whose disappearance might be a sign of broader changes in professional life.

Models of Professional Organizations

From these dimensions for defining professionals, sociologists in the 1950s and 1960s developed a model of professional tasks and work arrangements. This model rested on several key assumptions. First, researchers focused on a narrowly defined conceptualization of organizations, seeing them as primarily independent entities. They assumed that professional organizations were primarily rational, goal-oriented systems designed to carry out their core tasks effectively and manage whatever ancillary tasks were needed to support the core. At minimum, the model argued that organizations whose core activities were carried out by professionals (such as physicians in office practice settings or hospitals) used a different form of control than traditional bureaucracies. The authority necessary for defining and carrying out core tasks rested with the professional, whose performance was controlled by the knowledge, skills, and socialization received during extensive professional training. Professional performance was monitored, evaluated, or censured by professional peers.

However, this model was quickly recognized as inadequate to describe all of the activities needed to carry out all tasks performed within complex professional organizations, such as hospitals. Controlling performance also required more standard bureaucratic controls for the hotel-type service activities in hospitals, and even for some types of core work, such as coordinating patient care across different units within the hospital. And even professional staffs were dealing with a broader diversity of control mechanisms than this simple model acknowledged. Scott (1992), for example, discussed at least three models for embedding professionals in organizations: (1) *autonomous*, where professionals retain authority to control and evaluate themselves as a group (as in the traditionally structured law firm); (2) *heteronomous*, where professionals are subject to more line-authority control (exemplified by today's managed care organizations); and (3) *conjoint*, where professionals and administrators recognize their separate domains of expertise and power but also their shared benefits and need for collaboration.

Another very useful set of concepts for thinking about professional work comes from writings by Friedson (1986), and has been recently highlighted by Hafferty and Light (1995). Changes in the nature of professional work can occur in at least three ways. Changes in the actual *content*, or technical core, of professional work refers to the specific decisions made and procedures undertaken during the work process itself. Within medicine, the proliferation of clinical practice protocols (that identify which medical procedures should be used under specific conditions), or research on medical effectiveness, represent attempts to limit the individual practitioner's control over clinical decision-making. Changes in the *terms* of professional work refer to the characteristics of the professional's employment or work contract (rate of pay, hours, capitation arrangements), and changes in the *conditions* of work refer to the setting in which that work is performed, such as the organizational structures, staffing arrangements, and resources made available for professional practice. As Hafferty and Light (1995) point out, it is possible to control or change the content of professional work (the services provided to consumers) by controlling the terms and/or conditions under which that work is performed. This may well be true whether that work concerns medical practice, law, or the management of corporations.

SYSTEMS OF PROFESSIONS AND KNOWLEDGE CLAIMS

More recent students of professional practice have focused on systems of professions and knowledge claims (see Abbott 1988, 1991). These researchers generally do not study a specific profession in isolation, but focus on groups of professions making competing claims to the same task domain, or on the entire system of professional claims within a specific culture or society.

In this tradition the focus of research and writing is on the ability to claim jurisdiction over specific task domains in competition with other occupational groups. The place for understanding the knowledge claims of professionals lies not with the explanations and rationales given to consumers or relationships between professionals and the dominant interests of elites. Instead, the knowledge claims and prerogatives of professionals are best studied by looking at boundary disputes over occupational task domains (struggles between doctors and nurses; conventional medicine and chiropractic; lawyers and accountants; accountants and managers, etc.). It is these competitions that determine the prerogatives and (eventually) the relative prestige of professional groups. Relatively prestigious occupations rarely have their task domains challenged by competitors and (when they do) don't have much trouble winning these challenges. But far more numerous are occupations where professional task domains and prerogatives are continually challenged (teachers, nurses, pharmacists, psychologists, etc.). Through watching these competitions, researchers can study how task domains are controlled and how challenges to the conventional organization of professional work occurs.

Another variant of this focus on systems of professions can be found in the theory of countervailing powers, proposed by Light (1993, 1995) and others. The dynamics of change in the status of a profession is linked to a profession's location within a field of institutional and cultural actors. A profession or one of its competitors may gain dominance by subjugating the needs of other groups, which over time will mobilize their own resources and connections to counter this dominance. As will be seen in our discussion of theories of organizational change in chapter 5 below, the theory of countervailing powers parallels the framework and concepts of agency theory.

Research and writing on systems of professions points to the activities of professionals in work settings where multiple interests are represented at once. This is not only a more realistic portrayal of actual professional working life, but it is probably more descriptive of what is going on during this time of radical change in the organization of professional life. Research in this tradition also points to contests between occupational groups as the basis for knowledge claims and the larger legitimization that makes professional prerogatives and rewards possible.

Change Across Professions in the Terms and Conditions of Work

Many sociologists have studied specific professional and occupational groups in great detail. In fact, our own specialized review of past research on professions and occupations netted over 100 volumes. Even a superficial review of all these studies is beyond the scope of this volume. And we are more interested in tracing patterns of change across professions and the organizations where professional work is performed.

Although previous work on individual professions is important to establish the history of that group, it is difficult to extract useful information on specific issues (such as change over time in the settings in which professions work, or in the training required) from diverse studies undertaken for different goals, using different methodologies and different time frames. In later chapters of this book we will present detailed data on two of the classic free professions, doctors and lawyers, which directly address several of our most important arguments. However, we would like to get a broader perspective on how other professions have changed in status, power, and working conditions over the past 20 years. To do this, we turn to a bi-yearly volume published by the US Department of Labor, the *Occupational Outlook Handbook*. The *Handbook* provides forecast data (based upon Census information) for hundreds of occupations, focusing on a fairly standard set of variables, and it has done so over the past 30 years. The information is designed to provide job seekers with some idea of what the labor market for various jobs should look like in the near future. Although the *Handbook*'s projections are not infallible, they provide interesting data for our purposes. We do need to keep in mind that these descriptions are forecasts, not actual descriptions of occupational reality. But they are descriptions produced by the federal government, and as such they can be thought of as interesting historical qualitative data representing the Department of Labor's predictions on various professions' "fortunes" over time.

The tables 2.2–2.6 provide roughly 20 years of distilled forecasts, from 1980 through 1997, at about five-year intervals, for a selection of five traditional professions: biologists (representing one type of scientist), engineers, lawyers, pharmacists, and physicians. We limit our depiction to four key issues related to the terms and conditions of professional work, and the "systems" of other professional and occupational groups within which each profession works: (1) most commonly observed employment settings; (2) training and certification required for the profession; (3) the "outlook" for such professional jobs in the near future (similar to a summary of labor market demand for each group); and (4) listings of related occupational/professional groups.

The table for each professional is arranged over time, summarizing data from 1980, 1985, 1990, and 1996/7. The initial entries for each dimension in 1980 are presented in some detail. Then, as some indicators don't really change very much for some professions, the subsequent entries indicate only if the Department of Labor's descriptions have changed, and in what fashion.

Looking first at biologists in table 2.2, we find a division of science which was once linked closely to the university setting for a majority (60%) of all jobs. By the late 1990s that picture had changed, as a direct result of the explosion of both basic research and applications in biotechnology and genetics (most of these are within private sector firms). One-third of all biologists now work within the drug and biotechnology sector, one third within agencies of government (such as the NIH), and one-third within colleges and universities. Training requirements have stayed relatively stable, although there are now management-track jobs within applied research for which an M. Sc. or M.S. is suitable. The job prospects for graduates in biology have changed steadily from areas with emphasis on the environment toward jobs in biotechnology and genetics research. Similarly, the short list of related professional/occupational groups has gravitated toward medical science and clinicians.

For engineers, the change in work settings has not been as drastic (see table 2.3). The private sector (especially manufacturing, construction, and business) at about 47 percent and government (at about 14%) have been stable locations for most jobs in engineering. The small percent of engineers in faculty positions (5% in 1980) has dwindled steadily. Training requirements have not changed much during the past two decades. The *Handbook*'s description of job outlooks within engineering have consistently been good to moderate, with the most stable need tied to re-engineering of deteriorating infrastructure for transportation and utilities. Defense-related jobs have disappeared from these descriptions. The

Table 2.2 Biologists: work settings and job characteristics, 1980–1997 (extracted from *Occupational Outlook Handbook*)

1980	*1985*	*1990*	*1996–7*
WORK SETTINGS			
60% faculty in colleges/ universities 40% in fed/state/local government, private sector, nonprofit research organizations	Same as 1980	Same as 1980, 1985	33% faculty in colleges/ universities 33% federal/state/local government 33% drug industry – pharmaceutical and biotech establishments; hospitals, research and testing labs
REQUIRED TRAINING			
Ph.D. for college teaching, independent research, advancement to administrative positions; Masters for applied research; Bachelors sufficient for some non-research jobs	Same as 1980	Ph.D. – same as 1980, 1985 Masters for applied research and jobs in management, inspection, sales, service Bachelors – same as 1980, 1985	Same as 1990

JOB OUTLOOK			
Good for those with advanced degrees, more competition with lesser degrees; increase faster than the average for all occupations through the 1980s, because of increased attention to preserving the natural environment, medical research, growth in industry and government	Expected to grow faster than the average for all occupations through mid-1990s due to recent advances in genetics research, advances in biological technology, efforts to clean and preserve environment Better for those with advanced degrees	Expected to grow faster than the average for all occupations through 2000, mostly in private industry, continued growth in genetics and biotech research, growth due to efforts to clean and preserve environment Slow growth in federal government	Expected to grow faster than the average for all occupations through 2005, continued genetics and biotech research, growth due to efforts to clean and preserve environment, expected expansion in research related to health issues such as AIDS, cancer and the Human Genome Project
RELATED PROFESSIONS/OCCUPATIONS			
Conservation occupations agricultural scientists, biochemists, soil scientists, oceanographers, and life science technicians	Same as 1980	Conservation occupations, animal breeders, horticulturist, other agricultural scientist, medical scientists, medical doctors, dentists, vets	Same as 1990

Table 2.3 Engineers: work settings and job characteristics, 1980–1997 (extracted from *Occupational Outlook Handbook*)

1980	*1985*	*1990*	*1996–7*
WORK SETTINGS			
45% in manufacturing industries 36% in non-manufacturing – primarily construction, public utilities, engineering and architectural services, businesses and consulting 14% in government 5% faculty	48% in manufacturing industries 36% in non-manufacturing – engineering and architectural services, construction, public utilities, business and management consulting 13% in government 3% faculty	50% in manufacturing industries 36% in non-manufacturing – engineering and architectural services, construction, public utilities, business and management consulting 13% in government	47% in manufacturing industries 39% in non-manufacturing – engineering and architectural services, research and testing, business, communications, utilities, construction 14% in government
REQUIRED TRAINING			
Bachelor's in accredited engineering program, Graduate training for beginning research and testing positions Registration required for engineers whose work may affect life, health, or property, or who serve the public: degree, +4 years relevant work experience, State exam	Bachelor's in engineering, from accredited engineering program Flexibility between branches: civil, mechanical, electrical Graduate training for faculty position Registration required for engineers whose work may affect life, health, or property, or who serve the public: degree, +4 years relevant work experience, State exam	Same as 1985	Same as 1985, 1990

JOB OUTLOOK			
Increase slightly faster than the average for all occupations through the 1980s, mostly for replacement needs, much growth due to industrial expansion to meet the demand for more goods and services, design and construction of factories, utility systems, office buildings, as well as development and manufacture of defense-related products, scientific instruments, industrial machinery, chemical products and motor vehicles, energy related activities, environmental problems	Good through 1995, increase faster than the average for all occupations through 1995, mostly for replacement needs, develop and manufacture defense-related products and improve transportation, energy-related activities, environmental problems	Increase faster than the average for all occupations while the number of degrees granted in engineering is likely to decline through the year 2000, improve deteriorating roads, bridges, water and pollution control, and other public facilities	Good through 2005, improve deteriorating roads, bridges, water and pollution control, and other public facilities
RELATED PROFESSIONS/OCCUPATIONS			
Environmental scientists, life scientists, physical scientists, mathematicians, engineering and science technicians, and architects	Physical scientists, life scientists, engineering and science technicians, and architects	Same as 1985	Same as 1985, 1990 plus computer scientists, mathematicians

Table 2.4 Lawyers: work settings and job characteristics, 1980–1997 (extracted from *Occupational Outlook Handbook*)

1980	*1985*	*1990*	*1996–7*
WORK SETTINGS			
Private practice, government, house counsel in public utilities, transportation firms, banks, insurance, real-estate agencies, manufacturing firms, welfare and religious organizations, business and nonprofit organizations	Same as 1980	Same as 1980, 1985	Same as 1980, 1985, 1990
REQUIRED TRAINING			
For license: 3 years college, graduate law school; 46 states require Multistate Bar Exam, 38 states require Responsibility Exam, graduates receive J.D. or LL.B. Advanced degrees may be desirable for specialty, research, teaching	Same as 1980	Same as 1980, 1985	Same as 1980, 1985, 1990

JOB OUTLOOK			
Expected to grow faster for all occupations through the 1980s due to growth in population, business activities, government regulation, increases in publicly-funded legal services, growth of legal action in consumer protection, the environment, and safety issues	Expected to grow faster than the average for all occupations through the mid-1990s due to growth in population and the general level of business activities, growth of legal action in consumer protection, the environment and safety	Same as 1985	Expected to grow faster than the average for all occupations through the year 2005 due to growth in population and the general level of business activities, growth of legal action in employee benefits, health care, intellectual property, sexual harassment, the environment, and real estate
RELATED PROFESSIONS/OCCUPATIONS			
Abstractors, arbitrators, conciliators, hearing officers, patent agents, title examiners, legislative assistants, FBI agent	Arbitrators, legal examiners, journalists, patent agents, title examiners, legislative assistants, FBI agent, lobbyist, political office, corporate executive	Paralegal, journalist, legislative asst, FBI agent, lobbyist, political office, corporate executive	Same as 1990

Table 2.5 Pharmacists: work settings and job characteristics, 1980–1997 (extracted from *Occupational Outlook Handbook*)

1980	*1985*	*1990*	*1996–7*
WORK SETTINGS			
Community pharmacies, own their own business (25%) Others hold salaried positions in hospitals, pharmaceutical manufacturers, wholesalers, government and educational institutions, nursing homes	Same as 1980	Salaried positions in community pharmacies, hospitals, HMOs, home health agencies, and clinics	60% community pharmacies 25% hospitals 15% HMOs, clinics, home health care services, nursing homes, Federal Government
REQUIRED TRAINING			
License: 5 years beyond high school, graduate from an accredited pharmacy program, pass State exam, serve internship under licensed pharmacist Master's or Ph.D. for research Pharm.D, Ph.D., or Masters for administrative or faculty positions	Same as 1980	Same as 1980, 1985, plus: BA in pharmacy is minimum for positions in community pharmacies	License: at least 5 years beyond high school, graduate from an accredited college of pharmacy, pass State exam, serve internship under licensed pharmacies: BA in pharmacy Research: Masters or Ph.D. Faculty positions: Pharm.D.

JOB OUTLOOK			
Expected to grow faster than the average for all occupations mainly due to replacement, trend toward shorter working hours, population growth, increased life expectancy, greater demand for drugs, rising standard of health care, growth of health insurance programs Employment will rise more rapidly in hospitals	Expected to grow as fast as the average for all occupations through the mid-1990s mainly due to replacement, population growth, aging population. Employment will rise more rapidly in hospitals than community pharmacies, scientific advances making more drugs available, availability of health insurance	Expected to grow faster than the average for all occupations through year 2000 because of scientific advances making more drugs available; new developments in administering medicines; consumers seeking more information about drugs; increased demand in hospitals, HMOs, and other health care settings	Same as 1990
RELATED PROFESSIONS/OCCUPATIONS			
Pharmaceutical bacteriologists, pharmaceutical chemists, pharmacologists	Same as 1980	Scientists, pharmaceutical chemists, pharmacologists	Pharmaceutical chemists, pharmacologists

Table 2.6 Physicians: work settings and job characteristics, 1980–1997 (extracted from *Occupational Outlook Handbook*)

1980	*1985*	*1990*	*1996–7*
WORK SETTINGS			
Office practices, residents or full-time staff members in hospitals, remaining had administrative or research positions	66% office-based practice 25% residents or hospital staff 9% administrative or research positions	66% office-based practice 20% hospitals 14% administrative, research, government positions, other	Same as 1985
REQUIRED TRAINING			
License: 8 years post-secondary education, graduation from accredited medical school, pass licensing exam, 1–2 years graduate medical education 2–5 years for specialty training, 2 years specialty practice, specialty board exam To teach/research: masters or Ph.D.	Same as 1985	License: graduate from accredited medical school, pass licensing exam 1–6 years residency, final exam after residency for board certification To teach/research: masters or Ph.D.	4 years undergraduate, 4 years medical school, 3+ years residency; license: graduation from accredited medical school, pass licensing exam, residency, final exam after residency for board certification To teach/research: Masters or Ph.D.

JOB OUTLOOK			
Favorable through 1980s, greater percentage entering primary care specialties, including demand because of population growth and aging, broad health insurance availability	Expected to grow faster than the average for all occupations through mid-1990s because of population growth and aging, broad health insurance, public health, rehabilitation, industrial medicine, and mental health	Expected to grow faster than the average for all occupations through the year 2000 because of continued expansion of health industry; prospects good for family practitioners, internists, geriatric and preventive care; shortage in general surgery; less solo practice, more in group medical practices	Same as 1990
RELATED PROFESSIONS/OCCUPATIONS			
Audiologists, chiropractors, dentists, optometrists, podiatrists, speech pathologists, veterinarians.	Same as 1980	Same as 1980, 1985	Acupuncturist, audiologists, chiropractors, dentists, nurse practitioners, optometrists, podiatrists, veterinarians

list of related professions/occupations stays relatively stable, with the notable addition of computer scientists to the list in 1996/7. More recent entries may highlight the increased importance of this field to the future of engineering.

Table 2.4 summarizes the trends on work settings and job characteristics for lawyers. Although the list of work settings is extensive from 1980 onward, the *Handbook* did not provide estimates of the distribution of lawyers across these work settings over time. As we shall see in chapter 8, that distribution has changed. Training requirements have not changed at all, and the list of related professions/occupations is stable. The *Handbook*'s descriptions of job outlooks, however, show a change in the areas of legal specialization. In the 1980s, jobs were expected to expand in areas of government regulation, "legal aid," and consumer protection. By 1996/7, these three areas had been dropped to be replaced by an emphasis on employee benefits and health care (perhaps spurred by increases in medical malpractice, and more recently, denied benefits).

Pharmacy has experienced considerable change in both common work settings and training requirements (see table 2.5). In 1980, at least 25 percent of all pharmacists were owner/operators. By 1990, that type of work setting had all but disappeared; the entire profession had shifted toward salaried positions in "community pharmacies" (which includes chain stores), hospitals, and various health care organizations. Training requirements for any pharmacy position in retail shifted from training in accredited pharmacy programs to the BA in pharmacy from an accredited college of pharmacy. And only Ph.D.s in pharmacy could obtain faculty positions in such colleges (a good example of a professionalizing occupation, according to the trait theorists). Good job growth throughout this period has characterized pharmacy, but the source of that growth has also changed. In 1980, pharmacy jobs in hospitals were expected to increase; by 1990, that work setting had begun to transform into a demand for pharmacists in other health care settings, such as HMOs. Also, by the 1990s, pharmacy job growth was attributed to new developments in types of drugs and drug administration (linked to the growth in biotechnology), and increased demand for information about drugs from consumers. These changes correspond with a change in the focus on pharmacy from simple drug dispensing to consumer (and provider) education.

Finally, table 2.6 summarizes many of the trends we have previously mentioned linked to medicine. Although not highly detailed, the *Handbook*'s descriptions of work settings for physicians shows stable numbers in office-based practice, but a decline in the percent of physicians in hospital-based employment. We suspect this reflects the contraction within the hospital sector nationwide since the shift in Medicare/Medicaid reimbursement strategies in the mid-1980s. More jobs are indicated in other organizational settings, including administration, research, and government positions. Within the row on training requirements, residencies have become longer. Faster than average job growth continues through the mid-1990s, and better job growth in the primary care specialties was indicated during the 1990s (family medicine, internal medicine, geriatrics, and preventive care). The lists of related professions is stable from 1980 through 1990, but in 1996/7 we see the addition of acupuncturists and nurse practitioners. These two groups of related occupations are actually only symbolic of the increased types and numbers of auxiliary medical occupations that have been described elsewhere, such as physician assistants, physician extenders, nurse-midwives, and others.

Summary

In this chapter we have reviewed early definitions and theories of "professions" based on an accumulation of appropriate traits, through the development of more sophisticated theories concerning the types of organizations where professionals work, and the power relationships within systems of professions. This brief review has been done to illustrate how conceptual thinking about professions and professional work has changed dramatically. The second half of this chapter has briefly reviewed descriptive data from the Department of Labor on five traditional professions, considering each as a class of occupations. Here we have focused on questions concerning how job settings, training requirements, the market outlook, and related groups of other professions/occupations have changed over the past 20 years. These descriptive data are only illustrative, but the patterns we see underscore that indeed, change in professional work is widespread.

This brings us to chapter 3, where we look intently at the history of managerial work. As with early concepts of the professions, and later theories of professional powers and systems of professions, the history of management can be traced using the concept of autonomy as a sensitizing concept. With that tool, change in managerial activities can be seen as a progression of steps toward increasing the professional autonomy of managers.

3

Managers and Managerial Work in the Twentieth Century

When people think of managers these days they usually think of people who make decisions about what a company should do and how they should do it. The concept of "manager" itself conjures up a variety of contrasting images from foremen on the shop floor of a manufacturing plant, to supervisors on a sales floor of a department store, to a gray-suited financial manager communicating on a worldwide network with assistants and associates through computers and cellular phones.

Perhaps more diverse than the contrasting working conditions and working lives these managers experience is the diversity of activities they engage in. Most people think of "management" as an abstract category of people who make decisions about what business firms should do. But the act of management encompasses a wide variety of things that are actually "managed"; people, communications, raw materials, financial assets, and fixed capital.

In this chapter we seek to develop the idea that managers have been attempting (with varying degrees of success) to attain professional status. We trace the development of management in terms of this attempt at professionalization, and assess the extent to which relatively recent changes in organizational forms have aided the professionalization of managerial jobs.

This chapter develops a professional autonomy perspective to explain the development of managerial ideas in the United States. Our perspective combines insights on managers' behavior from the organizational literature with theories of the development of professions to explain changes in managers' activities.

Scholars have attempted to explain the historical development of management as an economic category and set of occupations. Many of these scholars have searched for mechanisms to explain managerial activities and historical shifts in organizational forms spawned by shifts in prevailing practices. For example, Braverman (1974) suggests that managers are motivated by a desire to control the work process. Threats to managers' control (e.g., pro-union legislation) lead to new activities to re-establish managerial dominance of the production process. Barley and Kunda (1992) offer a different perspective which suggests that shifts in rational and normative ideology explain surges in new managerial activities. Rational ideologies emphasize control, efficiency, and technical dimensions of management. Normative ideologies focus on people, work groups, and corporate cultures (Barley and Kunda 1992).

Others seek to explain changing managerial activities as a function of managers' desire to increase efficiency in the face of shifting economic climates (Chandler 1977; see Williamson 1975). But we suspect that managers (like other professional groups) are motivated by more than the desire to control others and increase efficiency. We think managers are also motivated by a desire to reduce uncertainty and increase autonomy and freedom of action in their working lives. These desires resemble those of other would-be professional groups. In this chapter we examine managerial work from a standpoint we label *professional autonomy*.

Our next section outlines the basic elements of our professional autonomy perspective. We apply this perspective to successive historical shifts in management activity. Using professional autonomy as a sensitizing concept, we then advance tentative ideas of what the next management activities will look like in chapter 4. We label these new activities "neoentrepreneurialism." We then discuss the organizational and research implications of this new managerial paradigm.

We should say a word about the scope of this chapter. Our intention here is not to explore every event that could affect managers' actions over the past 150 years. Instead, we want to focus on the sensitizing concept of professional autonomy to enlarge our understanding of managers' activities. We focus on a few major historical events that we believe have affected the autonomy of managers as a group. But first we develop the idea that managerial work can be studied as a professional project.

MANAGEMENT AS A PROFESSIONAL PROJECT

We defined the term *professional project* in chapter 1. Professional projects is a phrase coined by Abbott (1988) and refers to those activities used to further the professional aspirations of occupational groups. Professional projects are;

- activities that define the tasks of an occupation (what people actually do on the job);
- activities that define these tasks in ways others in the workplace will understand and respect;
- activities that defend an occupation's activities against other occupations that seek to control the same set of tasks.

Examples of subtle (and not so subtle) day-to-day activities that people do to protect the professional aspirations of their jobs abound. Doctors don't empty bedpans. Nurses, as part of their attempt to project a more professional image, have balked at emptying bedpans as well, leaving this task to orderlies and other unskilled hospital workers. Lawyers and accountants have been sparring for at least 20 years over the right to provide corporate financial advice. Teachers and principals engage in constant workplace negotiations over the limits of teachers' autonomy in the classroom.

But professional projects are more than pragmatic fights over day-to-day work tasks. Professional projects also involve the development of explanations and accounts of why people do what they do on the job. These involve both pragmatic descriptions of what is actually done that others will recognize as important ("I didn't reveal my client's whereabouts on the day in question because those statements are protected by lawyer–client privilege") and abstract statements about what jobholders should do and what their orientations should be toward their work ("Our only agenda is the best interests of the patient").

Precise definitions of professional work are elusive (for a review, see Freidson 1986). As we saw in chapter 2, some writers compare specific occupations to abstract sets of traits that they claim characterize professions, traits such as certification and the establishment of training schools (see Wilensky 1964). Others emphasize the ability of specific occupations to control training, decision-making, and compensation, paying particular attention to the lobbying activities of professional associations (such as the American Medical Association, see Derber and Schwartz 1991). In this book we adopt a definition that combines insights from the work of Freidson (1986) and Abbott (1988). Most professional projects attempt to (1) *enhance autonomy and freedom of action* for occupational members (sometimes referred to as "defining professional prerogatives," see Freidson 1986); and (2) *defend a specific set of tasks* from encroachment by competing occupational groups and stakeholders (see Abbott 1988).

Drawing on this literature, we suggest that the professional project of managers would involve (1) enhancing freedom of action within the firm, and (2) defending their work activities against encroachment by competing occupational groups and organizational stakeholders (i.e., employees and owners). Managers' desire to preserve freedom of action reflects the notion that they possess a set of interests that are distinct from owners (i.e., investors) and employees (Jensen and Mackling 1976). Managers owe their existence to the increasingly complex environment that confronted entrepreneurs and investors during the nineteenth century. Managers gained autonomy as investors faced greater difficulties in determining if managers were truly representing their interests (see Chandler 1977; Jensen and Mackling 1976). As business firms grew in size, managerial freedom of action could be defended by defining managers as "professional trustees" who represent the financial interests of the firm. The professional project of managers highlights the distinctive expertise necessary to produce the appropriate strategic mix of capital and human resources that produces success for the firm (and by definition, investors).

The managerial professional project also involves defending managerial tasks against employees and other nonsupervisory workers as well. Our perspective suggests that this defense occurs through the creation of new ideologies and rationales for maintaining or expanding professional autonomy.[1]

In sum, we view historical changes in management activities as the product of professional projects by managers who wish to increase their freedom of action in response to environmental shocks and stakeholder actions (e.g., Abbott 1988). We contend that autonomy was enhanced through four mechanisms: scientific management, human relations management, human resource management, and neoentrepreneurialism. Each of these is identified with a specific management paradigm and a specific historical era. In the section that follows, we begin by discussing the organizational landscape as it existed in the United States during much of the 1800s. From there, we examine the rise of the first three of these successive managerial paradigms (scientific management, human relations management, human resource management) through the sensitizing lens of professional autonomy. We develop the fourth mechanism, neoentrepreneurialism in chapter 4. A brief outline of our historical argument is provided in table 3.1.

Table 3.1 Factors contributing to management paradigm change

	SCIENTIFIC MANAGEMENT	*HUMAN RELATIONS MANAGEMENT*	*HUMAN RESOURCE MANAGEMENT*	*NEOENTRE-PRENEURIALISM*
EXTERNAL SHOCKS WHICH LEAD TO PARADIGM	Growing capital requirements with rising industrialization	Great Depression Labor legislation Immigration and urbanization	Change in capital markets to promote stability and efficiency Declining unionization Portfolio investment theory Rise of top managers from finance backgrounds	Rising global competition Skilled labor diversification Steep declines in unionization among employees Further investment diversification Management compensation tied to short-term stock fluctuation
CHANGE IN MANAGERIAL AUTONOMY	Dependence on skilled workers and/or subcontractors	Legislation-sponsored increases in union bargaining power Constraints on employment-at-will Growth in collective bargaining	Human relations approach is not isomorphic with portfolio investment theory Placated employees no longer necessary	Rapid capital movement Reduced environmental beneficence Competition for skilled workers

MANAGEMENT ACTION	Time and motion studies Job redesign Replacement of skilled workers and/or subcontractors with unskilled workers	Greater focus on human behavior and interaction within the firm Employee-centered supervision Concern for employee needs Internal labor markets Bureaucratic employment practices	Treating employees as human capital (similar to physical capital) Conglomerate is managed as a portfolio of investments Performance goals are thrust on enterprise managers Parts of conglomerates are acquired and discarded	Hiring temporary workers Contingent workforce Subcontracting Network organizations Outsourcing
CHANGE IN STAKEHOLDERS' LEVEL OF DEPENDENCE	Loss of knowledge monopoly by skilled workers Expanded pool of potential employees Greater labor market discipline	An initial decrease in employee firm-specific uncertainty, though this becomes reversed with the onset of ILMs Increase in investor risk due to uncertainties surrounding production	Firm-specific risk rises for SBU employees	Greater firm-specific dependency for unskilled employees
CHANGE IN STAKEHOLDER ACTION	Rising support for unionization Investor incorporation Lower employee investment in human capital	Employees begin unionizing at first, though union support declines as ILMs become more prevalent Investor diversification	Employees with marketable skills begin "opting-out" of traditional employment contracts	Skilled workers continue to reduce firm-specific dependencies by diversifying contractual ties

Entrepreneurialism, 1860–1910[2]

As late as the mid-1850s, firms were owned by individual entrepreneurs. Corporate organizational forms existed, but their use was limited to public works ventures (Hurst 1970). Most businesses were owned and managed by the same person who supplied much if not all of the money to fund the venture (Berle and Means 1932).

The dominant form of employee organization was the "inside contract" (see Stone 1974). Entrepreneurs would contract with individual craft workers to perform different operations associated with the production process. The craft worker would then hire assistants to actually perform the work outlined in the contract. The contract was referred to as "inside" because entrepreneurs contracted with their own employees to do the work. In sharp contrast to entrepreneurs, who often invested their life savings in a single firm, craft workers possessed vital human capital skills that were portable (see Marglin 1974; Stone 1974; Montgomery 1979).

By the late nineteenth century, the capital demands of rapid industrialization required investments greater than individual entrepreneurs could manage. As a result, the corporate form was beginning to emerge as the preferred arrangement of for-profit enterprises (Berle and Means 1932). Corporate organizational forms separate the suppliers of capital (investors) from those who have responsibility for the investors' money. This split produced the professional domain that came to be occupied by managers (Berle and Means 1932; Abbott 1988; Munzer 1990).

The historical developments affecting employers had quite a different impact on employees. In the beginning of the nineteenth century, the prevailing philosophies governing the work relationship were freedom-of-contract and employment-at-will. In theory, employees and owners could negotiate the terms of employment as well as end the employment contract at their discretion. Attempts to violate this practice were viewed as criminal behavior detrimental to owners and society at large. This was apparent in the *Philadelphia Cordwainers* case of 1806, where a group of shoemakers unionized in an attempt to increase their wages. The owner of the company sued and the court found the shoemakers guilty of criminal conspiracy. However, the *Commonwealth v. Hunt* decision of 1842 made it more difficult to apply the notion of criminal conspiracy to labor union activity.

In most inside contracting arrangements, entrepreneurs possessed little or no knowledge of how jobs were performed. The skills required to perform necessary tasks were largely controlled by craft guilds or learned through apprenticeship from other craft workers (Wren 1994). Due to the almost proprietary nature of craft knowledge, employees possessed a great deal of freedom and autonomy (Stone 1974). They were not dependent on the success of one particular firm and the short supply of craft workers meant that they could easily move from one firm to another. Craft workers were, in effect, independent contractors.

From Entrepreneurialism to Scientific Management, 1910–1940

As firms grew and investors were less involved in the day-to-day operations of specific firms, managers became a vital intermediary representing the interests of owners in the production process. The growing ranks of managers began looking for ideologies and paradigms that would allow them to assert themselves as aspiring professionals in an increasingly complex organizational world. Investors sought to tie compensation schemes for managers to returns on their investments so that the interests of managers and investors would coincide (see Edwards 1979; Kaufman 1993). But both groups were dependent on mobile, skilled craft workers. The inability to control the work pace of craft workers is one of the rationales many analysts give for the development of scientific management (see Braverman 1974; Edwards 1979).

Scientific management was a culmination of a number of independent developments brought together and popularized by Frederick Taylor (1856–1915). From his writings on the Midvale Plant, which culminated into a treatise on the subject in 1911, Taylor described many of the problems associated with production in terms of a lack of efficiency on the part of workers. He believed that these inefficiencies were due to variations in work methods. Taylor felt that these inefficiencies could be reduced by studying the work process itself so that more efficient methods of production could be devised. Managers would record these efficient procedures for the purposes of training both present and future employees. With all of the workers following standardized procedures based on the conservation of time and motion, worker productivity would increase.

As any student of the history of management will attest, Taylor's ideas gained widespread acceptance. Taylor's 1903 book, *Shop Management*, introduced many basic themes of scientific management. By 1910, Dartmouth University began teaching courses on scientific management (Wren 1994). A year later, Taylor's book, *The Principles of Scientific*

Management, was published. By 1921, variants of this method of managing could be found in factories throughout the world (Wren 1994). Though the rapid growth of Taylor's ideas can be attributed to the productivity concerns of investors, we suggest that another reason for the quick acceptance of this method was that scientific management reduced managers' reliance on skilled employees and increased their professional autonomy.[3]

Under scientific management, craft workers no longer had proprietary knowledge over their own work. The process of time-and-motion studies, job redesign, and training invested in scientific management allowed managers to shift new job opportunities toward unskilled workers who could perform simple, repetitive tasks. The labor force available for factory work increased. Because workers under scientific management were unskilled, interchangeable parts of a big, interdependent production process they were easily replaceable. This allowed managers to make greater productivity, hours, and wage demands, which served to stabilize the production process. Managers could lessen their dependence on skilled employees and reduce the uncertainty of returns to investors.

FROM SCIENTIFIC MANAGEMENT TO HUMAN RELATIONS, 1940–1970

From around 1910 through the 1930s, scientific management was a major impetus for managers' actions in the United States (Wren 1994). However, during this same period a number of social, political, and economic changes would affect key organizational stakeholders (i.e., investors, managers, and employees). In this section, we discuss these events in terms of their effect on the professional autonomy of managers. We suggest that such changes would ultimately highlight the limits of scientific management and create the impetus for human relations approaches to management.

From 1910 to 1930, much of the political environment was occupied with the debate over the legality of union activity. In the 1908 Supreme Court decision of *Loewe v. Lawlor*, otherwise known at the Danbury Hatters' case, the court ruled that union efforts to boycott an employer constituted restraint of trade under the Sherman Act of 1890. The effect of this decision was to make unions subject to antitrust laws, which seriously restricted union power. Recognizing the position of increased risk in which labor now found itself, Congress passed the Clayton Act of 1914 in order to relieve unions from the threat of injunctions. This recognition can best be exemplified by the remarks of Rep. Kelly of Pennsylvania, made during the debate of the Clayton Act:

> We must decide whether wealth is to rule or manhood, whether this nation is to be one of equal rights to all or special privileges to a few, whether honor and ability is to weigh in the selection of officials or cringing submission to corporate capital. . . . The free workers of America own themselves and their labor power. . . . They may act together for the protection of their rights and interests, and it is a sham and a fraud to say that they may organize without the power to use means necessary to make organization a vital force in demanding and securing justice. (Congressional Record 1914: 9086)

Although the Supreme Court in the 1921 case of *Duplex Printing Press v. Deering* found that the Clayton Act did not apply in cases where there was restraint of trade, the passage of the Act is nonetheless important because it signifies legislative admission that workers' dependence on a specific workplace was rising.

During the mid-1920s, the social structure of work in the United States was also changing. Millions of Americans were leaving farms and moving to the city in search of a better life (see Bogue 1959). This, combined with the continued immigration of foreigners into metropolitan areas (Bogue 1959), had a dramatic effect on workers. As the available labor force for factory work increased, the bargaining power of employees declined. With less ability to make wage or job security demands, and with heightened competition for jobs, employees found themselves increasingly dependent on the whims of specific employers.

The Great Depression would alter workplace environments still further. In the early 1930s, the unemployment rate in the US rose to approximately 25 percent. Congress, showing concern for labor, passed the Norris–La Guardia Act in 1932. This Act strictly limited the use of injunctions against unions and outlawed the use of "yellow-dog" contracts (contracts stating that the worker could not join a labor union as a condition for employment). Though managers were now restricted from seeking judicial protection from strikes and boycotts, the loopholes in the Act and the economic climate of the depression meant that they could merely dismiss striking workers and replace them with others at a lower wage (Cihon and Castagnera 1988).

In 1933, the National Industrial Recovery Act (NIRA) was passed, which contained sections specifically intended to address these loopholes. When the Supreme Court found the NIRA unconstitutional in

1935, Congress moved that same year to pass the Wagner Act, otherwise known as the National Labor Relations Act (NLRA). The concern of Congress was again with the power of employees relative to employers. This is exemplified by Senator Wagner's opening remarks before debate on amendments to the bill, where he stated:

> It [the NLRA] is the next step in the logical unfolding of man's eternal quest for freedom . . . [W]ith economic problems occupying the center of the stage, we strive to liberate man from destitution, from insecurity, and from human exploitation . . . In this modern aspect of a time-worn problem the isolated worker is a plaything of fate. Caught in the labyrinth of modern industrialism and dwarfed by the size of corporate enterprise, he can attain freedom and dignity only by cooperation with others of his group. (Congressional Record 1935: 7,565)

In 1937, when the Supreme Court upheld the constitutionality of the NLRA, it signified the first time that both the judicial and legislative branches were in agreement regarding employees' increased dependence on the firm.

The timing of this convergence of views in no small way reflects the economic environment of the early twentieth century (1920–44). The growth of the corporate form reduced the number of potential employers in the labor market. In 1909 there was one small manufacturing firm for every 250 people in the United States; by 1929 there was only one for every 900 people. The increase in the ratio of people-to-firms (partially) is the result of the growth in the corporate form (from the speech of Senator Wagner, Congressional Record 1935) as well as immigration and the movement of labor from farms to the cities (see Bogue 1959).

With the Supreme Court's 1937 decision to uphold the constitutionality of the Wagner Act, the employment relationship changed dramatically. Employment-at-will was no longer the only doctrine that governed the association between employer and employee. Instead, unionization and collective bargaining became options available to workers. With the advent of forced bargaining, union contracts, and strike funds, managers were quite vulnerable to the whims of collectively organized workers. Further, government restrictions on managers' ability to bargain and terminate employees had the effect of increasing the degree of uncertainty associated with investment in a firm. The prospects of greater scrutiny from investors also affected managers' potential autonomy.

The thrust behind the Wagner Act was to "level the playing field" between individual employees and the economic power of business firms. Scientific management was an excellent method for managers to defend their professional domain when they were threatened by a lack of knowledge of job skills, but it offered very little help against legislated union bargaining power.[4]

THE HUMAN RELATIONS APPROACH

The human relations approach to management is usually tied to the results of the 1929 Hawthorne Studies (Sherman and Bohlander 1992; Wren 1994). This approach focused on aspects of social interactions that affected firm performance. Managers were supposed to be sensitive to the needs and feelings of their employees as well as able to recognize the individual differences between them. This approach also emphasized the need for increased worker participation and employee-centered supervision (Sherman and Bohlander 1992; Wren 1994).

The human relations approach was radically different from its predecessor, which stressed the use of time-motion studies to achieve uniformity and maximum efficiency. Given the prevailing legal environment of the late 1930s, the continued exclusive use of scientific management would only exacerbate existing tensions between managers and employees and increase the uncertainty of continued, stable profits (which would invite unwanted attention from investors). What managers needed was a method that would appease workers in order to prevent them from exercising their newly-created rights. Through focusing on such areas as the needs and feelings of workers, managers hoped to avoid any costly confrontations (Bendix 1956; Braverman 1974) and stabilize firm output (Gillespie 1991).

FROM HUMAN RELATIONS TO HUMAN RESOURCE MANAGEMENT, 1970–1990

From the passage of the Wagner Act to the late 1950s, unionization in the United States increased rapidly: in 1935, 13.2 percent of the nonagricultural work force was unionized; by 1960 this figure had grown to over 30 percent (Hamermesh and Rees 1988). However, after 1960 the percentages began falling (Freeman and Medoff 1984; Hamermesh and Rees 1988). A number of reasons have been suggested for this decline, ranging from continued government intervention to institutionalization of union efforts to successful "union-busting" on behalf of corporations (Cihon and Castagnera 1988; Hamermesh and Rees 1988). As union membership began decreasing after 1960, the bargaining power of employees started to decline as well. This loss of power was one of the major contributors to increased freedom of action on the part of managers since World War II.

Another factor which contributed to employees' increase in firm dependence during the 1960s, and greater managerial autonomy, was the development of internal labor markets (ILMs) within firms. An ILM consists of well-defined job ladders, with movement up these ladders dependent upon the acquisition of firm-specific skills (see Althauser and Kalleberg 1981; Pfeffer and Cohen 1984). The development of ILMs was the result of complex institutional and environmental interactions between government intervention in manpower activities, industrial unions, and growing personnel departments. Government intervention by the War Labor Board during World War II and War Labor Board publications provided models for personnel practices that encouraged isomorphism among firms (Baron et al. 1986). Other measures, such as the government-led effort to reduce turnover and new demands to analyze and justify labor needs, provided strong incentives for firms to establish and extend personnel departments. Industrial unions were ambivalent about some aspects of ILMs. Many of the same provisions that increased management's control over the work process protected workers from layoffs and arbitrary treatment (see Gordon, Edwards, and Reich 1982; Baron et al. 1986).

In an ILM an employee joins the organization at a particular point-of-entry and moves up the organization by way of a highly-defined job ladder. As workers progress through the organization, they acquire skills that tend to be highly specific, applicable only to the firm at hand (Pfeffer and Cohen 1984). Workers become tied to their current organization because movement to new organizations would result in decreased wages (changing organizations would entail entering the new organization at the bottom of the job ladder because the new firm would require skills different from those acquired at the previous firm).[5]

Simultaneously, other events were unfolding which would dramatically affect investors' exposure to and scrutiny of specific managers. Post-depression regulations had made the stock market much more efficient in terms of access to information, reducing the risk associated with stock ownership. Moreover, the expansion in the amount of stock traded and the number of companies available for purchase further reduced the firm-specific dependence of investors by increasing capital mobility.

However, an important event in decreasing the dependencies of investors came in 1952, when Harry Markowitz published his work on "portfolio selection." Markowitz suggested that by focusing on the standard deviations of stocks, as well as the covariance between them and the market, investors could diversify away nearly all the risk inherent in any one stock, exposing themselves only to the risk of the overall market. Investors could now exercise control over a number of firms without being exposed to the risk of any one.

By the 1970s, internal labor markets and decreasing unionization had drastically altered the relationship between employees and managers. The continued development of the stock market and the growing use of portfolio investment theory lowered the scrutiny of investors toward specific firms. A less powerful workforce and diversified investment capital gave managers greater autonomy to promote their distinctive professional goals.

Another development during the 1970s was the gradual shift in the backgrounds of top executives within the managerial profession. Prior to the 1970s, the ranks of top management were filled with individuals whose training and corporate background involved marketing, sales, and engineering. However, beginning in the 1970s, a growing number of top executives with finance backgrounds were being selected for key executive positions. We suggest that as this cadre of managers grew, portfolio investment theory began to emerge as the organizing mechanism for large firms (see Fligstein 1990). The human relations approach was structured on a different set of principles that were not isomorphic with the new financial tools of top management. Further, the human relations approach was designed to pacify employees in response to newly-created union power. But decreasing union ranks and ILMs were making this pacification unnecessary. We believe these occurrences, along with the disjuncture in operating rationales between top executives and mid-level personnel managers contributed to the rise of human resource management.

The initial conception of human resource management can be traced to the 1958 writings of E. Wright Bakke, though it would take over ten years for this approach to replace human relations as the dominant approach to personnel managers' thought and practice. The basic concern of the human resource view is not the personal happiness of the workers but the attainment of productive work (Bakke 1958). The employee is viewed as another input into the production function in much the same way as a manager would view raw materials or machinery (hence the use of such terms as "human resource" and "human capital").

Human resource management to a large degree mimics the underlying tenets of portfolio investment theory as practiced by top financial managers. The decision by top managers to diversify financial assets was based on the notion that profit for the whole was more important than maintaining the individual parts of the organization. Top managers would add and discard firms based on their financial contribution to the overall corporation while the welfare of the individual firms under the corporate umbrella was downplayed. Human resource management viewed employees in a similar fashion. Workers were no longer seen as important in and of themselves (as in the human relations approach). Rather, employees were viewed in the context of their contribution to the specific firm and decisions to add or discard employees were based on this heuristic (Sherman and Bohlander 1992; Wren 1994).

Personnel managers increased their autonomy and relative standing by aligning their decision-making rationale with top financial managers, the ascendant group at the top of most managerial hierarchies (see Donaldson 1963; Monsen and Downs 1965; Baumol 1967; Fligstein 1990). In effect, we are arguing that most of the changes involved in the shift from human relations to human resource management were invisible to nonsupervisory employees on a day-to-day basis. What did change slowly was the implied contract between managers and employees regarding their place within the larger corporation.

SUMMARY

In chapter 4 we move on to discuss a fourth and more historically recent management paradigm, neoentrepreneurialism. But first, we need to recall the counterpart to this story, the changes occurring in professional work and the work settings where professional work is performed. We have now reviewed the development of the concepts of professions, professional projects, management, and managerial work. Through both this chapter and chapter 2, the concept of professional autonomy has been key to the growth in status and power of both groups over time. And, as we suggested in chapter 1, we can now see how convergence has developed between professionals and managers on a number of dimensions.

First, both professionals and managers are increasingly subject to a similar level of external oversight and less than complete autonomy.

Actually, a more accurate way to put this is that the autonomy of managers has increased, due to shifts in relationships among organizational constituents, and the ascendance of human resource management paradigms. On the other hand, professionals of all sorts have lost autonomy over time, so that their work is now subject to external oversight within organizational settings. Second, both managers and professional workers are increasingly viewed as "labor pools" from which replacements can be found, or as a set of functions and expertise that can be outsourced rather than carried within the organization's structure. As we will see in chapter 4, both of these trends have continued.

Further, both groups (managers and professionals) find themselves in closer contact within the worksite, or when outsourced, dealing with each other in a semi-competitive fashion. Each group is usually intent upon defending their own prerogatives and defining "turf." Neither group wants to give the advantage to the other, so professionals will struggle to protect their own areas of expertise, and managers will maneuver professionals so that they are either "controllable" within the firm's structure, or restricted to formalized transactions as an external subcontractor. However, outsourced professional expertise can become somewhat unpredictable and more difficult to control. Again, a particularly relevant example comes from the struggle between managed care organizations and physician groups. Physicians have become so threatened by the restrictions of managed care over medical decision-making that calls for physician unions are once again on the rise. This will be examined in more detail in chapter 4.

Finally, in chapter 7 we will also explore the extent to which both managers and professionals have become increasingly diverse groups, which thus leads to more difficulty for either group to present a "solid front" to the other, or to wield the kind of power exemplified by Starr's (1982) description of the institution of medicine from World War II until the late 1970s. And the sources of diversity range from demographic characteristics to specialization and interest diversity.

NOTES

1 Ideologies are ways of thinking that justify the existing distribution of resources. Managers at the same time are defending managerial autonomy from oversight by investors. Managers (collectively) do not want to simultaneously gain decision-making freedom over people only to watch their authority over investment allocation decline.

2 All dates are approximations derived in large part from Wren (1994).

3 Our account is at variance with some discussions of scientific management that point to the standardization of managerial work scientific management methods created as well (see Form 1987).

4 For excellent brief discussions of the effect of the Wagner Act on union organizing and militancy, see Rubin (1983) and McCammon (1992).

5 There are a variety of reasons given for why ILMs exist. For discussions of this issue see Kalleberg and Berg (1987), Althauser and Kalleberg (1981), and Wallace and Kalleberg (1981).

4

The Neoentrepreneurial Workplace

Almost since the beginning, sociologists of the workplace have been concerned with the creation of more humane working arrangements. In both classical and contemporary sociology, students of the workplace have taken for granted that (1) there would be workplaces to study, and (2) if one visited those workplaces, there would be people working there to talk to. Although students of social stratification have pointed to rising unemployment, spatial mismatches in employment opportunities, and a growing subculture opposed to wage labor (see Clogg 1979; Kasarda 1989; Mead 1991; Wilson 1997), even this policy-oriented work suggests that conventional life in western culture is centered around a physical workplace with steady (or reasonably steady) employment as an expectation.

Beginning in the late 1980s, journalists and policy analysts began to question whether these two rock-bottom assumptions behind most of their research and writing were warranted, and, depending on their answer, whether they should re-examine their assumptions to account for new and radically altered workplaces.

The laundry list of changes identified over the past two decades have very serious implications for the future careers of professionals and managers, and most analysts share a basic description of these changes that is not difficult to sketch out. Writers vary widely on the optimism or pessimism they attach to these trends; one man's new opportunity is another woman's new uncertainty. But few analysts doubt that the workplace of the 1990s and the twenty-first century is turning into a different organization than the one preceding it.

The workplace of the 1990s is characterized by (1) *flatter organizational hierarchies*, as new information technologies eliminate the need for most layers of middle management, (2) the growing use of *temporary workers* employed on an as-needed basis to perform specific jobs for the duration of single projects, (3) the extensive use of *subcontracting and outsourcing* to small firms to produce parts and provide services that used to be provided in-house by permanent employees, (4) *massive downsizing* of the permanent workforce resulting from flatter hierarchies and the replacements of skilled workers by machine tenders, (5) a *postunionized bargaining environment* where unions have no place and no structural ability to gain a foothold to bargain with employers, and (6) *virtual organizations* that exist, not as distinctive structural or geographical locations but as technologically driven webs of interaction. These changes have led to a new neoentrepreneurial workplace that has challenged managers and professionals to re-examine their roles in the division of labor.

NEOENTREPRENEURIALISM: THE EMERGENCE OF A NEW PARADIGM?

These changes in work arrangements have occurred in the past 20 years and they show no signs of reversing themselves. Presently, the human resource management perspective is the dominant paradigm governing the relationship between organizational constituents, as we reviewed in chapter 3. It is practiced in some form in virtually every major firm in the United States and taught in nearly every business school. However, the conditions which led to the rise of this paradigm in the 1970s have changed substantially; environmental forces have continued to alter relationships between organizational stakeholders. In this chapter, we discuss the current state of these relationships. We suggest that the changes which have taken place over the past 20 years (since the adoption of human resource management) have affected managerial autonomy to such a degree that a new paradigm is poised to emerge. We call this new paradigm *neoentrepreneurialism*. We summarized the relationships between significant stakeholders in chapter 1 (figure 1.2) and we reproduce this figure here for convenience.

The trends which gave rise to the human resource management approach in the 1970s have continued over the past two decades, further altering the relationships among organizational constituents. These trends are incorporated in the six characteristics we outline as part of the new workplace of the 1990s and beyond. Let's take a brief look at each of these characteristics and their implications for professional and managerial work.

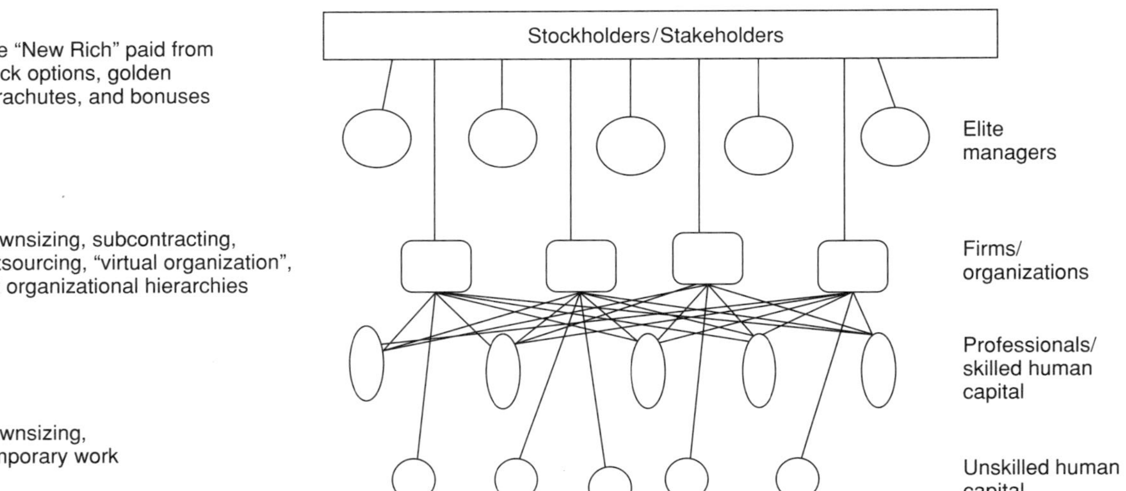

Figure 4.1 A model of the neoentrepreneurial organization of managerial and professional work

A post-unionized working environment

The unionization of the workforce, which began a slow decline from a mid-1960s peak of 32 percent of the civilian workforce in the US, now stands at roughly 9.2 percent of the non-governmental, nonagricultural labor force (Baird 1990; United States Bureau of Census 1997; for an analysis of this trend, see Cornfield 1986). Many writers speak of the decline in the social contract between employers and workers (see Edwards 1993; Rubin 1999). This social contract promised continuous employment in the form of a stable career in exchange for loyalty and commitment to a single business firm. Business firms had a stable geographic and temporal existence that encouraged managers to develop long-term relationships with specific employees.

The traditional bastion of unionized work in the United States has been in skilled crafts and among manufacturing operatives. But if one looks at trends in employment in these occupational groups (presented in figure 4.2) these are precisely the areas that the increasingly globalized economy of the United States is disinvesting in. Declines in these occupational groups are only exceeded by declines in Forestry and Fishery occupations. Much of the employment growth from 1992–2005 will be among professionals, managers, technical workers, and service employees. These are occupational groups with relatively high and low earnings, which some researchers believe foretells the coming of a polarized labor market in the twenty-first century (see Dunkerley 1996).

Richard Edwards (1993) has studied the decline of unionization and collective bargaining for two decades and claims that the central problem with regard to asserting workers' rights in the new workplace is a work regime that is outmoded and too rigid to adjust to the new realities of the globalized marketplace. What is this present regime? A system of statutory rights that is dictated by federal mandates, enforced by agencies of the federal government (like the National Labor Relations Board), and interpreted by judges through the courts. This system is unworkable and unsatisfactory because it is too cumbersome for both employers and employees, too easily avoided or shirked by employers, and renders solutions that are untimely and not very effective at alleviating persistent workplace problems. Statutory employment rights systems assume a modicum of employer good will, "local dependence" (to borrow a term from Logan and Molotch 1987) and intent to uphold the law. Once global competition and union decline are in full stride, employers lose what little incentive they have to comply with statutory

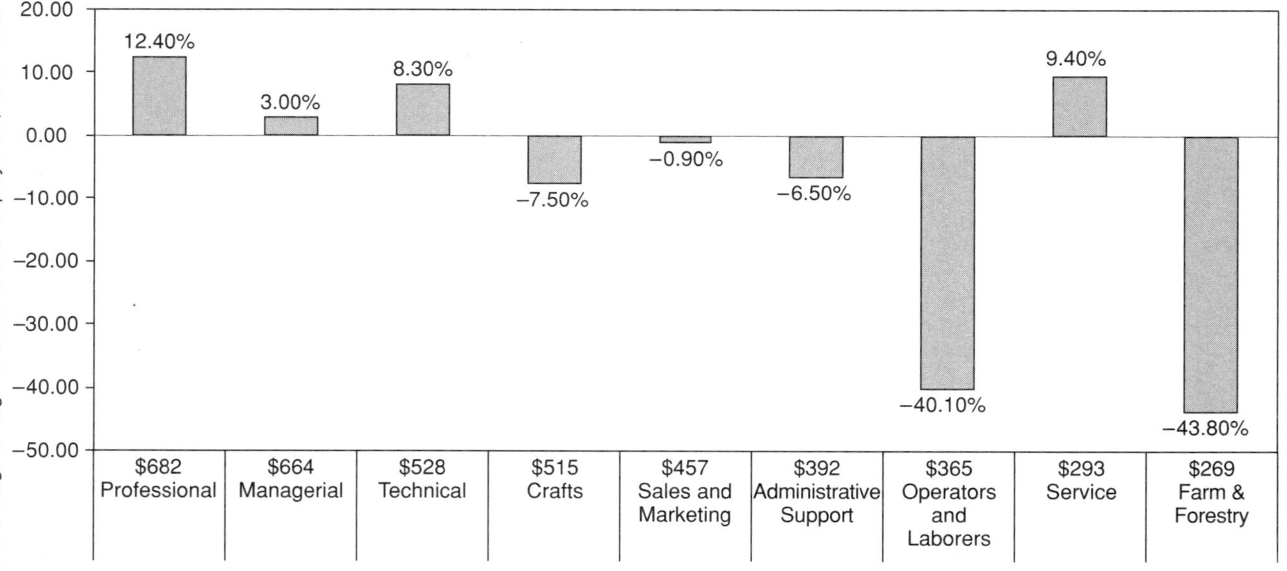

Figure 4.2 Job growth and decline in a polarized labor market
Source: *Business Week*, October 17, 1994 pp. 80–1.

workplace rights and gain every incentive to violate these rights and wait for the snail-paced courts to bring them in line. The present set of employer attitudes toward workplace rights remind us of an age-old statement by a prominent football coach concerning National Collegiate Association Rules regarding student-athletes, "they'll fire me for losing long before they'll fire me for cheating."

Other evidence of the decline of the influence of collective bargaining and unions can be seen in long-term trends in the effectiveness of strikes (see figure 4.3). At one time strikes were an effective weapon against employers who refused to bargain in good faith with union representatives or otherwise attempted to impose terms of employment that workers felt were unsatisfactory. But the evidence since the 1980s suggests that strikes now lead to further declines in employment and earnings among nonsupervisory workers even as they lower employers' net revenues.

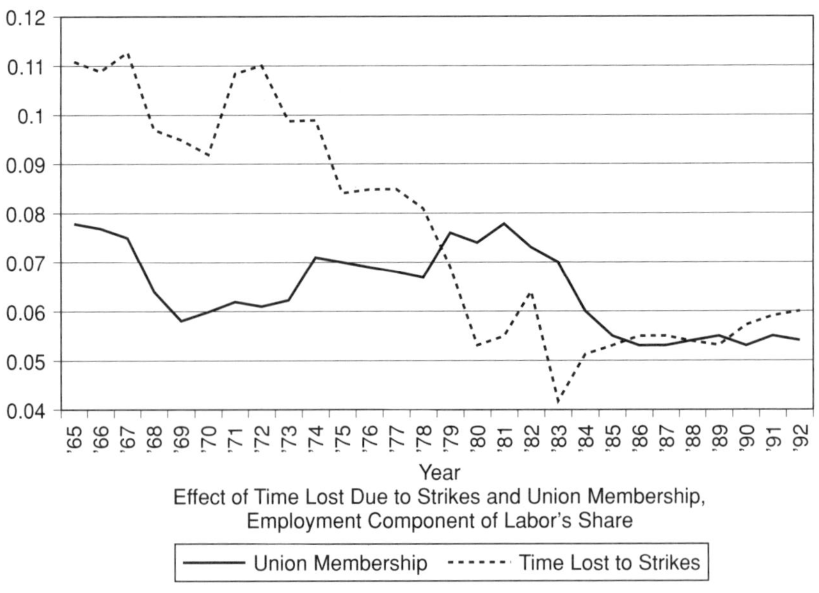

Figure 4.3 The long-term effects of strikes: lower wages, less employment, lower net revenues for employers

Source: Wallace, Leicht and Raffalovich 1999, pp. 280–1.

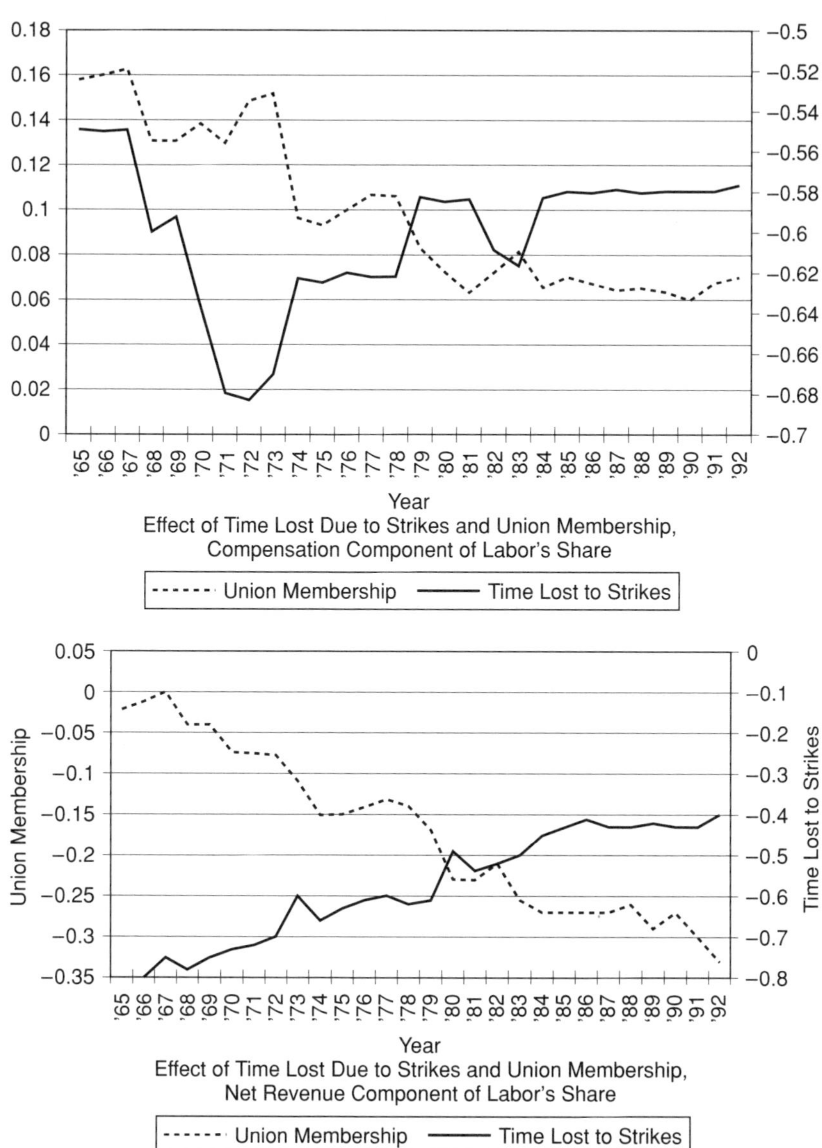

0.18
0.16
0.14
0.12
0.1
0.08
0.06
0.04
0.02
0
−0.5
−0.52
−0.54
−0.56
−0.58
−0.6
−0.62
−0.64
−0.66
−0.68
−0.7
'65 '66 '67 '68 '69 '70 '71 '72 '73 '74 '75 '76 '77 '78 '79 '80 '81 '82 '83 '84 '85 '86 '87 '88 '89 '90 '91 '92
Year
Effect of Time Lost Due to Strikes and Union Membership,
Compensation Component of Labor's Share
Union Membership
Time Lost to Strikes
Union Membership
0.05
0
−0.05
−0.1
−0.15
−0.2
−0.25
−0.3
−0.35
Time Lost to Strikes
0
−0.1
−0.2
−0.3
−0.4
−0.5
−0.6
−0.7
−0.8
'65 '66 '67 '68 '69 '70 '71 '72 '73 '74 '75 '76 '77 '78 '79 '80 '81 '82 '83 '84 '85 '86 '87 '88 '89 '90 '91 '92
Year
Effect of Time Lost Due to Strikes and Union Membership,
Net Revenue Component of Labor's Share
Union Membership
Time Lost to Strikes

Figure 4.3 *(cont'd)*

The net result of the long-term changes that have culminated in the arrangements of the new workplace is well-summarized by Castells (1996):

> What made possible this historical redefinition of the relationship between capital and labor was the use of powerful information technologies and of organizational forms facilitated by the new technological medium. The ability to assemble and disperse labor on specific projects and tasks anywhere, any time, created the possibility . . . of the virtual enterprise as a functional entity . . . the extraordinary increase in flexibility and adaptability permitted by new technologies opposed the rigidity of labor to the mobility of capital. It followed a relentless pressure to make the labor contribution as flexible as it could be. Productivity and profitability were enhanced, yet labor lost institutional protection and became increasingly dependent on individual bargaining conditions in a constantly changing labor market. (p. 278)

How globalized and virtual has the workplace become?

Another element which has drastically altered the dependency exposure of investors and employees, and hence the autonomy of managers, has been the growth in global competition. In the 1970s, global markets were in a rather embryonic stage of development. Because of this, US firms were relatively unaffected by international competition. Today, with the creation of the EC, NAFTA, and GATT, global markets have become much more efficient. Investor returns are no longer tied to firms in specific countries. Further, the conditions of global competition favor factions of management who lessen their dependence on investments in high-wage labor (see Fligstein 1990). This has had the effect of forcing US firms to adapt to global economic changes more quickly.

Figures 4.4 and 4.5 present information on the rise of global financial flows. The sheer volume of cross-boarder financial flows (figure 4.4) is now greater than the domestic gross domestic products of many developed nations. The average daily transactions on the world's stock exchanges (figure 4.5) increasingly involves investments outside of the world's three financial capitals, New York, Tokyo, and London. The value of world exports has also risen considerably in the past 20 years, as has foreign investment by the nations of the developed world (figure 4.6). The evidence increasingly suggests that capital operates in a

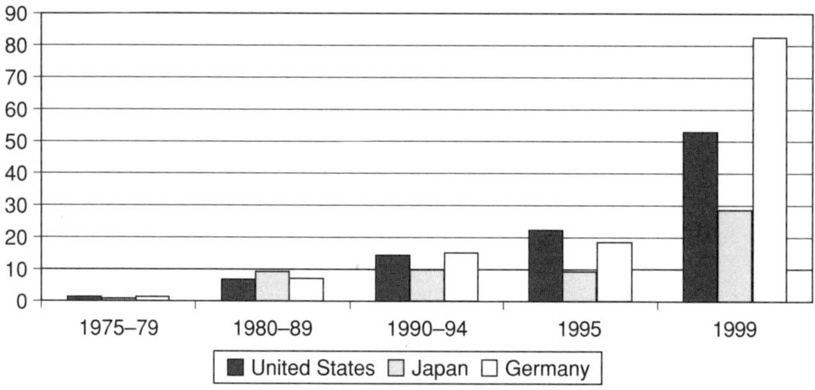

Figure 4.4 Sales of stocks between residents and nonresidents (transborder financial flows), 1975–1999 (percentage of GNP)

Source: Bank of International Settlement 70th Annual Report, 2000, p. 90.

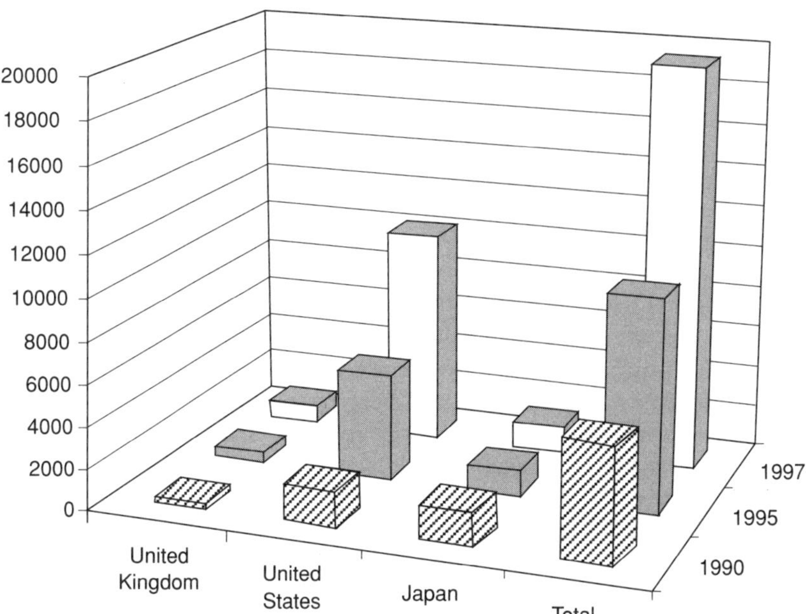

Figure 4.5 Total annual turnover of company shares on stock exchanges, 1990–1997 (in billions of US dollars)

Source: Adapted from *Statistical Abstract of the United States*, 1999, p. 859.

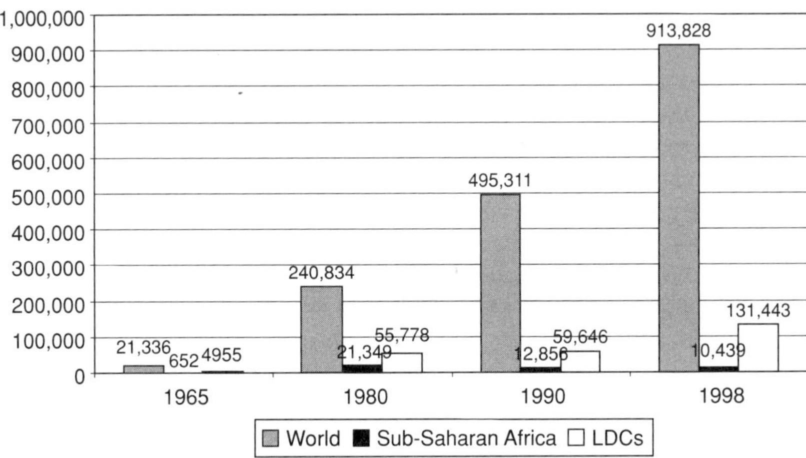

Figure 4.6 Value of exports to the United States from world, Sub-Saharan Africa, and less-developed Countries, 1965–1998 (in millions $US)

Source: US Census Bureau, International Trade in Goods and Services, December Issues.

global environment where the best returns can be calculated over a short time horizon and investors can move money to almost anyplace in the world.

There also is increasing evidence that the United States and the world is electronically connected via the internet and electronic mail (see figures 4.7 and 4.8). The internet now stretches to every portion of the globe with the exception of parts of sub-Saharan Africa, and even there limited forms of e-mail service are available. The United States increasingly exports information to other world trading centers to every region of the world, and the volume of information exchange between major trading centers in the United States has skyrocketed as well.

Employment Downsizing and the Relentless Drive for Efficiency and Productivity

Financial and physical capital have not had many problems in adapting to the demands of global competition. Managers can sell-off units, move their products to another market, or transfer funds from one area of the

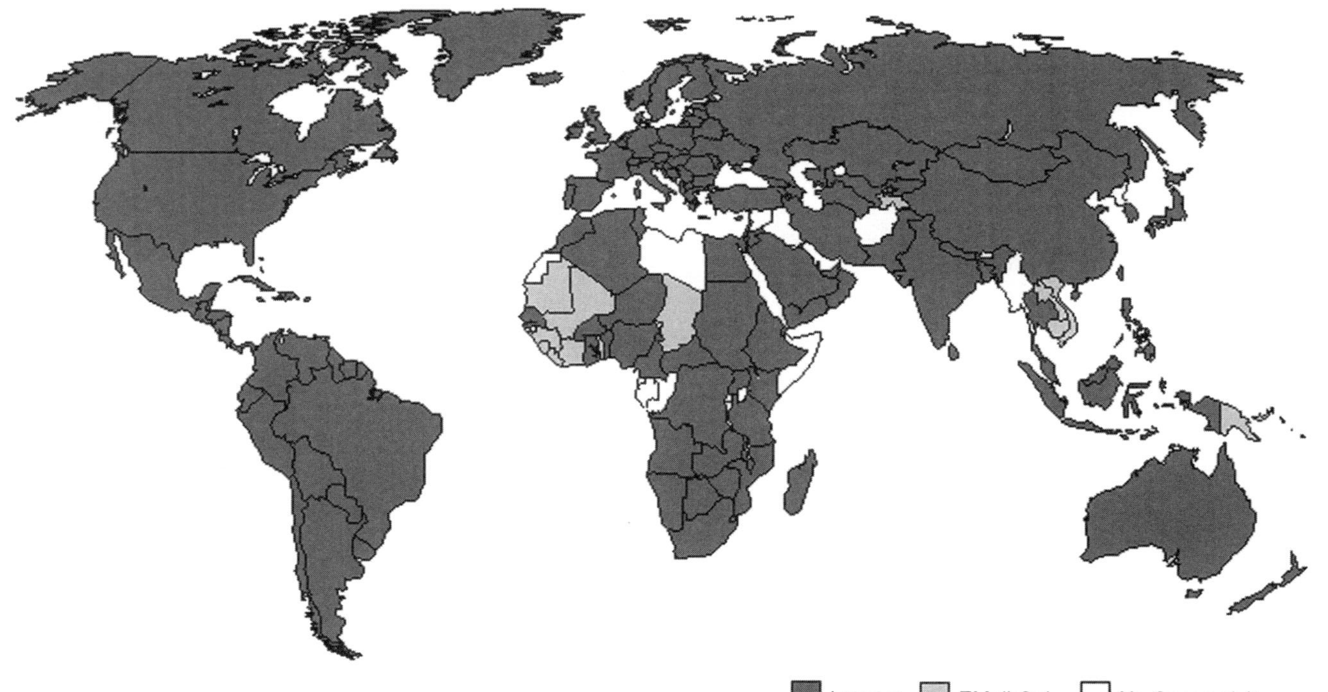

Figure 4.7 International connectivity via Internet and e-mail

Source: Copyright © 1997 Larry H. Landweber and the Internet Society.

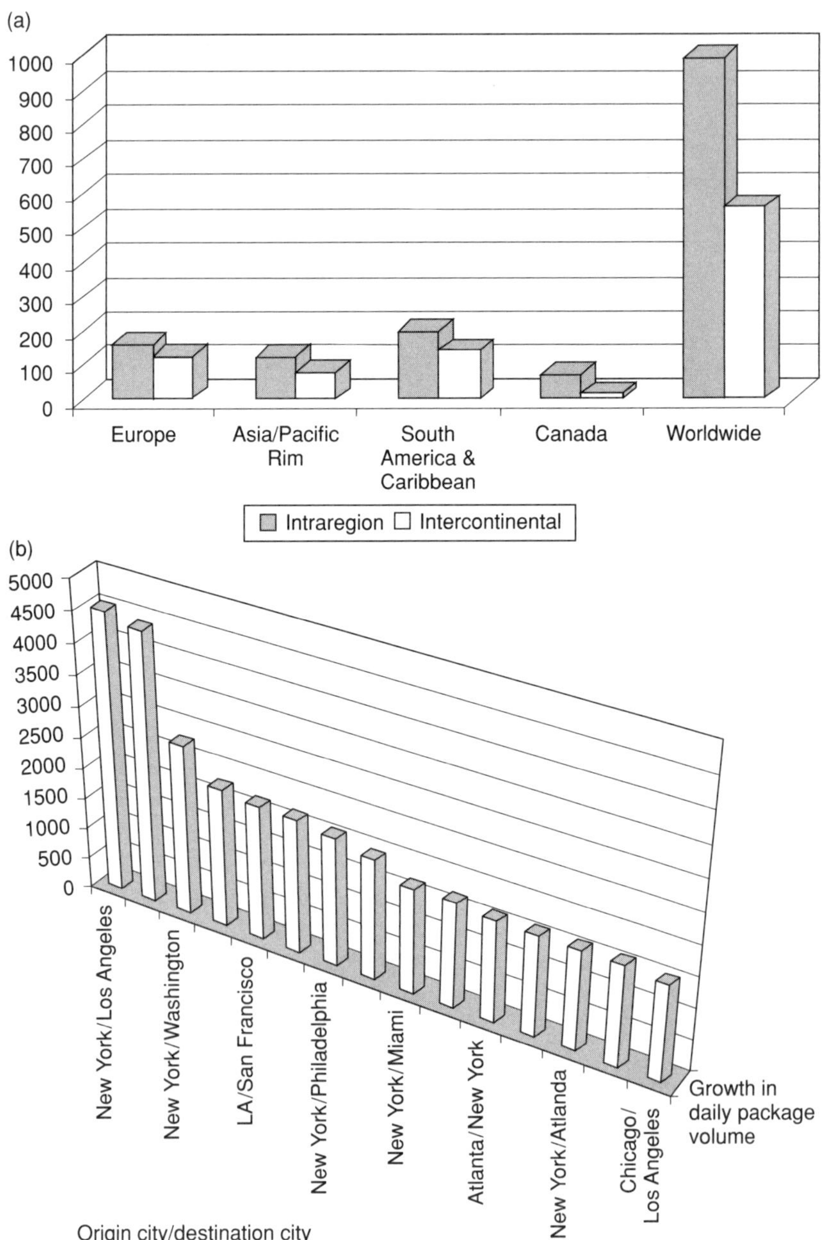

Figure 4.8 (a) Daily movement of information by air worldwide and by major world regions; (b) Largest absolute growth in information flows between US Cities, 1982–1990 (adapted from Michaelson and Wheeler, 1994, p. 97)

Source: adopted from *UPS Facts*, 2001.

world to another, all in order to achieve quick investment returns. Human capital has not adapted so easily. Employees cannot be effortlessly transferred from one area of the world to another depending on the whims of the market. However, as managers continued to dismantle ILMs and make rapid staffing changes in response to global markets, employees became more susceptible to fluctuations in the market for their firms' product.

In response to this uncertainty, we believe that a split is occurring in the employee ranks. In order to obviate much of this increase in firm-specific dependency, high-skilled employees have begun "opting-out" of traditional employment contracts (see Handy 1989). Instead of remaining beholden to a particular firm, these workers are beginning to resemble independent contractors with renewable contracts, or in some cases multiple contracts with various firms. We suggest that this action by high-skilled labor is an attempt to reduce their dependence on specific firms in the face of managerial staffing actions (e.g., downsizing). Announcements of corporate downsizing are now so prevalent that they scarcely gain special attention from the business or popular press (evidence on the prevalence of corporate downsizing is presented in figure 4.9), and job tenure among working men in the United States is declining (figure 4.10).

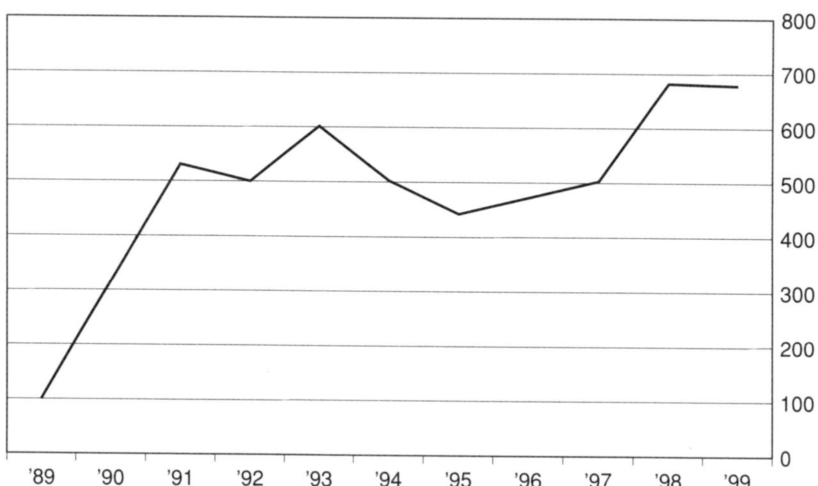

Figure 4.9 US job cut announcements (in thousands)
Source: *The Economist*, January 29, 2000, p. 90.

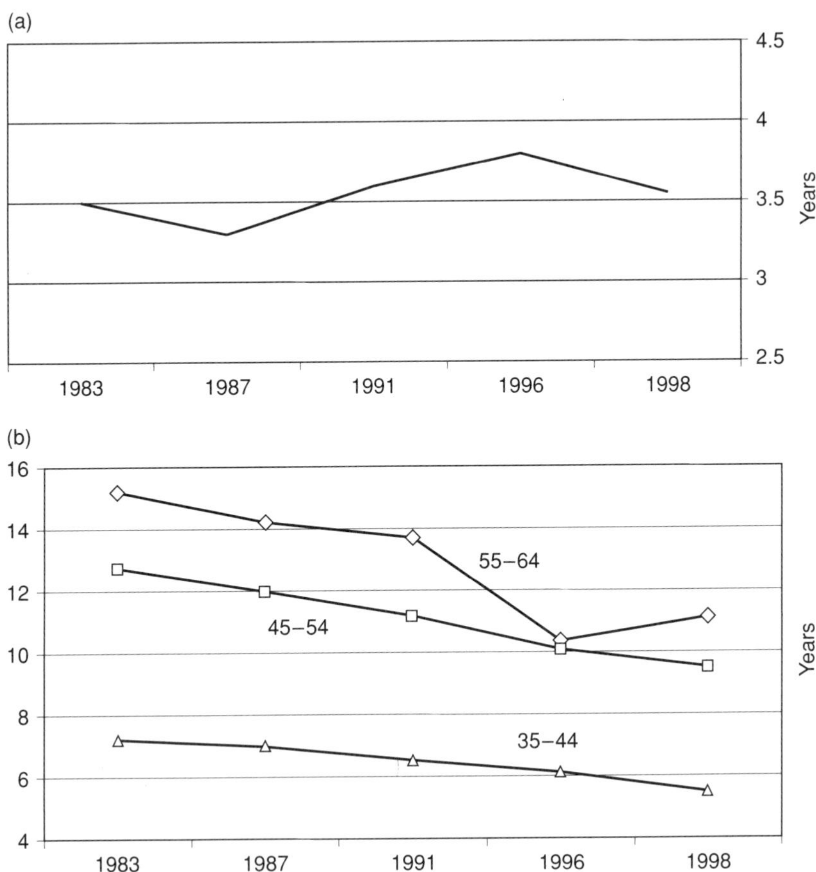

Figure 4.10 (a) Trends in job tenure: median years of tenure with current employer (employees 16 years and over); (b) median years of tenure with current employer (for men at different ages)

Source: *The Economist*, January 29, 2000, p. 94.

The trend in downsizing is by no means confined to the unskilled or even to the middle management ranks. Chase and Chemical Banks in New York dismissed 53 lawyers from their in-house legal staff after the companies merged in 1995 (*New York Times* 1996, p. 61).

However, the effect this has on managerial autonomy is rather pronounced. In today's economy, managers need high-skilled labor in order for their firms to compete effectively. However, as mentioned previously global competition favors firms who lessen dependence on high-wage labor (see Fligstein 1990). The human resource management paradigm worked well for managers throughout the 1980s and early 1990s, as managers could alter staffing levels depending on the demands of the global market. But, when high-skilled labor began opting-out of traditional employment contracts, a firm's talent pool became less predictable. Given management's need for high-skilled labor, a decrease in predictability serves to reduce the autonomy of managers in the firm.

Skilled workers in the newly-globalized economy are clearly in big demand (see table 4.1) and there has been considerable growth in the demand for managers (see figure 4.11). A growing number of these workers are self-employed, and turnover among skilled workers can be very high; in California's Silicon Valley, employee turnover in high-technology industries among skilled workers is close to 20 percent per year (*The Economist*, January 29, 2000, p. 90). In addition, there is some evidence that both employment and layoffs are growing at the same time. Although the United States has created over 100,000 jobs per month over the past two years, almost 300,000 people have filed new unemployment claims *each week*. Most workers are experiencing unemployment between jobs in addition to changing jobs themselves.

In addition to these changes in employment there is considerable evidence that there have been changes in compensation away from the traditional yearly raise and toward bonuses, stock options, and other forms of deferred compensation. Figure 4.12 shows how a typical employee stock ownership plan works. The American Productivity and Quality Center and the American Compensation Association reported

Table 4.1 United States: percentage change in employment by occupation, 1960–1998

	1960 level	*1960–1970*	*1970–1980*	*1980–1990*	*1990–1998*	*1970–1998*
Managers	10.6	–0.06	0.69	1.56	1.7	3.95
Professional and technical	11.21	2.96	1.88	0.94	1.38	4.2
Sales	6.6	–0.43	0.17	5.6	0.12	5.89
Clerical	14.67	2.77	1.17	–2.92	–1.69	–3.44
Crafts and operatives	30.81	–0.2	–3.53	–5.06	–1.05	–9.64
Semiskilled services	12.52	–0.17	0.97	–0.35	–0.1	1.22

Source: US Bureau of Labor Statistics, *Employment and Earnings*, various years.

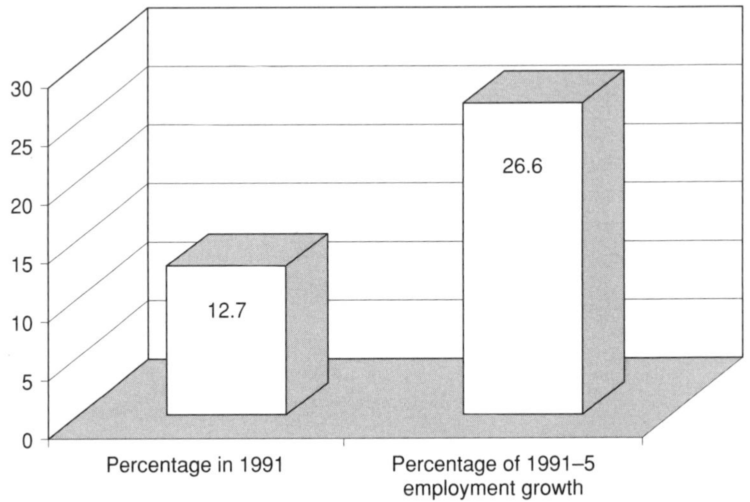

Figure 4.11 Managers as a percentage of nonfarm employment in 1991 and as a percentage of 1991–5 employment growth

Source: Reprinted from Gordon 1996, p. 54.

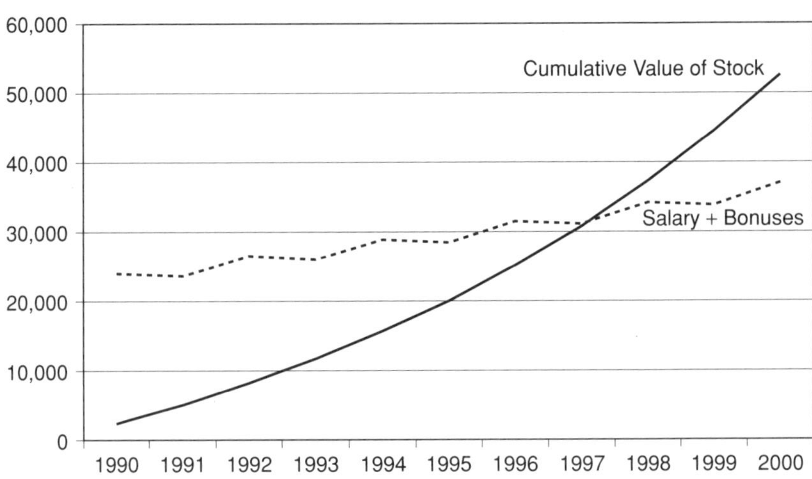

Figure 4.12 1990–2000 growth in salary + bonuses and stock value in a hypothetical employee stock ownership plan

Source: Boyett and Conn 1992, p. 141.

that, as early as 1987, more firms were moving toward nontraditional compensation packages that combine bonuses, stock options, and lump sum payments in place of traditional pay raises (reported in Boyett and Conn 1992).

The rising use of temporary, part-time, and subcontracted workers

In addition to reducing full-time employment, increasing numbers of firms in the United States are resorting to part-time and temporary employment to replace former permanent employees. About one in ten workers (around 12.5 million people) now work as either independent contractors or in some sort of temporary position (*The Economist* January 29, 2000). There has also been serious growth in the number of firms that claim to use temporary workers of some kind (see figure 4.13).

Ironically, the growth of contingent, temporary employment relationships is not confined to unskilled workers. Growing numbers of managers and even professionals are working as temporaries. *The Executive Recruiter News* reports that some 125,000 professionals work as temporary employees every day and that professionals are the fastest growing group of temporary workers (see Rifkin 1995). Eighty-nine percent of the firms

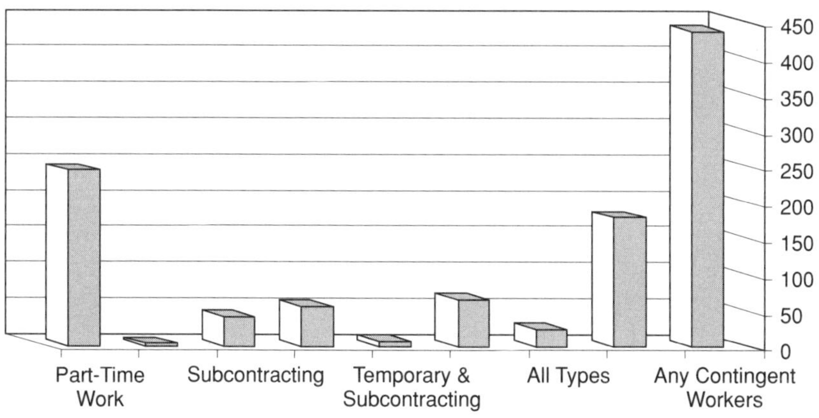

Figure 4.13 Organizations' use of contingent workers

Note: Unweighted sample, N = 614.

Source: Kalleberg et al. 1996, p. 264.

employing professionals in the National Organizations Study report hiring contingent workers (Kalleberg et al. 1996).

A typical description of these new employment arrangements is provided by Icarian, a Silicon Valley firm that specialized in "just-in-time" delivery of employees of all kinds to needy firms:

> within hours, claims Doug Merritt, Icarian's boss, he can summon not just secretaries and assistants but free-lance engineers (for $90–$200 an hour), technical writers ($75–$150), marketing directors ($200–$500), and chief executives ($300–800). . . . Mr Merritt says that business people are becoming ever more like film actors, with talent agents who offer package deals for their "stars." . . . (*The Economist*, January 29, 2000, p. 90)

Dick Ferrington is a 48-year-old employee-training expert who has worked as a temporary for seven of the past nine years. Mr. Ferrington makes close to $100,000 per year without benefits. He has worked recently as an interim vice president for human resources at Scios Nova, a Silicon Valley biotechnology company, where his contract lasted six months. When Mr. Ferrington is between temporary jobs, he hunts for new assignments from his home with a computer, modem, and fax (Rifkin 1995, p. 95).

With the dramatic changes in the relationships among managers and significant stakeholders over the past 20 years, we believe that the US is on the verge of entering into a new paradigm of employment relations. The impetus for such a movement is the change in managerial autonomy resulting from reduced environmental slack associated with global competition and the managerial staffing actions that resulted from it. These actions permanently altered employment relationships as employment became more temporary and contingent (see Sherman and Bohlander 1992). Recent downsizing efforts have been directed toward skilled human capital; skilled employees that globally competitive firms need but cannot retain in long-term employment relationships (see Korman and Associates 1994). We suggest that human resource management is ill-equipped to handle these changes for it will only continue to exacerbate tensions between managers and high-skilled labor, causing further reductions in managerial autonomy. What managers need, and what we see emerging, is a new paradigm of employment relations that grants greater autonomy to managers in the face of environmental changes and stakeholder actions. We label this new paradigm *neoentrepreneurialism*.

Neoentrepreneurialism is a change in the mindset of the employment relationship, where workers are viewed not as employees but as independent contractors. This new paradigm is the result of managements' desire to attract high-skilled, high-wage labor in a manner that allows managers to respond quickly to fluctuations in the global market. By constructing the employment relationship in this manner, managers are able to tap into larger pools of skilled labor, thereby making staffing more predictable. Furthermore, by designing employment contracts to be project and/or time specific, managers preserve their flexibility of action in firm-level decisions. In total, this emerging ideology allows managers to maintain their autonomy in light of factors which were impacting on their task domain. As a result of this paradigm, what we envision is a situation one sees in figure 4.1 (p. 63); growing numbers of firms, skilled workers, and investors in networks of contractual relationships that resemble a diversified investor's stock portfolio. Workers with different types of skilled human capital, then, will return to their former entrepreneurial status as "inside contractors" with groups of investors and small firms housed under a loosely-coupled corporate umbrella (Handy 1989; Boyett and Conn 1992). Hence the term neoentrepreneurialism.

IMPLICATIONS OF NEOENTREPRENEURIALISM

We believe that neoentrepreneurialism will have profound effects on two specific actors within organizations: mid-level managers and unskilled workers. We believe that the role of mid-level managers under neoentrepreneurialism will almost completely disappear. These functions either will be outsourced like the remaining skilled human capital or will be eliminated entirely as supervisory requirements are reduced. The key issue for the managers that remain will be their ability to motivate and coordinate a temporary and contingent workforce whose composition may change from job to job (Handy 1989).

Neoentrepreneurialism will profoundly affect organizational culture as well. With temporary arrangements for both high- and low-skilled employees (the former through contracting and the latter through turnover and termination), the existence of a distinctive corporate culture will be difficult to maintain at best. Indeed, this new paradigm leads one to question whether the cultivation of an organizational culture is even desirable. Given the flexibility that organizations require in responding

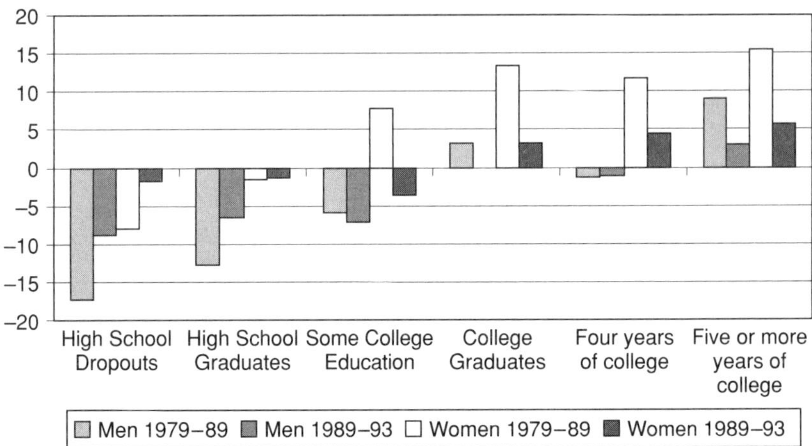

Figure 4.14 Rising earnings gaps by education: percentage change in real hourly earnings, workers' ages 25–64
Source: Gordon 1996, p. 179.

to global competition, one wonders if notions of loyalty and commitment will only serve to impede a firm's adaptability.

For unskilled workers, the result of this new, evolving management paradigm will be quite different (see figure 4.14). Unskilled workers may return to their role as "assistants" of skilled human capital, a position a vast majority of factory workers occupied in the nineteenth century. Here we see little but the continued creation of temporary, unskilled work with low pay and few benefits. Under neoentrepreneurialism, only those with human or financial capital are enfranchised players in the system. Actors without human or financial capital will see little in the way of firm investment in their future and (in some cases) work will be subcontracted to offshore facilities (Boyett and Conn 1992). The increasingly global nature of neoentrepreneurialism means that the different functions and linkages portrayed in figure 4.1 (p. 63) may not occur in the same country.

SUMMARY

Our perspective also has implications for management as a professional project. Specifically, the development of neoentrepreneurialism represents a definitive step in the direction of permanently professionalizing management. The rapid development of business consulting and fee-for-service compensation that is the hallmark of the subcontracting process represents the definitive step in the direction of further professionalization for management. Indeed, one can see this development placing professionalized managers on par with physicians and lawyers in their ability to establish and maintain independent, fee-for-service practice delivery to corporate clients. In this sense, personnel management under neoentrepreneurialism may be headed in the same direction as auditing services in accounting.

Our endeavor has just scratched the surface of the possibilities for examining changes in managerial paradigms and the incentives that managers as professionals have in instituting these changes. But they highlight what we consider to be the central change in the work environment for the managers that are left in the globalized business firm of the twenty-first century; the growth of a collaborative, nonbureaucratic work environment where managers are expected to bring together distinctive groupings of finance and human capital to produce specific products in very rapid periods of time. By itself, none of the evidence we've provided "proves" that managerial work is becoming more like professional work. But the changes discussed above have profoundly altered the meaning of managerial activity and given managers prerogatives to alter traditional work agreements in ways that would have been unthinkable as late as 20 years ago.

We now turn to a discussion of theories of organizational change in the professions. Traditional professional work is changing rapidly as well, which is part and parcel to our argument that managerial and professional work are "changing places."

5

Theoretical Models of Professional Work

Why Use Theories at All?

Some readers might question the need to apply theory to the study of the changing context of professional work. But as we have seen in our attempts to discuss the historical development of professional occupations, it is not even possible to describe the phenomenon without resorting to theory. Without a theory it is impossible to answer many of the most basic questions about professional life, let alone the researchers' motivations for studying it.

To illustrate this point, let's take a few basic questions about professional life and explore them:

1 Why study professions apart from other occupations?
2 Why do professionals enjoy relatively high rewards and social status?
3 Is the typical career of the average professional changing?

These appear to be simple empirical questions. But there are deeply embedded theoretical assumptions behind each one.

Question (1) asks us to discuss the *distinctiveness* of professional work. The answers to questions regarding this distinctiveness may be couched in mundane, everyday terms, but the answers all reflect broad templates of how social stratification operates. Even the answers that parents give to questions about their children's futures have this quality ("get all of the education you can . . ."; "marry a doctor . . ."; "I would be proud of my daughter if she became a lawyer . . ." etc.). If professional work is worthy of separate attention, then there must be something unique about professional work that people can easily identify. Theory gets us beyond the idiosyncrasies of specific professions to describe what constitutes professional occupations as a class of phenomenon worthy of study.

Question (2) asks us to isolate the mechanisms through which professionals acquire status and privilege. Almost all the answers to these questions involve responses to the question "why?" To answer these questions in almost any form, one must resort to theory. If we discover common themes as we attempt to describe professional life, we can place specific examples into general classifications that summarize the experience of large numbers of cases. These classifications then provide a "roadmap" for the study of new cases.

Let's take the simple question, "why do physicians make so much money?" There are several explanations that can be derived from popular theories concerning how and why money and power are distributed across different groups in our society. Physicians have made extensive educational investments that are rewarded because education increases productivity (a human capital explanation). Physicians perform a service that is close to a core value of most societies; physicians' income is simply the latest in a series of historically prestigious rewards given to those involved in healing (a functionalist explanation). Physicians are compensated well because they constitute a professional monopoly. Monopolies often lead to the collection of "rents" from consumers (market and power theories). Physicians' earnings are a manifestation of power domination. Those who traffic in dominant scientific and cultural themes are rewarded by elites interested in maintaining cultural hegemony (a postmodern explanation). Each of these explanations appeals to a theory of rewards in a system of social stratification.

Question (3) requires an appeal to theory in two respects. Change in professional careers implies that there have been typical careers in the past. Descriptions of these typical careers require a theory of careers and the lifecourse (a description of "what one should be doing" at different times when pursuing a specific career). The description of what one should be doing at different stages of a career usually carries normative weight; imagine attempting to practice medicine without a degree from an accredited medical school. The stakes involved include far more than whether or not you would harm patients (after all, doctors often do a fair amount of harm to their patients in the course of treating them). At stake is the capacity to define specific career paths as normative.

Most occupational groups attempt to institutionalize a career path. Institutions are regular patterns of behavior carried out by large numbers of people and oriented toward some core value of society. Changes in career paths challenge the institutional norms of professional work. We think this question has significance because the practices surrounding professional work and the "typical" career patterns of professionals are extensively institutionalized. There are numerous government and private organizations that monitor professional life and practice; consumers expect professional practice to "look" a certain way, and they expect professionals to follow normal career paths. For example, corporate clients and long-term individual clients of law firms expect the firm to recruit from certain law schools (thus guaranteeing a standard level of service style and quality). They also expect that older associates and partners will supervise the work of younger associates. And they expect older partners to manage their most important affairs. Finally, professionals themselves develop strong commitments to institutional norms through socialization, and through their lengthy training periods in professional and graduate schools. Institutional practices often represent the collective wisdom that has emerged over a period of years or decades (see Stinchcombe 1997).

In short, theories provide the basic frames through which we try to describe and study professional life. We will consult a number of theories as we examine changes in professional life in the 1980s and 1990s. As discussed in chapters 1 and 2, these changes have influenced professionals and professional work in a number of ways. Our central problem is not merely deciding which theory is appropriate but at what "level" the change in question has had an effect or has been observed. We will focus on theories that explain change at three levels of analysis: the professional career, the organizational settings in which professional work is performed, and the profession as a whole (as an important institution within society, valued both for the function it performs as well as the norms, values, and patterns of social life it may represent). Each of these three levels of analysis represents a "focus" or "frame" through which professions can be studied, similar to the three levels of analysis familiar to students of organizational behavior and organizational theory: the micro level (the individual performing the work, and that person's job history or career over time), the meso level (the organizational structures surrounding, supporting, and providing patterns to that work), and the macro level (the market, industry, or sector within which those organizations operate, compete and interact). We begin at the micro level.

THEORIES OF CAREERS

One of our basic assumptions in this book is that we need to think about professionals and the organizations in which professional work is performed together. As introduced in chapter 1, professional careers provide a useful window for studying both change in professions and change in organizations simultaneously. Careers are orderly progressions of jobs that represent changes in responsibility, status, and authority. It is through the professional career that the benefits of professional life (status and money) are accrued. Career paths trace the training outcomes (degrees, location of first job, choice of specialty) and job transitions of individuals over their working lives. Professional career paths among the traditional professions have been very slow to change; in fact, many of those careers (doctor, lawyer, academic) have themselves become highly institutionalized – until the last decade or two. Now that the demography of some professions has begun to change, and the range of organizational settings for professional work has expanded, career paths have probably become more diverse, and perhaps linked to individual characteristics such as gender and race. We will examine this issue with data on doctors and lawyers in chapters 6–8.

At this point, we need to consider which theories about careers may be helpful in untangling how professional careers might have (and still are) changing. For this task, we can turn to several theories from research on job mobility in large organizations: contest mobility, sponsored mobility, tournament mobility, and gender queuing.

Under a contest mobility model, candidates for jobs or for promotions within firms are expected to compete openly, and decisions are made after a fairly extended period of time, such as after a probationary period. Classic examples of contest mobility within professions can be found in university tenure systems and large law firms. Within universities, assistant professors are hired under the assumption they will go through six years of hard work to build up their scholarly portfolios and teaching skills, after which they will be evaluated for promotion and tenure. Some will achieve tenure; many will not. Within large law firms, a similar probationary period is experienced by newly-hired associates, and the larger the firm the more likely a number of associates will be hired at the same time. After about six or seven years, they are all reviewed, and only a few will be promoted to junior partner.

Sponsored mobility models differ in a number of critical ways from contest mobility models. Under sponsored mobility, individuals are selected for promotion soon after they begin, and the "anointed" or preselected can either short-circuit the usual probationary period, or enjoy a relatively stress-free probationary period. Both "old boy networks" and "mentoring" are examples of this type of model, and both have been found in management ladders within the private sector, and postwar university tenure systems. They are far less common now, although hooking up with the right mentor in almost any professional setting can make a big difference in terms of having an inside source of information on how the system works and how to increase the odds of promotion.

A combination of these two systems is found in the *tournament mobility model*. This model is historical in the sense that careers are viewed as a sequence of competitions with each competition affecting subsequent promotions in an individual's career. Winners at each selection point have the opportunity to compete at higher levels of the organization, with no assurances of further movement upward. Losers are often excluded from further competition opportunities for higher positions. This model places great emphasis on the role that early promotions play in affecting subsequent promotions. Employees receiving early promotions will have greater opportunities for later promotions. This type of model has been commonly seen in the legal profession (Nelson 1988; Hagan 1990), in management tracks in large corporations (Rosenbaum 1984; Ospina 1996), and in the federal civil service (DiPrete 1989). It is an interesting question whether one or the other of these mobility models will apply to large managed care organizations where physician-administrators are increasingly common. (For more on mobility models see Spilerman 1977; Rosenbaum 1979, 1984; Althauser and Kalleberg 1981; Stewman and Konda 1983; White 1970.)

An alternative (and actually, complementary) model of professional job mobility can be found in gender queuing theory, developed by Reskin and Roos (1990). This model borrows from Thurow's classic work on social inequality (1975), and postulates that employers typically rank potential employees according to their overall desirability. This ranking or "queuing" of potential employees becomes a gender queue through several overlapping processes. First, jobs carry gender labels, and workers rise and fall in the employer's desirability ranking based on the gender label attached to any specific job. Second, employers use gender as a proxy for other characteristics associated with productivity and superior job performance (such as commitment to work, likelihood of quitting, etc.), and sort individuals on the basis of group characteristics. Third, some employers fear that men's productivity will decline if they have not previously worked with female co-workers (or female supervisors). Fourth, some large employers are not particularly concerned with minimizing their labor costs (particularly organizations with professional employees, see Stinchcombe 1990), and would prefer to hire "known" and "reliable" employees – such as white male graduates from the same elite schools where they have always recruited. All of these processes lead employers to place men ahead of women in hiring and promotion queues.

In addition to the queuing of workers by employers, employees themselves construct queues of desirable jobs (Jencks et al. 1988). Men and women both tend to value the same dimensions of work (England 1982), but employers still control access to jobs. As jobs become less desirable, men will leave them for better jobs, and employers may then need to move further down their preference queue to find employees. Women will benefit from this movement, but they will move into jobs that are less desirable than those men move into. Because of the initial existence of the employer preference queue, women's job mobility will be slower and will peak faster than men's job mobility both within and across firms.

The observable results of gender queuing (combined with sponsored and tournament processes) can be found in glass ceilings in management, "mommy tracks" in law, and university professorates where all the full professors and all the senior deans are men, some associate level professors are women, and both men and women compose the most junior ranks. It is possible, however, for pressures from within the organization or from the environment to alter employer queues (through affirmative action programs, where they still exist) so that women (and minority workers) move up the employer's preference ranking (DiMaggio and Powell 1983). The processes of organizational change that can lead to structures and promotion practices that block or promote women and minorities are examined in the next section. These same organizational structures and processes are having an increasingly significant impact on the careers of professional employees across a wide variety of professions.

Theories about Change in Organizations

The study of change in organizations has usually adopted one of two basic models. Change is either conceptualized as the outcome of a rational, strategic process of decision-making in which the organization actively chooses one course of action over another (usually in response to environmental threat), or change is the outcome of environmental selection processes that are outside of the control of any individual organization. These two basic models are usually referred to as the rational choice and population ecology (or selection) models.

Conceptualizations of the environment have also evolved into two categories of environmental constraints or characteristics: technical and institutional environments (Meyer and Scott 1983, 1995; Stinchcombe 1997). Contemporary, *or neo-institutional theory* has made important contributions to our understanding of how the environment of organizations shapes organizational strategies and structures (see Scott 1995 for a particularly thorough treatment). Technical environments involve aspects of the organization's task environment related to the production and market exchange of goods and services; institutional environments encompass the elaborate rules and requirements to which organizations must conform if they are to receive the social and political support and legitimation needed to survive. All organizations are subject to both technical and institutional constraints, with varying levels of intensity. Professional organizations often experience strong pressures from both contexts, such as health care organizations, banks, and to some extent, pharmaceutical firms (Scott 1992). Health care organizations, for example, must respond to the technical demands of modern medicine and calls for cost and quality control, as well as the broad array of governmental regulations and requirements, professional expectations, and certification processes. Many other professional service organizations, such as schools, law firms, and mental health clinics, confront highly constrained institutional environments but weaker technical pressures.

The notion of organizational change as *strategic choice or adaptation* has been a popular one, in that it attempts to explain organizational behavior in terms of monitoring, anticipating, and responding to changes in the environment. Strategy has been used to predict internal structural change, diversification of product or service lines, and involvement in interorganizational alliances, joint ventures, networks, or consortia (see work by Williamson 1985; Chandler 1990; Powell 1990; Schlesinger 1998). One area of strategy research in which there has been renewed interest and which is particularly relevant to professional organizations is on the *role of governing boards* in the strategic management process. Governing boards have long been ignored in the application of organizational theory to various public and private sector firms, often because of the postwar environment of growth and plush resources. For example, observers assumed that most hospital boards performed either a purely external linkage role (Pfeffer 1973), or a symbolic role (as was often the case with university boards of trustees, or nonprofit foundations), and had little to do with long-term strategy formulation or day-to-day operation of the organization. Such a passive role is no longer defined as appropriate for health care, educational, or philanthropic organizations, and the performance and vitality of governing boards, as well as their relationships to CEOs, are increasingly scrutinized as factors involved in strategy formulation, both for internal management and linking strategies (such as board interlocks; see Mizruchi 1982; Domhoff 1986; Fennell and Alexander 1989).

The *resource dependence* framework also assumes that the organization has some active role in responding to environmental influences, but focuses specifically on the linkages developed between organizations in order to acquire needed resources (Pfeffer and Salancik 1978). This perspective has been developed by a number of organizational theorists, and includes work on political economy by Zald (1970), and power dependency (Emerson 1962; Thompson 1967). The basic assumption of resource dependence theory is that relationships of power/dependency develop between organizations because less powerful organizations need to align with resource-rich organizations to ensure access to needed resources. This is a familiar type of strategy in the public sector and among nonprofit organizations.

Two important economics-based variants of resource dependence include *agency theory* and *transaction cost analysis*. Agency theory applies to the problem of motivating and controlling cooperative action between two actors, a principal seeking to achieve some outcome, and the agent whose assistance is needed in order to reach the goal of the principal. Economists assume that both parties are motivated by self-interest, and the problem arises in being able to ensure that each is doing his/her fair share. This approach has been applied to the study of acquisitions and mergers, board and managerial relations, and is quite suitable as a framework to investigate relationships between managers and professional employees (Jensen and Mackling 1976; Fama 1980; Eisenhardt 1989).

Agency theory is closely related to *transaction cost analysis* (Williamson 1975). Transaction cost analysis offers an alternative explanation for when and why organizations are likely to integrate with other organizations. In this theory, organizations are viewed as systems for managing exchanges or transactions. There are costs involved in any negotiation or exchange. To the extent that transactions are frequent and critical to the organization, the organization benefits from trying to control them by incorporating them internally into the organization or creating more formal linkages to the other organizations involved. For the study of professional organizations of the late twentieth century and the new millennium, this approach has clear advantages for examining decisions to outsource professional services, contract with professional groups, or vertically integrate.

The *population ecology* or selection approach uses a completely different perspective on what causes change in organizations, and a different level of analysis as well. Selection theorists focus on organizational populations, rather than on the actions of individual organizations, and they define environmental forces as the catalysts for all significant population level changes in form or type. The actions (or inactions) of managers are much less important in this perspective, and the timeframe for change is much longer. The study of population-level dynamics of organizational growth, variation, replacement, and survival unfolds over decades rather than years, and the need for systematic population-level longitudinal data is crucial. Because of the difficulty of identifying such longitudinal databases on professional organizations, the number of empirical studies using this perspective is somewhat limited. The best opportunities have been found in health care, where longitudinal databases on populations of health care providers do exist (see work by Alexander and Amburgey 1987; D'Aunno and Zuckerman 1987; Ricketts et al. 1987; Christianson et al. 1991; Renshaw et al. 1990).

PROFESSIONS AS INSTITUTIONS

At this level of analysis we are interested in examining professions at a macro level of analysis: as institutions within society that cross organizational boundaries. Institutions are broadly defined as social forms with a fixed or distinctive character, one that provides meaning as a vehicle of group identity or as a "receptacle of vested interests" (Broom and Selznick 1973). Professions as institutions, then, represent identifiable structures of knowledge, expertise, work, and labor markets, with distinctive norms, practices, ideologies, and organizational forms. Theories at this level tend to focus on the knowledge systems or power relationships that shape those institutions.

Liberal/technocratic theories

Some theories of professional life explain the professions as a product of distinct role demands in postindustrial capitalism (Bell 1976; Inglehart 1990; Manza and Brooks 1999). These theories claim that the demands of an increasingly technological society increase demands for highly educated people to fill complex jobs. The rise of technological complexity leads to the search for qualified people to fill these highly specialized roles. The process of filling and enacting these complex roles creates a technocratic professional elite that applies their knowledge to a broad spectrum of problems. The susceptibility of wider sets of problems to technocratic solutions has led some in this group to predict the "end of ideology" (see Bell 1976).

The tone of most liberal technocratic analyses of professional life is decidedly functionalist. The spread of technology creates roles and the demand for highly educated people. But there have been recent developments that offer other interpretations within the liberal/technocratic framework. Recently, authors have spoke with some alarm about the creation of a globalized, highly technocratic economy (see Rifkin 1995; Wilson 1997; Gordon 1996; Massey 1996). While these writers don't claim that educated people have a conspiratorial agenda (that is left to power explanations of professional life) they do suspect that the consequences of an increasingly technical, globalized economy are far from the utopia portrayed by some of the more strident supporters of the "end of ideology" thesis (Toffler 1990; Naisbitt 1994). These writers point to massive social and community dislocations, rising economic inequality, residential segregation, and the concentration of the poor and unemployed in cities as consequences of a technologically sophisticated economy that demands a highly educated workforce. Labor markets increasingly exert a global reach as nations compete for scarce pools of highly educated labor. The result of this international competition is a "brain drain" from the less-developed world to the developed world and rising residential, social, and cultural segregation of urban areas (see Bradshaw and Wallace 1996; Massey 1996). Some writers in the liberal/technocratic tradition even describe the possible creation of a "global overclass" of economically prosperous, highly educated scientists, technicians, and financiers who will increasingly share a common, segregated, elite subculture (Massey 1996).

The other variant of liberal/technocratic models closely examines the changing social and cultural links of professionals and highly educated workers. The purpose of this investigation is to discover whether or not professionals and experts are starting to occupy distinctive positions in the social structure of advanced capitalism (see Inglehart 1990; Manza and Brooks 1999). Many of these investigations discuss the existence of a "new class" of economically prosperous, postmaterialist, socially liberal citizens with distinctive worldviews and political orientations. These orientations do not fit easily into traditional liberal or conservative ideologies (see Giddens 1994). The empirical evidence for this "new class" is considerable, but researchers disagree about the political and social implications (see Brint 1994).

Criticisms of liberal/technocratic theories tend to focus on the benign roles assigned to technology and economic development in the creation of professional roles. The impression one gets from early work in this tradition is that persistent problems of postindustrial development produce unconscious role demands and that professionals are the natural and inevitable solution. Scholarship in the sociology of work since the 1970s has questioned whether many aspects of the contemporary division of labor are natural or inevitable (see Braverman 1974; Littler 1982; Edwards 1979; Form 1987). Others don't think there is any easy one-to-one relationship between specific technologies and specific ways of organizing the division of labor (see Burawoy 1979, 1985). These criticisms apply to the creation of skilled professional work in addition to the division of labor among unskilled and skilled craft workers.

Recent research on the "new class" cannot be dismissed so easily. While some in this area are agnostic concerning the existence of jobs with specific bundles of role expectations and are content to study the consequences of occupying these positions for other aspects of social life, others examine whether professional roles increasingly are under attack and whether defense of professional "life space" constitutes a basis for distinctive political organizations (see Castells 1996; Manza and Brooks 1999).

Regardless of the criticisms, liberal/technocratic theories ask us to examine closely the role that expert knowledge plays in the larger social order. The variants either ask us to take professional roles for granted and study the consequences of their spread, or they ask us to question whether the larger role of technical knowledge is changing in a globalized world and (if so) how. Shorn of its functionalist/evolutionary assumptions there is still much to be said for this tradition.

Power theories

Power theories of professionals and professional activity shift our focus toward the prerogatives and status accruing to professionals. There are several variations on the basic themes that power theories use. All power theories of professional activity begin with the observation that professionals possess considerable power and social status. Contrary to expertise or liberal/technocratic theories, power theories are skeptical that professional status and prerogatives flow from the mere possession of exert knowledge. Instead, the rewards of professional life are a product of conscious attempts by professionals or their patrons to extract economic and social "rents" from consumers or to exercise social control. Where power theories diverge is with regard to the benefactors of the monopolization of professional knowledge and whether professional knowledge constitutes a distinctive, superior way to understand the increasingly technical problems of late modernity.

Some power theories locate professional power within the organization of the professions themselves. These theories claim that professional interest groups attempt to gain control over the supply and production of new professionals as well as control over the locations and conditions of professional work. Professional associations exert this control by enforcing stringent educational requirements that bear only a marginal relationship to the performance of professional roles. Attempts to create licensed monopolies also falls under attempts to regulate the supply of professionals, driving-up prices and limiting practice to accepted and established methods. These theories assume professional groups extract financial and social rents from their knowledge for the benefit of the status and autonomy of professionals themselves.

A slight variant of this first group of theories claims that the organization of professional work and labor markets serves a "social closure" function. In addition to restricting the supply of professionals in order to keep demand and fees high, this variant of power theories claims that educational and licensing requirements are part of a larger agenda to limit professional practice to high-status social groups (Protestants, whites, and men). This group of theories claims that economic rents are extracted from consumers of professional knowledge because social rewards generally move in the direction of occupations with high-status occupants. Typically, this variant of power theory is used to explain gender and racial inequality within subfields of the professions in addition to examining the relatively privileged position of professionals themselves.

Yet another variant of this first group of power theories attempts to explain inequality among specialty groups within the professions. These theories point to the increasingly skewed distribution of professionals in the direction of glamorous and visible subspecialties that do not necessarily reflect what the distribution of professionals would look like if the "service ideal" were truly operative. For example, the distribution of power and influence in medicine is skewed in the direction of drastic interventions that fight the advanced stages of serious, potentially terminal diseases. The provision of basic preventive care and the promotion of public health have taken a backseat in the prestige and rewards of medicine. In law the subspecialties that are most highly rewarded represent transactions that protect the interests of highly visible and prestigious corporate clients. Lawyers more interested in public interest and constitutional law are consigned to a professional life of lower compensation and prestige. The only explanation for these skewed rewards and the distribution of professionals across specialties is that professionals are pursuing compensation and prestige much like incumbents of occupations that lack service ideals.

But is that the only reason for the observation that rewards and compensation are not equally distributed across specialties within professions?

Marxist variants of power theories suggest not. In addition to the motivations of individual professionals, Marxist scholars suggest that the structure of professional incentives is tilted toward specialties that service the rich and powerful. Through the funding of scientific and medical research, and the financing of rewards through professional fees, professionals are encouraged to take up subspecialties that have paying customers. Since, for example, basic health care is not a problem among the affluent, medicine has oriented itself toward drastic interventions designed to prolong life rather than more modest goals of basic health-care for all. In the legal profession, the compensation available from commercial real estate transactions, lawsuits, and protection from government regulations dwarf by several times over the compensation of lawyers in family or criminal law. In the minds of these scholars professional work exists to serve the interests of elites, both by providing services geared toward them and by acting as instruments of social control over the rest of the population.

Yet another variant of power theories questions whether professional knowledge is distinctive or valuable (see Illich 1982). This postmodern variant of power theory views the very existence of professional knowledge as an expression of power and domination. Not only are the knowledge claims of professionals dubious, but also those claims privilege scientific and technical knowledge at the expense of intuitive, practical knowledge. The end result of this process is the political and social disenfranchisement of nonprivileged groups.

A distinctive substream of postmodern professional theories makes a series of claims that are the opposite of those made by other theories in this tradition. Rather than questioning where professional prerogatives and prestige come from, what the knowledge claims of professionals lead to, or the links between professionals and other dominant groups, this group of scholars asks whether the control and prerogatives of professional work have shifted away from professional groups toward superordiant organizations that do not represent the interests of professionals themselves (see Larsen 1977). These writers suggest that professional prerogatives have been under attack by an increasingly skeptical public and by other occupational groups seeking to control costs. In this variant of power theory, an educated, knowledge consuming, and quasi-organized set of consumers are seeking to reorganize professional services. This reorganization constitutes a direct threat to professional prerogatives similar to the deskilling and proletarianization of an earlier era.

The strengths of most power theories lie in the decoupling of knowledge from the specific organizational forms attempting to use it. Clearly, there are manipulative practices engaged in by professional societies that are designed to increase the compensation of professionals apart from the social utility of the services professionals provide. The claims that the distribution of professionals across specialties reflects the interest of elites is not necessarily in dispute either. The weaknesses of this perspective lie in its overemphasis on the behavior of elites and relative lack of emphasis on the actions of average consumers. While elites might drive the market for highly visible and glamorous specialized professional work, nonelites accord a great deal of authority and legitimacy to the professions that cannot be easily summarized by the manipulative tactics of professional groups or the hegemonic control of elites (see Starr 1982). While the rise of professions as important and prestigious occupations is certainly linked to the actions of organized professionals themselves, these processes are discussed as if their success is taken for granted and that success in professionalizing an occupation is relatively easy. But research on the history of professions is replete with stumbles and pitfalls of professional groups that aren't sure how to organize or rationalize professional identities. This active stumbling around by professionals themselves, and the eventual consolidation of some professional claims over others, is almost certainly a product of a more complex set of forces than the manipulative capabilities of professionals or economic elites.

Further, most power analyses of professional prerogatives assume that the knowledge claims of professionals work as a legitimizing activity. They typically use medicine and law as examples of deeply entrenched, legitimized professions that serve primarily an elite clientele. But this perspective has difficulty explaining why these same professional groups are under attack and the predominant organizational forms for the delivery of services are changing. One would presume that professional dominance and elite sponsorship counted for more than it apparently does.

SUMMARY

In the next three chapters, we attempt to show the utility of applying an institutional approach to the study of changes in professional and managerial work. We return to theories of professions as institutions in our concluding chapter, summarizing our analysis and discussion of the place of managers and professional in the elite division of labor. Chapter 6 more closely examines these changes in the organizational context of managerial and professional work with an eye toward furthering our understanding of some of the connections between them.

6

Change in the Organizational Context of Managerial and Professional Work

The major thesis of our book is that the work that managers and professionals do is starting to look more similar to each other. We think that the economic and political events of the 1980s have helped to move the relationship between managers and professionals toward convergence in organizational forms. This convergence is (to a great extent) unintentional and (probably) unconscious on the part of the participants involved.

We base our thesis on the behavior of elite managers, their perceptions of their prerogatives (the activities they believe they are entitled to control, based on their own judgments as managers), and our perceptions of developments in the creation of team-oriented, streamlined, nonbureaucratic workplaces that elite managers are helping to create.

Our thesis also is based on perceptions of change in professional work. The 1980s have witnessed an exponential growth in concerns about accountability and prerogatives exercised by professionals. The resulting growth in external controls is unnerving to most members of the professions and has disrupted traditional professional routines that other significant stakeholders have come to rely on.[1] Almost all professional groups now have significant committees within their professional associations that monitor "the state of the profession," including (but not limited to) working conditions, compensation, organizational oversight, credentialing issues, and competition from other occupational groups. The discussion of unionization among physicians and other healthcare professionals is the most visible sign of concerns about the effects of organizational oversight on professional conditions and standards of work.

While we doubt that you (or we) will ever see managers and professionals explicitly discussing this convergence in the organization of work, we think that this convergence may be one of the more central trends of the early twenty-first century workplace. This trend (if it continues) would be very significant because it affects those usually thought of as the privileged entrants to the labor market; those with the credentials and education to command considerable earnings power, considerable autonomy, and considerable responsibility from their jobs.

We also doubt that you will find a "smoking gun" among managers; managers talking in terms of expanding their prerogatives. Part of the reason that we doubt that you will find this in significant public discussions about managerial work (and especially elite managerial work) is because a well-developed ideology that justifies managerial activity has existed for quite some time. Managers (and the business community generally) have taken a critical view of economic trends since the 1970s and the role that the federal government has played in regulating business activity. In the minds of many (including significant segments of the business press writing for the *Wall Street Journal*, *Fortune*, *Business Week*, and *The Economist*), the 1980s and 1990s are seen as a return of managers to their rightful place as producers of profit for investors in an environment that was increasingly shorn of regulations over financial transactions.

However, if one looks hard at the trends, doesn't it appear that managers are exercising prerogatives over their work that look more like those professionals have traditionally claimed for themselves? We highlight several 1980s trends that we think shed light on this issue.

DEINDUSTRIALIZATION – THE PURSUIT OF PROFIT COMES TO THE FOREFRONT

Most of us know (at least from newspapers and the personal accounts of friends and relatives) that the 1980s was a time of serious economic restructuring in the US economy and in most of the world's developed economies.[2] These changes go under a variety of names but social scientists often refer to these changes under the term deindustrialization.

Deindustrialization is the systematic disinvestment in a nation's manufacturing capacity and infrastructure (see Bluestone and Harrison 1982). Like many diseases, deindustrialization has numerous "symptoms" that are indicators of a general trend toward declining emphasis on manufacturing activity. Taken together these symptoms usually point to an economy that is engaging in deindustrialization.

The most obvious symptom of deindustrialization in the 1980s was mass layoffs of manufacturing workers. These workers usually made better-than-average wages in manufacturing jobs. The difference between layoffs during the deindustrialization phase and layoffs that have occurred at other times in the manufacturing sector of the economy is that this latest round of layoffs appears to be relatively permanent. Nonsupervisory workers were losing jobs that they had little prospect of getting back. They also have little prospect of finding jobs with similar wages and fringe benefits without extensive retraining.

Plant closings often accompanied mass layoffs during deindustrialization. Announcements of plant closings often were met with disbelief and (in some cases) anger and outrage. In many cases the plants that were closed in the 1980s had been operating in their present locations for decades, and it wasn't unusual for families to all work in specific plants for several generations. Sometimes plant closings represented a permanent change in the mix of products that a corporation was going to market. At other times plant closings in one place were accompanied by plant openings someplace else, usually someplace with more favorable labor costs and fewer business regulations. Plant closings tend to be more devastating than layoffs because local communities and business leaders start to look feverishly for new tenants for industrial property that normally falls into disrepair as the plant prepares to close (see C. Perrucci et al. 1988).

Another symptom of deindustrialization is only noticeable by relatively perceptive people who pay attention to overall industry trends. Declines in capital investments produce a situation where employees are required to maintain productivity goals with outdated and (in some cases) worn out machinery. The diversion of capital from the replacement of machines to other uses is usually a sign that a corporation is disinvesting in a production process. It is usually just a matter of time before specific plants become uncompetitive because the machinery used is not in good repair and is not producing at the rates produced by newer facilities in other locations (sometimes in very distant parts of the world, see Porter 1990).

A related symptom of deindustrialization is the phenomenon referred to as "milking." When a corporation "milks" a plant they run production at full speed but they invest the profits from the existing operation in a new operation at another location. Once the new location is on-line and ready to run, the days are numbered for the old operation. At some point (usually after an initial competition between the new and old facilities) the old facility is closed, leaving the new facility to produce the product at a brand new site.

Finally, the 1980s were especially characterized as a time when corporate takeovers were rampant. The deregulation of the financial industry in the United States produced considerable changes in investment vehicles, changes that make the production of quick profits more likely and that de-emphasized the production of long-term profitability for stockholders. From the standpoint of deindustrialization, the most pertinent method for financing corporate takeovers was to take on greater levels of corporate debt in an attempt to buy pieces of other corporations. This would often lead to "stock swaps" at inflated prices. These stock swaps would increase the compensation of corporate executives whose stock option benefits were tied to the price of specific stocks. The desire to raise capital to participate in contests in the "market for corporate control" often led corporations to cut their subsidiaries into separate functioning parts to be sold off individually to the highest bidder. The long-term profitability prospects for most of these divested subsidiaries are not good (see *Academy of Management Journal* 1998), but the short-term profits made from the divestiture made handsome profits for the company doing the divesting.

None of these trends by themselves provides support for our thesis that professional and managerial work is becoming more alike. But we think that the roles that managers have played in these changes have put the spotlight on managerial prerogatives and the effects that managerial decision-making has on the lives of other significant stakeholders in specific production operations. As communities, politicians, and citizens question the decisions that managers make, managers have had to justify their specific decisions and their presumed rights to make such decisions without outside interference. This has put managers in a similar position that professionals find themselves in when they defend their prerogatives against those who complain about costs, quality, and accountability.

Capital flight and global capital flows

The economic changes in the 1980s and 1990s involved far more than the layoffs of some nonsupervisory employees and the closing of some manufacturing plants. Some have argued that these economic changes were accompanied by *capital flight*; the systematic flow of investment capital from traditional uses toward new uses in an internationalized, global economy.

The ability of finance capital to relocate to wherever investment returns are the highest is one of the hallmark characteristics of the new global economy (see Castells 1996). The capital that is moving from place to place at seemingly breakneck speeds comes from increasingly diverse sources as well, as our presentation and data in chapter 4 makes clear (see Castells 1996). While much investment capital still originates in the United States and the other industrialized countries of western Europe and Asia, that capital is increasingly crossing national borders. There is considerable debate about whether investment capital is (as a whole) moving from the relatively developed northern hemisphere toward the relatively undeveloped southern hemisphere (see Wallerstein 1997; Biggart 1999). But few analysts and observers doubt that financial capital increasingly moves around the world in search of better and more lucrative short-term returns.

The movement of financial capital is fueled by computer technology, financial deregulation, the lowering of trade barriers (through such agreements as NAFTA, GATT, and organizations such as the World Trade Organization and the World Bank), automated production processes that can be set up quickly just about anywhere, and large differences in labor costs, regulations, and militancy (see Florida and Kinney 1993). The ability to continually monitor investments has helped to fuel a global frenzy for high short-term financial returns. The time horizons for evaluating "good returns" to productive investments has shortened, and the ability to instantly move money from one national market to another has accelerated the speed with which new investment opportunities can be pursued (and old opportunities can be divested).

Supporters of this trend laud the new investment opportunities as a major producer of economic growth, new jobs, and new opportunities for integration into a truly global economy where everyone has a chance to participate. These new opportunities include new opportunities for skilled labor to move internationally across what were once insurmountable barriers, and opportunities for people from isolated areas to have access to jobs and financial opportunities that have long been closed to them.

Detractors point to rising income inequality and social and economic stability that results when investors "troll" the world looking to make a "fast buck" (see Korten 1999). Most detractors suggest that economic growth in new locations is rarely (if ever) equitably distributed, and the disruptions of traditional ways of life often leave a majority of the population worse off than they were before their exposure to the economic engines of the developed world (see Korten 1995). Others point to developmental distortions in underdeveloped parts of the world that will prevent their economies from ever looking like the economies of the developed world (see Frank 1966; Wallerstein 1997).

The increased volume and velocity of capital flight has left communities in an escalating competition for investment opportunities. This competition has had numerous consequences from the "brain drain" of educated people from undeveloped communities to developed ones, the "overurbanization" of central cities in rapidly developing regions of the world, to the race by local and regional governments to provide incentives to investment capitalists that reduce their factor costs, taxes, and regulatory exposure (see Leicht and Jenkins 1998).

Elite managers are increasingly at the forefront of those who claim that the ability to control and make decisions about investments is the driving force of market economies and is essential for the welfare of everyone. The very real human consequences and responsibilities for layoffs and plant closings have been combined with claims about investment decisions. Both decisions are critical to other constituencies in market economies. This control has given elite managers serious power to decide the fates of individual employees, communities, and the workings of governments and national social stratification systems. The increasingly voluminous claims that such decisions should be made "without interference from outsiders" has increased our perception that managers are making claims of expertise over a significant dimension of social life that is similar in tone and consequence to claims of autonomy and prerogatives among professionals.

The changing managerial project

Earlier we discussed extensively the concept of the professional project. Professional projects encompass all attempts to establish and defend the jurisdiction over a decision domain against potential competitors. Here our major argument is that pressure by investors to find continually higher returns has driven much of the deindustrialization that we've seen (see Biggart 1999). As investors have become more impatient, managers have increasingly asserted their prerogatives regarding when and how to invest, when to choose opportunities, and when to relocate operations to other communities or nations. They have become more strident in their insistence that other stakeholders cannot interfere with these decisions or else aggregate profits will decline and the consumption pie will not grow for everybody.

This claim of (more or less) absolute control has pitted elite managers against "rank-and-file" middle managers, employees, local government officials, and communities. These stakeholders often claim that they're "out of the loop" or "out in the cold" as managers make decisions that have big effects on their lives (see *New York Times* 1996). Managerial claims of prerogatives over investment and employment decisions have become increasingly strident as other stakeholders question corporate decision-making. But managers insist that their decisions are based on their understanding of business climates and are an essential part of their responsibilities as representatives of investors. Managerial opponents point to the ability of managers to "line their pockets" through short-term capital manipulations, stock sell-offs and other schemes that raise managers' compensation, but do not improve the performance of the company (see Gordon 1996).

The end of the social contract between the classes

These increasingly strident claims on both sides of the issue of economic restructuring has led some researchers to claim that there has been a severing of the social contract between the classes. But what did this contract actually involve and was the contract real or simply inferred from established patterns of behavior?

Industrial capitalism after World War II was based on a simple, though fundamental agreement between the social classes. Investors, in exchange for taking entrepreneurial risks with their money, were entitled to competitive returns to their investments. Employees, in exchange for diligent work on behalf of corporations, were entitled to relatively secure careers, some chances for advancement and promotion, pay raises, and fringe benefits. As long as productivity was improving and national and global economies were growing, employees could be provided with these guarantees and investors could make competitive returns on their investments.

But starting in the early 1970s, investors began to complain about falling rates of profit and shrinking returns to investments. Productivity growth seemed to be stalled. But employee expectations about steady careers, higher wages, and better fringe benefits were not stalled. The (seeming) inability to change employee expectations in the face of downturns in productivity is widely blamed for the "stagflation" of the late 1970s (see O'Connor 1973; Stein 1983).[3] This was not the only explanation for stagflation, but it was one that was most salient in the minds of many managers and investors. Organized labor, in particular, was blamed for negotiating contracts that provided liberal pay increases without productivity gains, elaborate fringe benefits, and complex (and inflexible) staffing plans that prevented new innovations in production activity.

Many investors and managers also blamed the government (and especially Keynesian Demand Management practices of the federal government) for discouraging savings and promoting excessive consumption that fueled the inflation of the late 1970s. Others claimed that the growing volume of government regulations over employment standards and investments was putting US investors and managers at a handicap in their increasing competition with foreign corporations.

Regardless of the explanation one accepted, productivity growth in the US in the 1970s fell to the lowest in the industrialized world. The major popular culprits for this decline were union work contracts and a social contract that exchanged extensive promises of future compensation for a lifetime of effort on the part of employees.

Investors increasingly demanded more flexibility in allocating capital and labor. The wave of merger and acquisition activity during the 1980s was part of a larger effort to produce greater short-term capital returns while reorganizing the economy away from the implied social contract that had governed relations between the classes for over 30 years.

The resulting dissatisfaction with stagflation and the growing chorus of complaints about the inflexibility of the current production system played a big role in the election of President Ronald Reagan in 1980. The Reagan administration campaigned on an explicit platform to "get government off of our backs" and to turn loose the entrepreneurial spirit of unregulated capitalism. The ability of the Reagan administration to dismantle various parts of government regulation has been debated ever since he left office in 1988. However, there is little doubt that the Reagan administration accelerated two trends that were underway before he came into office; the deregulation of strategic industries (including banking and finance) and the deregulation of labor markets.

The aggregate result of declining productivity and changes in the regulation of markets has contributed, we think, to gradual divorce of the social contract between the classes. Financial capital and the managers that represent them no longer need a stable, productive, and happy workforce to realize gains from their investments. For their part compensation, fringe benefits, and interesting work for employees are no longer tied to investment gains either. There is, then, increasingly less relationship between economic gains for investors and economic opportunities for everyone else. This has produced an environment where managerial prerogatives are increasingly (and stridently) questioned.

Professional Work and Changes in Workplace Skills

Professionals have faced a different set of challenges in the workplace. These challenges do not easily fit into ready-made terms like "proletarianization," "deskilling," "deprofessionalization," or "reprofessionalization." Instead, we see a myriad of forces affecting the future of professional work. Some of these forces act to increase the power, prerogatives, and status of professionals. Others act to decrease and constrain the use of professional skills with resulting declines in occupational prestige and (ultimately) compensation. Many of these changes are the result of various "crises" in professional work life. We argue that these changes have helped to make professional workplaces more like the workplaces managers aspire to control. We make this prediction (in part) because business managers have taken the lead in several challenges to traditional professional activities and prerogatives.

Professionals and the crisis of accountability

The economic crises of the late 1970s and early 1980s helped fuel an increased questioning of professional practices as professional fees for service have risen at several times the rate of inflation (see Congressional Budget Office 1997). We refer to the questions resulting from these economic changes as the *crisis of accountability*.

Increasingly, professionals of all kinds are asked to account for the expenses they bill for and incur. Nowhere has the magnifying glass of accountability been focused more than on health care costs and the billing practices of physicians. In the 1980s, employers started drastically reorganizing and downsizing their healthcare plans in an attempt to control employment costs. Many employers shifted from traditional insurance plans to HMOs and PPOs. Others simply eliminated health care benefits altogether. Employers and large health insurers began to ask serious questions about the services they were paying for, whether some procedures were necessary for the health of patients, and whether some procedures were overutilized because of the availability of traditional healthcare plans to pay for them.

Health insurers, facing a potential catastrophic decline in employers' business, began offering alternatives to traditional fee-for-service health care. These new organizational forms were designed to control costs, make physicians accountable for the procedures they performed, and to standardize compensation for procedures performed by different physicians. Many PPOs and HMOs went to "treatment protocols" that required relatively standardized procedures and billing norms, using "utilization committees" and other forms of managerial oversight to catch (and eventually penalize) physicians who strayed from organizationally proscribed norms. Medicare and Medicaid, the two largest components of the US Federal Budget after defense, went to prospective payment plans that paid fixed reimbursement prices for medical procedures. Health care facilities that could perform these procedures for less than the standard rate made money. Those that couldn't lost money.

Other professional groups besides physicians are facing increased scrutiny and calls for accountability that are altering the norms of professional practice. Pharmacies are increasingly automated and pharmacists rarely (if ever) mix their own medicines anymore (a once common practice). College professors increasingly must account for the number of hours they spend in classrooms in front of students and the time spent away from this activity is increasingly scrutinized and analyzed by administrators, boards of trustees, and government officials. Lawyers must increasingly justify the fees they charge, and often face clients who will "put out bids" for legal services and hire firms on a price-sensitive basis. Scientists must increasingly justify the "cost effectiveness" of their work amid a rising chorus of those who question the contributions of basic science to the betterment of the human condition (see Illich 1982).

The most effective challenges to professional authority, prerogatives, and compensation have come from large organized consumers like corporations. Individual consumers are rarely in a position to question the wisdom of professional practices, but corporations (through their control of access to clients and money to pay for professional services) have made considerable progress in reorganizing the delivery of numerous professional services to "lower costs" and "increase accountability."[4]

Professionals captured by clients or technologies

In a related trend, some professional groups have faced a situation where either consumers (clients) or new ways of performing work (technologies) will undermine professional prerogatives and status. We refer to these trends under the heading of professions "captured" by clients or technologies. Under *client capture* the consumers of professional work gain the ability to control the activities, timing, and costs of professional work. In effect the "consumer becomes sovereign" much as consumers search for (and price) other consumer goods and services. Under *technological capture* a new way of performing professional work (usually a machine or computer) gains control over the skills involved in delivering professional services. In both cases professionals find their work affected by consumer desires and technological dictates that are outside of the realm of the normal professional/client relationship.

Lawyers (arguably) are the prototypical example of a professional group that faces continual threats of "capture" by clients and their interests. Ideally, lawyers are "officers of the court" whose first loyalty is to the law and the legal system that defines and extends the law. In this role lawyers represent clients in their interactions with the system of the law, reconciling conflicting interests and coming to agreements according to prespecified frameworks. They also counsel their clients away from actions that are contrary to the law and that could (potentially) undermine the system of law.

Ultimately the practice of law is tied directly or indirectly to the overall functioning of the economy. Most lawyers regulate and control property transactions of some kind (deeds, wills, real estate, torts, corporate stock transactions, reorganizations, divestitures, mergers, labor relations, and product liability). In spite of the high visibility of constitutional law and the relationship between constitutional law and individual liberties and freedoms (witness the relative fame of Supreme Court decisions like *Miranda* compared to decisions like *Griggs v. Duke Power Company*), corporate clients and relatively routine transactions are the bread and butter of legal practice.

As legal fees rose in the 1970s at several times the rate of inflation, and as new sets of complex government regulations made the number and importance of legal transactions rise for corporations, large corporations (and some smaller ones) started to hire salaried attorneys to do routine legal work. This reduced the income that legal firms derived from corporate retainers and ultimately compromised the independence of lawyers in legal firms and those who were hired as salaried attorneys by corporations.

As the old saying goes, "if you have small debts, the bank owns you; if you have large ones, you own the bank." The same process has been working with the system of securing compensation for legal work. An increasingly educated, concentrated, and cost-conscious corporate world has started to "shop" for the legal services they consume. Both routine and nonroutine legal work is given to specialized practitioners who are increasingly dependent on one or a few clients for specific types of business. The net result of this process is that the client can dictate what types of services they want and how much money they will pay for them. The long-term professional relationship between clients and firms has been replaced by "one shot" shopping where each complex legal transaction is either "farmed out" to specialized firms that conduct specific types of transactions or "taken down the hall" to the "legal eagles" who will take care of the problem the corporation has. These changes are a far cry from the independent practitioner representing the legal system to clients who passively consume advice on how best to make their way through a system of specialized and esoteric knowledge.

Technological capture is threatening numerous professional work contexts from architecture to medicine. The increasing availability and decision-making capabilities of computers threatens to standardize professional decision-making and (more importantly) make some types of professional knowledge routinely available to nonprofessionals. In architecture, the increasingly sophisticated use of graphics programs (and the computational capabilities they contain) threatens the control that architects exercise over design specifications, technical specifications, and knowledge of building codes. These technologies raise the prospect of standardized, mass-produced designs that can be tailored to specific locations with little or no professional input. In law, increasingly sophisticated search engines and computer data bases (like westlaw. com) have altered the nature of legal research, rendering the ability to assemble and collate large amounts of information easier, faster, and much less labor intensive. In pharmacy, computers increasingly scan medications proscribed for specific patients for incompatibilities and potential complications. College professors face challenges from universities that offer "distance learning," a "talking head" on a television screen that broadcasts lectures and discussions around states, nations, and (increasingly) around the world. Even in medicine, traditionally the bastion of nuanced professional judgment and the exercise of decision-making prerogatives, expert knowledge systems threaten to do much of the preliminary decision-making for doctors during the diagnosis phase of medical practice, leaving the physician to apply treatment protocols outlined by computers that have eliminated a whole host of illnesses through the use of complex decision-making rules.

In most cases, client and technological capture threaten professionals with declining demand for their services as service provision is "stretched" by new ways of delivering services and clients "shop around" for the individual services they wish to consume. They also threaten professionals with lower compensation as the technological intensity of work replaces human intervention as the purveyor of the knowledge base on which the profession depends.

Professionals compromised by tight labor markets

One of the hallmark characteristics that define professional work is the extensive control over the labor market that most professions attempt to exercise. This control is usually exercised through a system of *credentialing* that certifies that only certain groups of people with specific sets of educational experiences are qualified to practice a profession. Implicitly (or explicitly) control over credentialing activities is also a mechanism for controlling the labor market for professionals and assuring that there is sufficient demand for professional services to keep qualified practitioners occupied and well compensated.

Professions can lose control over their labor markets through a variety of mechanisms, but most of this loss of control produces the same result; a tighter labor market with more practitioners going after the same (or a shrinking number of) clients. The major mechanism that produces a tight labor market is an oversupply of professionals. This can occur because the profession loses control over credentialing, either because they lose the exclusive right to provide a professional service or because other stakeholders in the profession have an interest in increasing the number and locations of training in professional practice.

An example of a professional group that is fighting for exclusive control over credentialing is nursing. Traditionally nurses in the post-World War II era have been trained in either two- or four-year programs, most of them run by traditional four-year colleges and universities and (occasionally) by non-profit hospitals (in the case of two-year programs). As the demand for nurses has risen and the starting pay for nurses with Bachelor's degrees has increased, hospitals have looked for other ways of filling nursing slots, including the substitution of noncredentialed hospital workers for nurses in traditional nursing roles. Many of these noncredentialed workers are trained by other hospital staff, paid a fraction of what a credentialed nurse would make, and have no formal license or exam to pass in order to perform nursing services. These changes in staffing on the part of hospitals have harmed the already tenuous claims that nursing has made toward professional status relative to other competitors in the health care domain.

Alternatively, a profession can lose control over the number of people that are appropriately credentialed. This is a fairly accurate description of the situation facing the profession of law in the United States. There have been a proliferation of law schools since World War II and the American Bar has shown relatively little ability to stem the increasing numbers of people who seek legal credentials. This, combined with changes in the provision of legal services that we just discussed, produces a situation where ever larger numbers of credentialed lawyers are looking for work. As you might suspect, the relatively loose labor market for lawyers is one of many things that has contributed to what many believe is a decline in legal ethics as practitioners compete to file frivolous lawsuits, perform unnecessary procedures, and otherwise engage in activities to "drum up business" (Kronman 1995). The production of new lawyers (and even new law schools) shows no signs of abating.

Labor markets that have too many practitioners attempting to perform the work available are tailor-made for producing professional conflict over declining resources, changes in professional practice norms as people desperately search for a "market niche," and breeches in professional ethics. But sometimes the overproduction of new professionals is the byproduct of other dimensions of the system of professions that are attempting to control a specific task domain. The work of college professors typifies this situation.

The supply of college professors across disciplines varies widely in relation to the number of slots available. Professors in the arts and humanities are in chronic oversupply, professors of social science tend to (approximately) meet the demand for their services, and professors in areas of professional practice (law, medicine, and engineering for example) are chronically in short supply. Part of what determines whether a labor market is "tight" or "loose" is the availability of competitive jobs outside of the academy. But another feature of academic labor markets that creates variability in demand for professional services is the substitutability of less credentialed people for Ph.D.s. Because college professors train their replacements in graduate programs, part of the training for most new Ph.D.s involves a stint as a teacher in a college or a university where one is doing graduate work. If a specific discipline isn't careful (and many haven't been since the overall shrinkage in the academic labor market in the 1970s), the people that college professors train can become perfect substitutes for trained professionals. The temptation to do this is all the greater because (1) graduate students are much less expensive on university budgets than professors, (2) graduate students usually must teach as part of their training, and (3) almost all universities and colleges want to have graduate programs as an institutional sign that they are at the forefront of advancing knowledge in specific disciplines.

The result for many disciplines is a chronic oversupply of those studying in a discipline relative to those who can be employed as college professors. If the pipeline is especially "narrow" at the top, there can be hundreds or thousands of people employed as temporary teachers without the prospect of ever finishing their graduate work or obtaining a professorial position. Much like Henry Ford's "five dollar day," the existence of this reserve pool of would-be college professors compromises the professional prerogatives of the current college professor corps.[5]

Professional competition: substitution versus complementarity

Central to the concept that there is a system of professions is the idea that different occupational groups compete for control of specific task domains (Abbott 1988). This competition occurs in both formal arenas (through lobbying for changes in certification and legal control over work tasks) and informal arenas where actual tasks are divided up between professional groups. One of the central challenges to professional groups is the creation of rival occupational groups that compete for the same task domain and groups that "chip away" at, or provide complementary services to, an established professional group.

There are numerous examples of competition like this, especially in workplaces where multiple professional groups are hired to perform the same or highly similar tasks. Hospitals are a typical workplace where different professional groups come together and compete for different roles in the provision of healthcare services. The advertisements that trumpet the "team of professionals at Mount Crumpet Hospital . . ." (and similar advertisements) are designed to give consumers the perception that numerous people will come together and work in harmony toward the single goal of producing healthy patients. While, publicly, interactions between health care service providers appear to be this way, these harmonious public interactions are hiding what (often) are serious professional conflicts over who has control of specific tasks and skills.

The typical (and most public) example of the substitution versus complimentarity problem surrounds the physicians role and competition with nurse midwives, nurse practitioners, licensed nurses of various sorts, physician extenders, and medical technologists for control over different domains of medical decision-making. Traditionally, the physician was viewed as controlling all major healthcare decisions; other groups that helped patients were viewed as "paraprofessional" groups that took orders from physicians that described specifically the type of care that the paraprofessional would provide. The crisis created by rising healthcare costs has thrust many of these paraprofessionals toward the forefront of making more strident demands for independence, claims that are aided by the fact that fees and costs of paraprofessional work are usually much lower than fees and costs of professional work.

Another (and more publicly visible) example of conflict over the same task domain is the conflict between clinical psychologists, psychiatrists, and social workers over the provision of services for the mentally ill. Clinical psychologists and psychiatrists are at the center of the debate over the effectiveness of drugs versus counseling and therapy as methods for treating mental illness. Social workers often claim the unique ability to solve the practical problems of patients and are uniquely situated to help their patients develop coping skills, and social workers (increasingly) are claiming "family therapy" as a task domain that they wish to control. Conflicts between each group can become especially acute if all three are employed at the same work site.

The final example of competition versus complimentarity is the increasingly tenuous relationship between accountants, lawyers, and financial analysts. Some law firms have moved in the direction of providing multifaceted business consulting services that impinge on the task domain usually occupied by accountants. These new legal tasks include attempts by lawyers to pass judgment on financial solvency. Almost as controversial has been the hiring of accountants by law firms as part of an omnibus legal team that provides legal and CPA services to corporate clients. When such firms also provide financial and investment advice, financial analysts and bankers find their task domain impinged upon and attempt to fight back by claiming exclusive perspectives and expertise in the evaluation of the investment process.

Obviously not all of these potential conflicts end up as knockdown, drag-out fights over the exact same tasks. Often a set of related professional groups work out a division of labor that allows them to function as complementary parts of a professional and paraprofessional team. The ever-evolving relationship between psychiatrists, psychologists, and social workers is an example of this. Psychiatrists increasingly see themselves as treating chemical imbalances in brain functioning. As more and more mental illness is connected to physiological changes that affect brain functioning, this is a task domain that physicians seem uniquely capable of claiming. Clinical psychologists, by contrast, increasingly view themselves as resolving personal conflicts and conflicts surrounding individual identity and mental functioning. These problems seem uniquely susceptible to the "talking cure." Social workers view themselves as helping to produce and monitor concrete adjustments to new and challenging social situations, offering practical advice and referring clients to different support systems that communities and local governments are able to provide. In spite of the continuing controversy over the effectiveness of different treatment regimens, there is evidence of an emerging complementary division of labor in the treatment of mental illness.

Professional Work in Changing Contexts: The System of Professions in Hospitals[6]

As a concrete example of the types of changes in professional and managerial work that we've discussed, we offer an analysis of data provided by the American Hospital Association.[7] These data provide a relatively comprehensive look at the growth and decline in the fortunes of different occupational groups that worked in hospital settings during the 1980s. Many of the trends we discuss here have continued or accelerated since then, but we have a relatively thorough understanding of changes in hospital care during this time period and we use it as an example of the broader changes we've discussed.

The health care industry is undergoing the broadest set of changes seen since the advent of modern medicine in the early twentieth century (see Starr 1982). From prospective payment systems to the health insurance crisis and President Clinton's aborted health care reform proposals, the organization of health care delivery in the United States has been shaking at its foundations.

One issue that researchers haven't addressed is whether these changes have affected the relative fortunes of different professional groups. The sociology of occupations and professions has a long history of examining the effects of technological and organizational change on the relative standing of occupations within industries and firms. We draw heavily on this prior research in our presentation here.

The classic model of hospital organization has emphasized different domains of authority claimed by physicians and administrators. In recent years the relationships linking physicians to hospitals have become far more diverse and range from the traditional independent physician with hospital admission privileges, to more formalized employment by the hospital or a health maintenance organization (HMO), to preferred provider contracts and physician joint ventures that directly link physicians to hospitals through financial partnerships. Nurses also have made claims to a primary role in patient care as part of the core technology of hospitals and the number of allied health occupations working in hospital settings has increased drastically. Professional managers have increased both in number and importance within medical care organizations.

In our simplified analysis, we focus on these three occupational groups most closely tied to hospitals for which there is reasonably accurate data over time; hospital administrators, nurses (RN's and LPN's), paraprofessionals such as physician assistants and nurse practitioners, and hospital-based physicians.

Changes in the hospital industry, 1980 to the present

Until very recently, the structure of health care delivery organizations was influenced by the medical profession and its control over federal and state regulations affecting delivery of and payment for health care. During the late 1980s and early 1990s, however, attempts at health policy formulation moved away from the objective of increasing access to hospital care and toward the objectives of containing costs and increasing competition among providers. Current proposals to modify the health care system now emphasize a combination of "managed competition" and broader access for the uninsured.

The hospital sector of the health care industry has experienced considerable contraction since 1980. The number of community hospitals has declined to approximately 5,400 from a high of 6,500 in 1975. This contraction has occurred through a variety of mechanisms, including mergers and closures. Between 1986 and 1988 alone, 342 hospitals closed, followed by another 191 closures in 1991. The general climate of the hospital market since the shift to a prospective payment structure in 1983 has been one of reduced resources, increased competition, and cost containment. Health care is now referred to as an "industry" rather than a "system," a subtle but significant symbolic change (see Mick and Associates 1990). Alexander and D'Aunno (1990) have suggested that the traditional normative structure of medical care delivery has begun to erode, and the institutional constraints on the medical sector have shifted toward an emphasis on efficiency, cost concerns, and the corporatization of medical care.

Against this background of general industry contraction and competition, the past decade has seen three major trends in health care organizations:

1 an increase in the diversification of organizational types and products;
2 change in traditional ownership and management configurations; and
3 the development of new interorganizational arrangements and governance structures.

Diversification has involved the creation of new organizations (for example, freestanding emergency care centers and out-patient surgery centers) that compete in markets traditionally monopolized by hospitals. Hospitals have diversified by moving away from the treatment of the very sick toward health promotion, geriatric programs, and vertical integration to provide all levels and intensities of services to the patient.

Of the many changes experienced by hospitals in the past few years, at least three can be classified as profound organizational changes[8]; *mergers*, *corporate restructures*, and *multihospital system affiliations*. Mergers combine two or more freestanding hospitals into one hospital. Corporate restructures divide up hospital assets and functions into separate corporations. Multihospital systems are combinations of two or more hospitals that are owned, leased, or managed by a single corporate entity (Humana, Hospital Corporation of America, etc.).

There is a serious and lively debate about whether these profound changes actually affect how hospitals perform or the outcomes they produce. From our standpoint we are less interested in whether such changes produce cost efficiency or increase the quality of patient care, though these are both laudable goals. Instead we are interested in whether these profound changes have affected the relative position of different, potentially competing, occupational groups that work in hospitals.

What does hospital reorganization have to do with the relative standing of professionals?

There is a growing consensus among most researchers that the effects of profound change in organizations are not uniform across occupational groups. The effects of technical and structural change appear to depend on several factors; (1) the motivations of managerial groups, (2) the ability of specific occupational groups to appeal to the institutional environment, (3) competition between occupational groups, (4) the ability of organizations to shield core activities, and (5) the technical environment and pressures for market efficiency.

Much research in the sociology of work suggests that technical and organizational changes are implemented to lower the skill requirements of jobs. This research normally focuses on skilled craft work, but has expanded in recent years to studies of office employees and other white-collar occupations.

Observers disagree about the motivations behind attempts to deskill work. Those who argue that efficiency motivates technical and organizational change claim that managers subdivide skilled employees' work to lower labor costs and increase profits. Managers (in this scenario) attempt to alter the relative demand for different occupational groups in order to tip the scales in the direction of cheaper, less skilled occupations.

Other observers have questioned the efficiency of deskilling as a managerial action. Instead, they claim that managers change organizational structures and technology to increase their own power and control. Changes are oriented toward furthering the interests of managerial groups regardless of whether these changes contribute to efficiency or not. Even in situations where several alternatives are equally efficient, solutions that promote the interests of managers are preferred.

Recent observations by managerial consultants regarding the obstacles associated with installing participative management schemes that give employees a say in making corporate decisions seem to correspond with this view. These studies point to the ability of managers to obstruct technical and organizational change that reduces managerial prerogatives or leads to downsizing of managerial staff. While there is little evidence that the effects of organizational and technological changes reduce the work skills of all employees in organizations, this perspective suggests that highly skilled workers will be the primary targets of organizational change as managers attempt to reduce costs, increase their control, or both.

Organizational researchers and scholars of the professions point to the institutional environment surrounding organizations as moderating the effects of organizational change on specific occupational groups. Occupations that succeed in classifying themselves as professions make appeals to core societal values ("health," "well-being," "quality of life," etc.) and key constituencies outside of organizations (customers, politicians, and private foundations) to help them in their attempts to control the conditions of work. Occupations backed by strong professional associations and clearly defined domains of professional expertise are able to deflect the effects of organizational change toward others who lack the ability to make these appeals. Most organizations that employ professionals have several occupations in open competition for jurisdiction over a set of work tasks. The relative demand for professionals combines with institutional expectations about professional employment to constrain the hospitals' ability to reorganize the work process as it chooses.

Regardless of the mechanisms involved, institutional approaches predict that less skilled and less organized occupational groups will be most affected by profound organizational changes, whether these effects are intended or not. In the medical sector the situation is complicated by an institutional environment that traditionally buttressed the power of physicians and their technical expertise. But recently, the values of corporate rationality have challenged this institutional definition by placing increased emphasis on cost control, corporate structure, and professional management of the hospital sector.

Alternative descriptions point to the ability of organizations like hospitals to buffer core activities from outside pressures. These observers view managers and core-technology workers as sharing the same interests in preserving core activities of the organization. Managers act as buffers to prevent environmental shocks from affecting the core activities of the organization. These buffering activities would protect skilled workers, but this protection would not be due to victory in an interprofessional competition. Instead, the favored position of core skilled workers is produced with the active cooperation of managers and others who represent the organization to outsiders.

Similar themes are developed by those who study the strategic management of organizational downsizing. This work suggests that, when organizations start to decline, managers will develop techniques to protect the organization's core mission and preserve minimal levels of morale among core employees as staff positions are reduced and departments are eliminated.

Hospital care is an industry where resources have been in decline and institutional values are shifting toward efficiency and cost containment. Our central question is simple to state, though it draws on the long observations of others we discuss above; *what happens to the relative size of administrative occupations, physicians, and patient-care workers as a result of profound organizational change?* Hospital administrators might be protected by recent shifts in values toward the "corporate ethic." Physicians still may wield the traditional institutional power base of the professional expert, and nurses may claim to be vital for patient care, the core technology of the hospital.

Based on prior observations in a wide variety of settings, we would expect organizational changes that were not directly geared toward downsizing management to benefit hospital administrators at the expense of physicians. We would expect changes that reflect managerial instability (hospital CEO turnover and consolidation into multihospital systems) to favor physicians at the expense of hospital administrators. These latter changes should also favor physicians at the expense of nurses. Declines and instability in the hospital's performance and resource base should favor administrators (who specifically claim the ability to fix these problems) at the expense of technical hospital personnel, and organizational decline and resource instability should increase the hiring of physician assistants, nurse practitioners, and other low-cost alternatives to physicians.

With our data we measure the relative standing of occupations by looking at the relative employment of different occupational groups, expressed as ratios (physicians/hospital administrators; nurses/administrators; nurses and physicians/administrators; and nurses/physicians). Because the hiring of nurse practitioners and physicians assistants is still a relatively new practice, we examine the probability that a given hospital will employ physician extenders in relation to the profound organizational changes that hospitals experience.

Table 6.1 presents some basic demographic information on the hospitals in our American Hospital Association data. From 1980 to 1988, around 10 percent of all hospitals identified themselves as for-profit. Nineteen percent were affiliated with medical schools. The average hospital had around 190 beds ready to accept patients. Forty-eight percent of our hospitals have experienced instability in their resource base, 5 percent have experienced decline, and 10 percent have experienced growth. The average hospital has had approximately two changes in CEOs over the eight-year period.

This table also provides evidence that hospitals have undergone profound organizational changes over the decade. Few hospitals (less than 1 percent) report participation in a hospital merger. Twenty-four percent report corporate restructuring activity. Twenty-two percent report affiliations with multihospital systems. Clearly this national sample of hospitals has undergone its share of change in resources and change in organizational structure during the study period.

Table 6.1 Basic demographic information on hospitals (AHA Survey, N = 4,488)

	Mean	*SD*
For-profit hospital	0.1	0.3
Proportion of services available	0.43	0.15
Medical school affilation	0.19	0.39
Hospital size	187.43	179.57
Instability	0.48	0.5
Decline	0.05	0.22
Growth	0.1	0.3
Leadership turnover	1.59	1.34
Merger	0	0.05
Corporate restructure	0.24	0.43
Multi-Hospital system	0.22	0.42
MD/Administrator ratio	0.49	2.71
RN/Administrator ratio	23.14	29.51
(MD + RN)/Administrator ratio	23.63	30.04
RN/MD ratio	85.22	133.3
Nurse practitioners and physician's assistants (= 1)	0.22	0.41

Table 6.1 also provides the baseline comparisons of the relative size of different occupational groups. On average there is one physician for every two hospital administrators, 23 nurses for every hospital administrator, 24 nurses or physicians for every administrator, and 85 nurses for every physician. Clearly the nurses as an allied health profession group outnumber physicians and administrators in our hospitals by a wide margin. Twenty-two percent of these hospitals employ nurse practitioners and physicians' assistants.

Are there zero-sum trade-offs between the employment of each occupational group? Table 6.2 looks at some basic correlation coefficients to address this issue.

All groups tend to increase in presence with the size of the hospital, which is not surprising. But do some groups grow faster than others?

The answer to this question is a clear "yes." As hospitals grow in size:

1 the number of physicians grows relative to the number of hospital administrators,
2 the number of nurses grows relative to the number of administrators,

Table 6.2 Correlations between measures of organizational change and occupational representation (AHA Survey, N = 4,488)

	MD/Admin. Ratio	*RN/Admin. Ratio*	*(MD + RN)/Admin. Ratio*	*RN/MD Ratio*	*Nurse Pract. or MD Asst.*
For-profit Hospital	−0.048	0.029	0.025	0.015	−0.098
Proportion of services available	0.193	0.308	0.319	0.397	0.397
Medical school affiliation	0.224	0.22	0.236	0.25	0.442
Hospital size	0.224	0.345	0.359	0.45	0.401
Instability	−0.032	−0.09	−0.091	−0.129	−0.056
Decline	−0.021	−0.046	−0.047	−0.05	−0.041
Growth	0.013	−0.036	−0.034	−0.041	−0.03
Leadership turnover	−0.016	−0.051	−0.051	−0.083	−0.049
Merger	0.053	0.026	0.03	0.017	0.055
Corporate restructure	0.036	0.077	0.079	0.141	0.125
Multi-Hospital system	−0.022	0.031	0.028	−0.035	−0.024

3 the number of nurses grows relative to the number of physicians, and
4 the hospital is more likely to hire nurse practitioners and physicians' assistants.

The number of nurses grows the fastest, followed by physicians and then administrators, suggesting that technical core activities are the first to expand as hospitals get larger.

Is there any relationship between profound organizational change, changes in hospital resources, and the relative employment of different health professionals? Table 6.2 suggests that the answer is a qualified "yes." Resource instability and decline clearly favor administrators at the expense of physicians and nurses, as does leadership turnover. Hospital mergers and corporate restructuring seem to have the opposite effect, favoring technical core professionals at the expense of hospital administrators. All of these results are consistent with the observations of other analysts in different contexts.

Figures 6.1 through 6.4 present graphs that depict the net effects of resource shifts and organizational change on the relative employment of

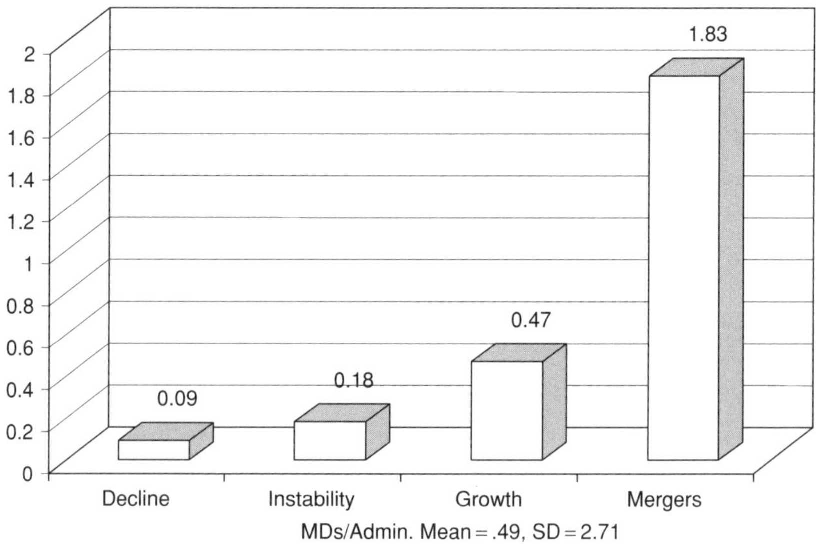

Figure 6.1 The effects of radical organizational change on the relative standing of MDs to hospital administrators (AHA Survey)

Note: Decline, instability and growth refer to changes in the number of in-patient admissions to hospitals, 1980–4 (see table A.6.1 for analysis details).

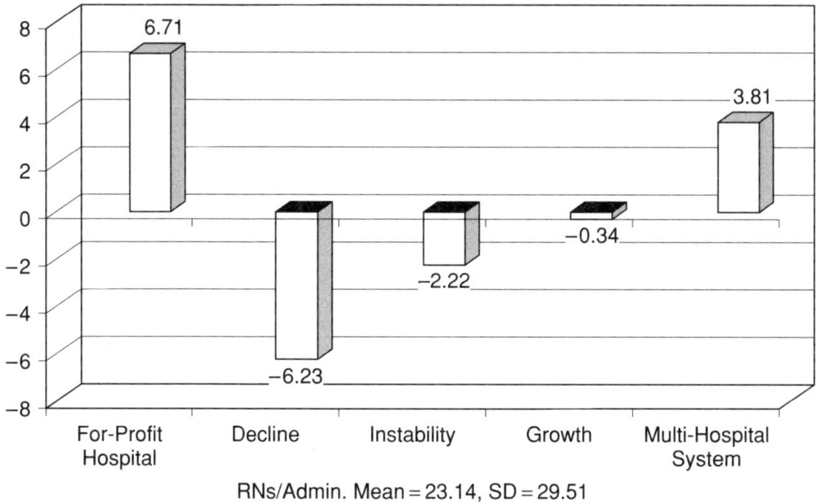

Figure 6.2 The effects of radical organizational change on the relative standing of nurses to hospital administrators (AHA Survey)

Note: See table A.6.1 for analysis details.

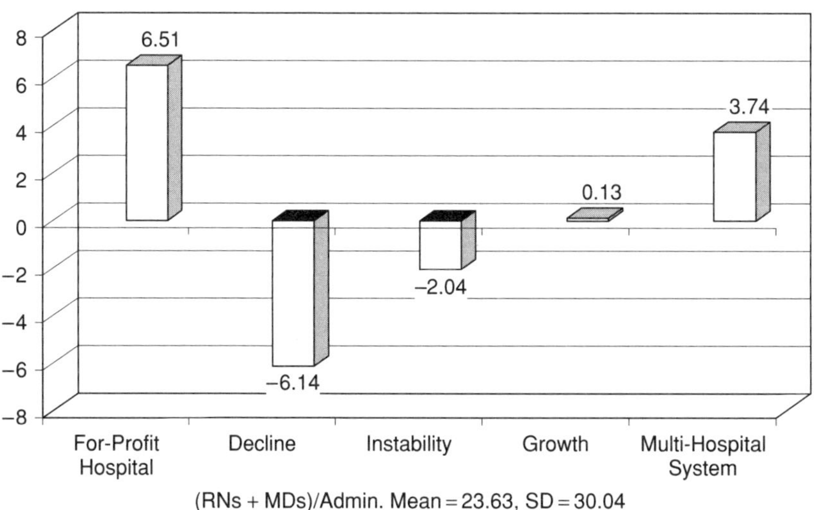

Figure 6.3 The effects of radical organizational change on the relative standing of nurses and MDs to hospital administrators (AHA Survey)

Note: See table A.6.1 for analysis details.

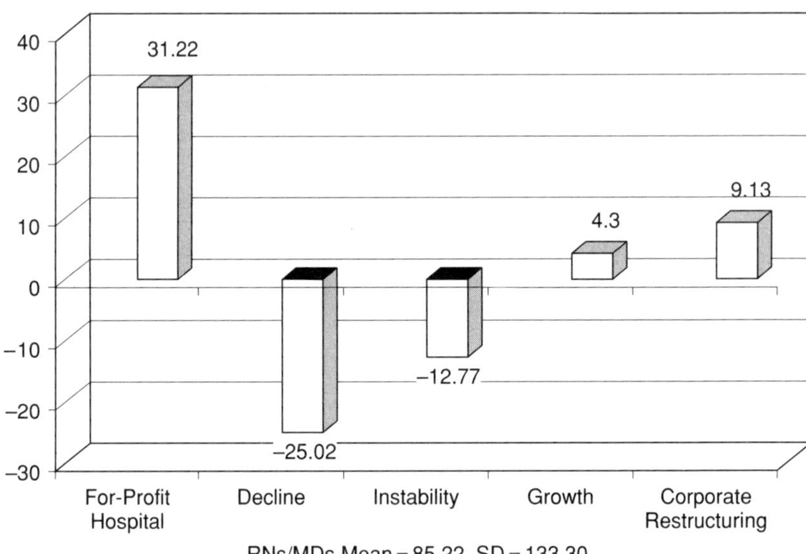

Figure 6.4 The effects of radical organizational change on the relative standing of nurses to MDs (AHA Survey)

Note: Corporate restructuring is defined as the segmentation of a hospital's assets into two or more separate corporations any time from 1980 to 1988 (see table A.6.1 for analysis details).

our occupational groups. There are clear shifts in the fortunes of our occupational groups based on the specific configuration of changes that the hospital has been through. Each of our figures looks at the results across each of the comparison measures we use.

In figure 6.1, there are clear differences between a hospitals' economic fortunes, the types of organizational change they pursue, and the relative standing of physicians and hospital administrators. Almost all of the changes favor physicians in this comparison. Specifically, resource growth and merger activity significantly increase the ratio of physicians to administrators, the latter by a quite large amount. The number of physicians increases roughly 183 percent in hospitals that undergo mergers.

The remaining figures tell a more interesting story in many respects. Figure 6.2 looks at the effects of profound organizational changes and changes in hospital resources on the ratio of nurses to administrators.

Figure 6.3 looks at these same effects on the ratio of technical core occupations to administrators, and figure 6.4 looks at these same effects on the ratio of nurses to physicians.

The figures present a clear and interesting order of relationships between occupational groups as hospitals respond to changes in their environment. Administrators clearly benefit from instability and declines in hospital resources. They are the group that is expected to "manage" these changes for the core activities of the hospital. Physicians are able to buffer their high prestige positions in the technical core of the hospital at the expense of nurses as well. Only two changes interfere with these trends. Multihospital system affiliations reduce administrative employment relative to technical core occupations, and corporate restructuring benefits nurses at the expense of physicians.

Finally, figure 6.5 suggests that instability and growth contribute to the hiring of nurse practitioners and physicians' assistants by hospitals. Clearly hospital administrators are looking for less expensive alternatives to physician-based care as resources shift. None of the measures of profound organizational change affected the probability of hiring physicians'

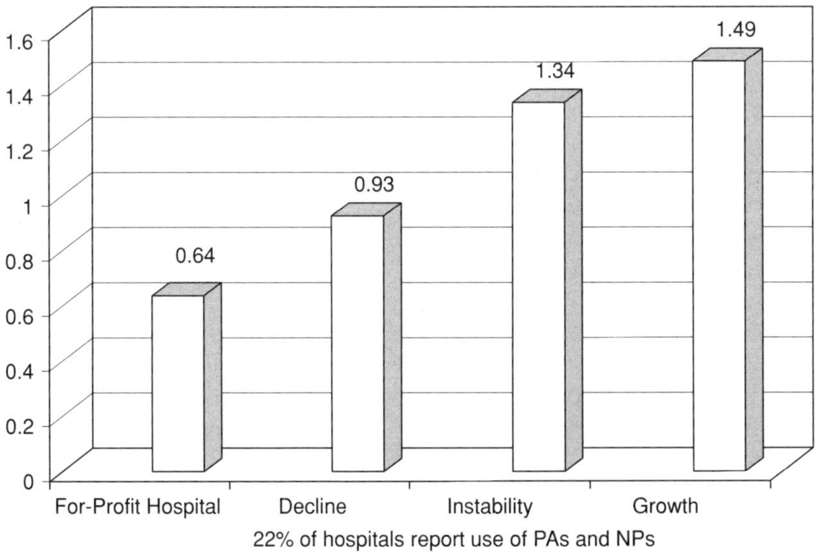

Figure 6.5 Odds of employing physicians' assistants and nurse practitioners (AHA Survey)

Note: See table A.6.2 for analysis details.

assistants or nurse practitioners net of the controls in our analysis (see Appendix, to this chapter, p. 130).

Overall, this brief exercise in the study of changing organizational arrangements and the relative standing of occupational groups in hospitals supports several conclusions. We suspect that these conclusions could be replicated in other settings where numerous professional and would-be professional groups compete for resources under conditions where the taken-for-granted resource base is changing and different groups are vying for institutional control.

First, as the hospital resource base becomes more uncertain, *hospital administrators expand their presence to deal with increased problems of strategic decision-making*. The activities of physicians are protected from sharp changes in the hospital resource base. The historically subordinate activities of nurses are not expanded at the same rate and may be reduced. These results support an institutional interpretation of hospital activity since the ability of technical workers to protect their activities from profound organizational change depends on their ability to appeal to an external constituency that provides legitimating and powerful professional norms. However, the same changes in resource base that expand the relative representation of physicians *also* expand the hospital's search for lower cost alternatives for patient care.

The larger environment supporting physicians seems to buffer them from bearing the consequences of many organizational changes. Only corporate restructuring appears to affect physicians' relative standing in hospitals. In fact, there appears to be a clear "pecking order" when it comes to bearing the consequences of organizational change. Physicians are at the top, almost never bearing the brunt of most of the organizational changes we've studied. Administrators are just below physicians, and nurses bear the brunt of most of the changes we've studied. The first two occupational groups enjoy considerable institutional protection. Administrators are protected because they are the occupational group that manages the increasingly complex environment of the hospital. Further, administrators and managers generally play a large role in defining institutional environments in the first place. Physicians are protected by traditional institutional norms that are violated only in rare instances as a last resort. Nurses, in spite of their changing roles, have none of these protections.[9]

Obviously, our preliminary study is not perfect. We don't deal with physicians that aren't employed by hospitals. We think that the experience of hospital-based physicians may be a sign of the effects of future health care reorganization as more physicians come under the umbrella of HMOs, PPOs, and other employing organizations, but we can't be 100 percent sure of that. There are probably other measures of the relative standing of occupational groups that are more appropriate than employment ratios (earnings ratios, for example). We find it difficult to believe that occupational groups whose jobs are being lost can claim they stand in a more favorable position in the division-of-labor compared to occupational groups whose numbers are increasing (see chapter 4), but there are other dimensions of prestige and standing that we can't address with the information we have.

There are several implications of this preliminary analysis for policy makers interested in monitoring the effects of changes in the organization of healthcare delivery. Our brief presentation suggests that discussions of the restructuring of hospitals and health care needs to be sensitive to some of the unintended consequences suggested by organizational theory. Organizational change usually leads to clashes of occupational groups with competing interests. In discussions of organizational restructuring in other contexts, managers and CEOs clearly have attempted to circumvent the process of organizational change to directly benefit their interests. Policymakers and healthcare activists should be aware of these potential consequences and help to construct appropriate incentives that produce intended outcomes (cost containment, increased access to care, and quality health care delivery).

As the hospital sector is reorganized, analyses of the type we've done here will be more vital to our understanding of what the consequences of reorganization will be for hospital workers. These analyses can also contribute to the evaluation of whether changes in the organization of hospital care are having their desired effects. The implications are far from merely academic, as anyone who has spent time in a hospital as a patient can attest. As the lessons from numerous other industries have shown, placing greater decision-making power in the hands of administrators often is not the way to produce greater cost efficiency and organizational performance (see Fligstein 1990). Nor will increasing the number of administrators improve the quality of hospital care. Through the analysis of the relative employment of different health care professionals we can begin to grasp what the day-to-day consequences of health care reform will be for hospitals and patients alike. Our next chapter looks at the consequences of the changing organization of professional work for the growing diversity of interests within professions.

APPENDIX: DETAILS OF ANALYSIS USING DATA FROM THE AMERICAN HOSPITAL ASSOCIATION

Our primary data sources in this chapter are the American Hospital Association Annual Surveys of Hospitals (1980–8). The AHA Annual Survey of Hospitals is administered in the fourth quarter of each year to all AHA registered and nonregistered facilities (N = 6,800). Except for minor modifications, the survey remained unchanged throughout the study period (1980–8). This survey covers areas related to facilities and services and their use, staffing, financing, and administration. The measure of mergers is taken from the AHA *Directory of Hospital Mergers* (1980–8) and the measure of multihospital systems are taken from the AHA *Directory of Multihospital Systems* (1980–8). The sample used in our analysis is the subsample of community hospitals (N = 4,488) with valid data on our independent and dependent measures. Our sample represents 77 percent of the population of community hospitals in existence in 1981.

It is important to remember that the 1980–8 period encompasses an era of radical change in the delivery of hospital services, including the onset of DRGs and an acute shortage of registered nurses (Secretary's Commission on Nursing 1988; Krasner 1989). This is an especially relevant period for studying the effects of organizational change on occupational competition in the health care industry.

Measuring the relative power of occupational groups

To measure the relative power of occupational groups within hospitals, we follow the research of Wallace and Kalleberg (1982) and use employment ratios to capture the relative representation of nurses, physicians, and administrators. In order to capture groups of physicians that are exclusively dependent on the hospital for their livelihood, we use the number of hospital-based physicians (such as radiologists, anesthesiologists, pathologists, and so on) as our measure of representation. We do this because attending physicians and MDs who have admission privileges with hospitals act in a quasi-independent entrepreneurial role. While hospital-based physicians are only a small number of the total number of physicians most hospitals interact with, they do represent the salaried portion of the medical profession with definite employment ties to the hospital. Ironically, many of the new alliances between third-party payers, hospitals, and physicians would place most physicians in the same dependent relationships that hospital-based physicians currently occupy. This is an issue we cannot address with this analysis. Further, most occupational disputes occur in the context of work organizations where professionals operate in the same domain (see Abbott

This appendix taken from Kevin T. Leicht, Mary L. Fennell, and Kristine M. Witkowski. 1995. "The Effects of Hospital Characteristics and Radical Organizational Change on the Relative Standing of Health Care Professions." *Journal of Health and Social Behavior* 36: 151–67.

1988). We argue that hospital-based physicians, administrators, and nurses and other occupational groups engage in inter-occupational disputes that are driven by changes in the context of health care delivery in the United States in the 1980s. These conflicts should be most intense among those who are most dependent on the hospital as their primary employer.

While relative employment size may not reflect organizational power in the face or organizational change, it is difficult to see how sparse or shrinking occupational groups could have occupational power relative to groups that are large and growing.

Measuring profound organizational change

Our analysis focuses on organizational changes that occurred in the 1980–8 period. Combining measures over a nine-year period gets at long-run organizational change while assuring that our measures of change precede in time with our measures of employment. Our measures of organizational change are:

1 *Merger* (= 1). This variable indicates whether a hospital has gone through a merger during the 1980–8 period.
2 *Corporate Restructure* (= 1). This variable measures whether the hospital has experienced corporate restructuring during the 1980–8 period. Corporate restructuring is defined as the segmentation of a hospital's assets and functions into two separate corporations (Fennell and Alexander 1993).
3 *Multihospital System Affiliation* (= 1). This variable measures whether the hospital was affiliated with a multihospital system during the 1980–8 period.
4 *Leadership Turnover*. This variable indicates the number of times a hospital has experienced CEO turnover during the period 1980–8. Leadership turnover creates considerable discontinuity in the strategy and structure of organizations (Pfeffer 1972; Meyer 1978; Carroll 1984; Singh, House, and Tucker 1986; Finkelstein and Hambrick 1990).
5 *Life-Cycle Changes*. Sampled hospitals were classified into one of four separate life-cycle stages; *growth*, *decline*, *instability*, and *stability*. These measures were based on the number of annual in-patient admissions to the hospital for the years 1980–4. Admissions are vital resources to the hospital that reflect the ability of the hospital to compete and grow in its market. The measurement strategy used here is detailed further in Alexander et al. (1993). Specifically, five-year patterns of change were examined to capture long-term trends as opposed to short-term aberrations, and the admission measures were standardized by mean changes for a given hospital's industry comparison group. These measures of hospital growth, decline, stability, and instability thus take into account industry-wide trends in admissions, and categorize individual hospitals on the basis of "net" or "real" change over and above national trends. The period 1980–4 was chosen in order to capture growth/decline at the early end of the study time period, and to represent admissions trends prior to most hospitals'

compliance with the prospective payment system (PPS), post-1984. The switch to prospective payment affected both admissions and length of stay, and the post-1984 period is characterized by large variances in hospitalization rates both within hospitals over time and across hospitals. The pre-1984 measure of life-cycle stage should depict more accurately the hospital's performance trends prior to the "shock" of PPS (Zajac and Shortell 1989).

In order to adjust for industry trends in admissions, nine mutually exclusive comparison groups were formed on the basis of ownership category and hospital bed size. Hospitals showing increases in adjusted admissions greater than 5 percent above the average for their comparison group in at least three of four consecutive year pairs (1980–1, 1981–2, 1982–3, and 1983–4) were classified as *growers*, while those showing decreases of more than 5 percent below reference group averages for three of the four-year pairs were classified as *decliners*. Hospitals showing at least one pair of consecutive years with admissions declining greater than 5 percent were classified as *unstable*. All other hospitals were classified as *stable* (the omitted category in our analysis).

6 *Control Variables*. Our analysis controls for several variables that may be related to organizational change and the relative power of occupational groups. Specifically, we control for hospital size (number of hospital beds, set up and staffed for use), for-profit status (= 1, non-profit hospitals = 0), affiliation with medical schools (= 1, otherwise = 0), and the proportion of services available (out of 21 listed in the 1985 AHA surveys) as a measure of product diversity. These measures represent general aspects of the hospital environment that could affect the relationship between our measures of interest and occupational representation.

Analysis plan

We use hierarchical regression in our analysis, first comparing across models that include (1) control variables only, (2) controls and life-cycle variables, and (3) all previous variables plus the organizational change variables. Given the infrequent nature of most organizational change events and the exploratory nature of our analysis, all organizational change events are included in the analysis at the same time, even though we initially hypothesized that only certain relationships should be present. Our equations take the form:

$$\begin{aligned}\text{Occupational Ratio} = a + BX &+ b_2(\text{Instability}) + b_3(\text{Decline}) \\ &+ b_4(\text{Growth}) + b_5(\text{Turnover}) \\ &+ b_6(\text{Merger}) + b_7(\text{Restructuring}) \\ &+ b_8(\text{Multihospital System}) + e\end{aligned}$$

Where X represents a vector of controls in our analysis (hospital size, for-profit status, medical school affiliation, and product diversity) and B represents the vector of regression coefficients associated with X. The results of this regression

Table A.6.1[a] The effects of organizational change on the relative standing of (1) physicians to administrators, (2) nurses to administrators, (3) nurses and physicians to administrators, and (4) nurses to physicians in 1990, unstandardized regression coefficients (N = 4,488)

Independent Variables	*MDs Adminstrators (1)*	*RNs Administrators (2)*	*RNs + MDs Administrators (3)*	*RNs MDs (4)*
Controls				
For-profit hospital[b]	−.20	6.71★★★	6.51★★★	31.22★★★
Proportion of services available	.57	18.80★★★	19.37★★★	87.08★★★
Medical school affiliation	.91★★★	.32	1.23	−22.66★★★
Hospital size	.20★★★[d]	.04★★★	.05★★★	.30★★★
Life-Cycle				
B_2 Instability	.18★	−2.22★	−2.04★	−12.77★★
B_3 Decline	.09	−6.23★★	−6.14★★	−25.02★★
B_4 Growth[c]	.47★★	−.34	.13	4.30
Organizational Change				
B_5 Leadership turnover	.05	−.47	−.43	−1.85
B_6 Merger	1.83★	−2.04	−.21	−62.72
B_7 Corporate restructure	−.10	−.97	−1.08	9.13★
B_8 Multihospital system	−.07	3.81★★★	3.74★★★	−3.14
Constant	−.46★★	7.80★★★	7.35★★★	.64
R^2 (adjusted)	.06	.13	.14	.22

★ $p \leq .05$; ★★ $p \leq .01$; ★★★ $p \leq .001$

[a] Taken from Leicht, Fennell, and Witkowski, 1995, table 2, p. 161.

[b] Not-for-profit hospital is the reference category.

[c] Stable life-cycle is the reference category.

[d] Coefficient × 100.

analysis are presented in table A.6.1. Figure 6.1 in the text is taken from equation (1), figure 6.2 is taken from equation (2), figure 6.3 is taken from equation (3), and figure 6.4 is taken from equation (4).

The employment of nurse practitioners and physicians' assistants is measured as a dichotomy (= 1 where these occupational groups are present, 0 otherwise), so the analysis of this variable is done using logistic regression. These results are presented in table A.6.2. These results are used to produce figure 6.5.

Table A.6.2[a] The effects of organizational change on the likelihood of employing physicians' assistants and nurse practitioners in 1990, odds ratios (N = 4,488)

Independent Variables	*Odds of Employing Physicians' Assistants or Nurse Practitioners*
Controls	
For-profit hospital[b]	.64*
Proportion of services available	29.55***
Medical school affiliation	4.03***
Hospital size	1.00**
Life-Cycle	
B_2 Instability	1.34**
B_3 Decline	.93
B_4 Growth[c]	1.49**
Organizational Change	
B_5 Leadership turnover	1.06
B_6 Merger	2.08
B_7 Corporate restructure	1.16
B_8 Multihospital system	1.00
Constant	.03***
Chi-Square	1,037.83***

* $p \leq .05$; ** $p \leq .01$; *** $p \leq .001$

[a] Taken from Leicht, Fennell, and Witkowski 1995, table 3, p. 163.

[b] Not-for-profit hospital is the reference category.

[c] Stable life-cycle is the reference category.

NOTES

1 A "stakeholder" is someone with significant interests in the activities of specific actors and institutions. They are either involved in the productive activity of actors and institutions in some significant way, they purchase the services the actors and institutions provide, or they are clients who consume the services produced by these actors and institutions. If we use law as an example, some examples of stakeholders who have some interest in the functioning of the legal profession would include other members of the criminal

justice system, corporations who pay for most legal work, law schools that train lawyers who enter the profession, judges (most of whom are lawyers themselves), political actors concerned with the functioning of the judicial branch of government, and political activists interested in promoting social change through changes in the interpretation of the law. There are others that we could identify, but in almost all cases the stakeholders in professional and managerial work stretch beyond those who directly pay for and consume the services that managers and professionals provide.

2 We use the term "developed" here in the limited and traditional way that most social scientists use the term. Developed economies are market economies with relatively high productivity, high consumption, high standards of living, and a demographically dominant middle class. We prefer the term "developed" to other terms such as "western" because many of the economies of East Asia (Japan, Korea, Taiwan, and Singapore, for example) meet our criteria. As with most social scientific uses of the term, developed does not imply moral, economic, or cultural superiority.

3 "Stagflation" is a term used to describe the simultaneous appearance of high inflation and high unemployment. There are numerous explanations for the late 1970s phenomenon of stagflation, and our account is not the only (or even the most plausible) one. However, many corporate leaders acted as if the explanation we describe was an accurate description of economic troubles in the US. Because they believed this explanation was true, they acted on it (rather than some other alternative). Hence we focus on the "cost push" explanation of inflation at the expense of the "demand pull" explanation (see Stein 1983).

4 Obviously, there is considerable skepticism concerning the ability of the changes imposed to increase the efficiency of service delivery, lower costs, and increase the quality of the professional product consumed. There have been few, if any, systematic comparisons of the quality or costs of professional care under different organizational forms. The belief in a more "business oriented" approach to the delivery of professional services stands as one of the great untested assumptions driving most calls for increased accountability.

5 Henry Ford revolutionized factory work by launching his famous "five dollar day" in January, 1914. The effects of offering this unprecedented wage to assembly-line workers were immediate and dramatic; potential employees flooded Ford's factory gates, allowing him to pick and choose the employees he wanted, work those whom he hired as hard as he wished, and firing those that could not keep up at will (see Blauner 1964).

6 This portion of our chapter is taken from Kevin T. Leicht, Mary L. Fennell, and Kristine M. Witkowski 1995, "The Effects of Hospital Characteristics and Radical Organizational Change on the Relative Standing of Health Care Professions," *Journal of Health and Social Behavior* 36:151–67.

7 See the Appendix to this chapter (p. 126) for a detailed description of the AHA survey, the measures we derive from it, and the analysis methods we use.

8 Our definition of profound organizational change draws from Hannan and Freeman's (1984) and Pfeffer's (1982) notions of changes in the core attributes of organizations. Criteria for defining such changes include: (1) changes in the stated goals of the organization, (2) changes in the forms of authority within the organization, (3) changes in core technology, (4) changes in the kinds of clients or customers to which the organization orients its production, and (5) changes in the fundamental identity or autonomy of the organization as they pertain to loss of organizational culture or power to control the organization's destiny (Fennell and Alexander 1989). Of the many changes experienced by hospitals recently, at least three are clearly definable as profound changes; mergers, corporate restructures, and multihospital system affiliations.

9 Obviously, the identification of nursing with traditional gender roles has played a large part in the relative lack of occupational power for nurses in the hospital sector (Heikes 1991).

7

Interest Diversity and Demographic Diversity among Professionals

Fragmentation of Interests among Professionals

In chapter 1 we briefly discussed one of the traditional myths commonly held about the classic free professions: each of the professions (like law or medicine) consists of a body of like-minded individuals who are equally dedicated to their work, to their identity as a professional, and to the profession itself as their most important reference group. One of the best examples of this notion of the profession as a unified front is provided by the profession of medicine.

Two of the classic descriptive histories of the profession of medicine provide us with a picture of the profession as a monolith. Starr's *Social Transformation of American Medicine* (1982) reviews the history of medicine from pre-colonial times up to the late 1970s. He traces the rise in power of the American Medical Association as the result of technical, political, and social changes in the practice of medicine, which left the AMA as the effective "mouthpiece," lobby group, and regulatory power over medical education. It became so powerful in part because its membership was so broad (and after 1900, membership in local medical societies became linked to membership in the national AMA), and in part because the members themselves were all alike: white males from predominantly the upper and middle class. Becker's *Boys in White* describes the microcosm of life in American medical schools and residency programs in the 1950s (Becker et al. 1961). Similarly, the power of that educational/socialization process is partly due to the similarity of the experience across all medical schools, and in part due to the fact that up until the late 1980s, everyone going through that process was demographically homogenous: white boys in white.

That monolithic homogeneity has begun to crumble, and in fact, Starr pointed to one early structural cause of the ensuing decline in the AMA's power in the late 1980s and through the 1990s: over specialization among the clinical "troops," and the differentiation within the profession of knowledge elites vs. practitioners. Within each medical specialty there has developed both a specialized professional association, and a technically demanding (and constantly changing) knowledge set. As specialized knowledge and specialist professional identification became increasingly important, the general professional group (the AMA) by default became less important to most practitioners. Not surprisingly, the political interests of specialist physicians are unlikely to be as well represented by the generalist AMA. This partially explains why membership within the AMA dropped to less than 40 percent of all practicing physicians by the early 1990s (Hafferty and McKinlay 1993).

Starr and others have discussed the fragmentation within medicine due to another dimension of professional stratification: the development of an elite, high status group of knowledge producers (university-based research and teaching faculty), vs. the rank and file knowledge consumer/user group, the community-based clinical practitioner (see Abbott 1988; Freidson 1994). An additional specialized interest group is perhaps represented by those described as administrative elites by Friedson (1986). These are physicians who have at least partly abandoned clinical practice in order to take positions within administrative hierarchies of the organizations where physicians practice. Most of these writers suggest that the different work foci of these three professional groups produce cleavages within the larger profession, which reverberate through issues such as professional identity, governance of the profession, and definitions of professional interests. Recent work by Hoff on the work loyalties of practicing physicians and physician administrators tells an interesting story about cleavages within and between these different physician roles. Physicians in administrative positions tend to report the same patterns of loyalties to patients, colleagues, and group, whether or not they are actually involved in patient care while performing administrative duties. Nonadministrative physicians, however, have very different evaluations of practicing and nonpracticing physician-administrators. Nonpracticing MD administrators are seen as having somehow abandoned the core values of the profession; they are described as no longer "in the trenches" doing patient care; as having lost an important base of legitimacy in the eyes of their clinical colleagues (Hoff 1997; see also work by Montgomery 1990).

In chapter 1 we raised the question of whether recent efforts to contain/control costs in medicine and other professions have helped to develop (or worsen) cleavages or conflicts within professions. Attempts to study this question are often confounded by the other diversification trend in professional work: increased diversification of the settings in which professional work is performed. There is simply too much that we do not know, such as: Are cost-control measures equally demanding in all types of professional work settings? Are all types of professional workers targeted by cost-control measures? We suspect not, because often "corporate restructuring" efforts tend to affect individual groups of professionals, and workers at the low end of the professional status structure, and have had little effect on the content and context of work for the most elite professional workers. Sometimes, the elite professionals find their autonomy enhanced as they are given responsibility for those cost-containment measures. This has been the case in many large HMOs or physician practices with physician administrators in control.

And finally, we really do not know to what extent interest-diversity among professionals is the result of changes in the demographic composition of professional workers over time, or the result of changes in the organizational arrangements within which professionals work. To what extent do these three sources of diversity (interest, demographic, and work-setting diversity) overlap?

We turn then to consider this basic question: Are the traditional professions becoming more diverse? And if so, on what dimensions: demographic (gender, race, ethnicity, socioeconomic status); interest diversity (subspecialization vs. general professional identity), or other status stratifications (content-elites, managerial-elites, vs. rank and file). Evidence on these various dimensions of diversity is very fragmentary, but one place we can begin to look for answers is also the most basic of the dimensions: demographic diversity.

To do this, we can use data on selected professions over time from the Current Population Surveys (CPS). The CPS tracks the numbers of people in the US who are job-holders in all types of occupations and professions, using a national probability sample of about 60,000 households, located in 2007 counties and cities, covering every state and the District of Columbia. These data are collected by the Census Bureau on a monthly basis, to provide estimates of employment, unemployment,

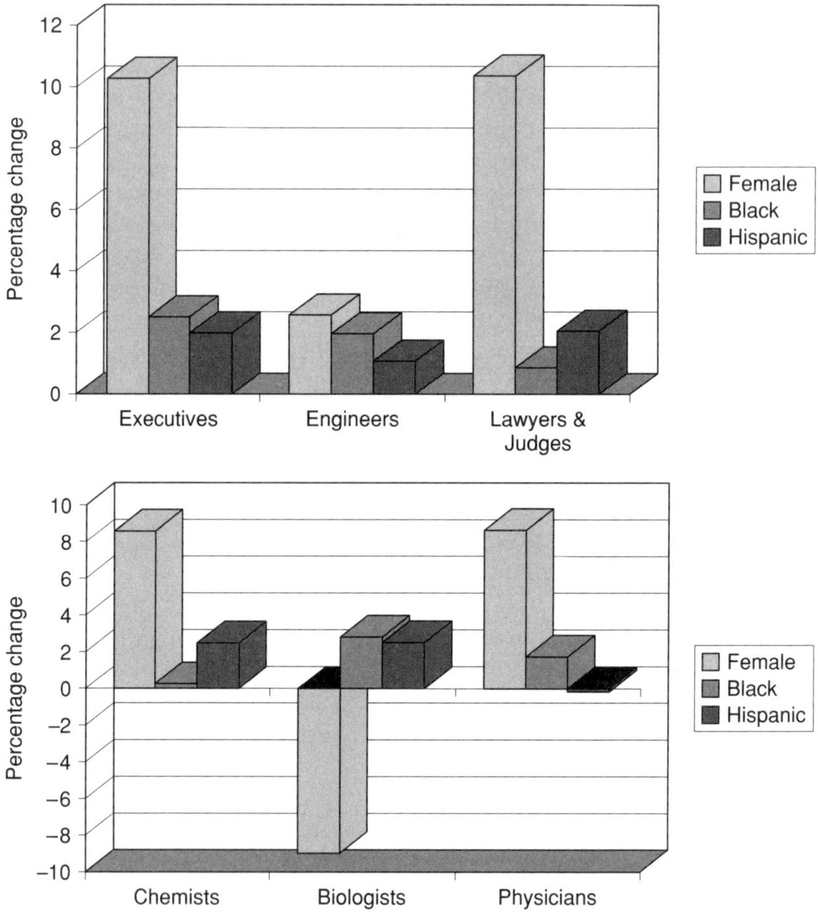

Figure 7.1 Change in the diversity of selected professions, 1983–1995 (CPS)

Source: Current Population Survey.

income, work experience, and worker demographics (age, race, gender, etc.).

Figure 7.1 provides a graphical representation of demographic changes in six different professions over the period from 1983 to 1995. These bars show the percent change in the proportion of each profession that is female, black, and Hispanic. The six professions we have chosen include: (1) "executives," which includes managers, top administrators, and executives; (2) engineers (all types); (3) lawyers and judges; (4) chemists; (5) biologists; and (6) physicians.

Taken as a whole, the demographic mix of these six professions has changed quite a bit, but the amount of change and the type of change is not similar across these professions. Women have clearly made the greatest strides, with about a ten percent increase in their proportions for executive jobs, and lawyers/judges, and a little less than that as chemists and physicians. The proportion of women has increased only minimally in the engineering profession (a 2.3% increase), and has actually lost ground among professional biologists (a decline in proportions of 9%).

The decline in the proportion of women in biology is particularly interesting, given the dynamics of growth in the biotechnology sector. In chapter 2 we reviewed Occupational Handbook data on the federal government's projections of growth in different professions over time. Nearly all of the growth in jobs for advanced degree biologists in the past ten years has been due to developments in genetics, pharmaceuticals, and biotechnology. At least one-third of all biology jobs are represented by this new high-tech industry in the private sector. Unfortunately, the CPS data does not allow us to determine which type of jobs within biology are biotech vs. traditional university and government lab jobs, and whether those sectors are segregated by gender. However, we would suspect that there may be a statistical relationship here.

Although women have increased proportionately in most professional fields, the story is quite different for nonwhites. Blacks and Hispanics have experienced only very small increases across all six professions – two percent or less since 1983.

So how do we interpret the CPS data to answer our question about demographic diversity among professionals? Well, yes, there is more diversity now than in the early 1980s. But it would be foolish to assume that the affirmative action programs that have recently been disbanded in many state university systems had come anywhere near to reaching their goals of proportional representation of women and minorities across the ranks of professional workers. Increases in the proportion of women in law and medicine have produced professions that are still overwhelmingly male (about 25% of lawyer/judges are women in 1997, and 22% of practicing physicians; US Department of Labor 1997; AMA Enterprise Information Base 1998), and these are two of the professions that have experienced the most dramatic increases in the proportion of women. Black and Hispanic representation in these elite professions lags well behind female representation.

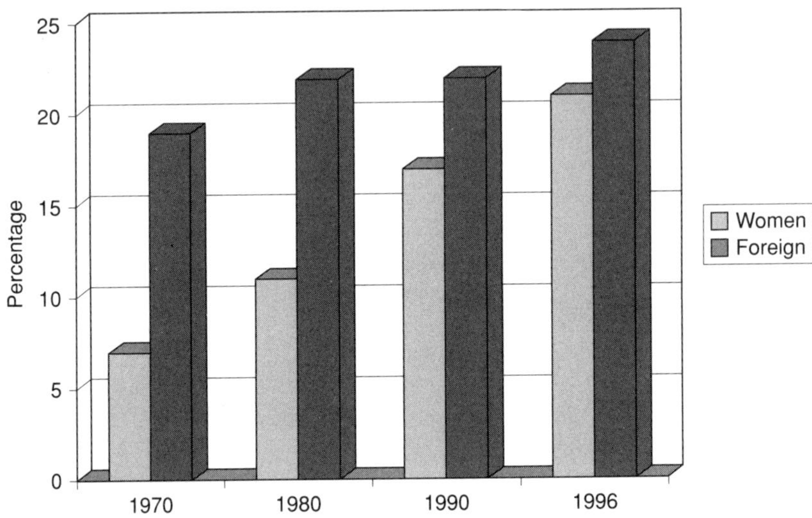

Figure 7.2 Change in the diversity of US physicians, 1970–1996 (AMA)

DIVERSITY IN THE PROFESSION OF MEDICINE

Let's look a bit more closely at one of these classic professions, medicine, and examine how the change in diversity has unfolded. Figure 7.2 provides breakdowns of the percentage of all US practicing physicians who are female or foreign-trained, since 1970. These data come from the AMA Enterprise Information Base (EIB), which houses the AMA Physician Masterfile. The EIB and Masterfile contains current and historical data on all physicians, whether AMA members or not, and includes data on graduates of foreign medical schools who reside in the US and who meet US educational and credentialing requirements to be recognized as MDs. An AMA EIB record is established when an individual enters medical school accredited by the Liaison Committee on Medical Education, or (for international medical graduates) upon entry into an ACGME-accredited program. The record for each physician contains data on medical school, year of graduation, gender, birth place, and birth date. Additional information on residency, licensure, board certifications, type of practice, practice specialty, and other career developments are included in the EIB record as the physician ages.

Foreign-trained physicians have actually provided a significant proportion of the US medical labor force since well before the 1970s. Figure 7.2 shows that that proportion is now nearly 25 percent, growing slowly but steadily from 17 percent in 1970. In 1970 the percentage of practicing physicians who were female was about 7 percent; the 1996 figure was 21 percent, a more rapid rate of change than the percentage that were foreign-trained. Information on race and/or ethnicity is not available using Masterfile data. However, in the mid-1990s, one of the recommendations made by the Council on Graduate Medical Education was to increase minority representation in medicine (COGME 1995), a recommendation that first appeared in their 1992 report. So it is probably safe to assume not much growth has occurred in the percent of physicians who are black or Hispanic. But in terms of gender diversity, the Masterfile data corresponds with the CPS data: the profession of medicine as a whole has become increasingly gender diverse, but the profession is still overwhelmingly male, and white male at that.

The data in figure 7.2 give us a picture of how the composition of the entire medical profession has changed on some indicators of demographic diversity since 1970. Figure 7.2 does not show us, however, anything about interest diversity, or about the individuals within the profession of medicine, or about how the careers of medical professionals may have changed over time. To do this, we need to look at cohorts of physicians who have graduated from medical school at the same time and try to trace the progression of their careers. The historical data on physicians from the AMA Masterfile allows us to begin that analysis.

CHANGE IN MEDICAL CAREERS OVER TIME

As we discussed in chapter 5, careers are orderly progressions of training experiences and jobs over the lifetime. The career path traces the training outcomes (degrees and locations) and job transitions (promotions, lateral and vertical moves) over an individual's working life. For most professional careers, we can think of the career path as a series of individual decisions, beginning with: where to go to school, which graduate or professional school to attend, whether to specialize and in what subfield of the profession, where to begin the job sequence (i.e., which job to accept once the degree is in hand), and whether to stay with the organization where the first job is located, or move to another, and when that should be done. As we saw in chapter 5, most theories of careers assume that earlier decisions affect the options open to individuals later in their careers, so for example, where you go to school can influence the type of job offers you get upon degree completion. Some decisions cannot easily be re-entered: once you've completed your advanced degree at one institution, you don't typically try again somewhere else. And, physician choice of specialty usually involves considerable investment of time, effort, resources, and opportunity costs. Although specialty changes do happen, the typical assumption is that physicians do not leave their chosen specialties (Ernst and Yett 1985; Colwill et al. 1997).

We can use the AMA Masterfile data to examine some of these career decisions, for physicians from different graduating cohorts. A *cohort* is defined as a group of people who have all begun some important life stage at approximately the same time point, such as the birth cohort of all children born in a particular year, or the cohort of all college freshmen entering college in a given year. Demographers and sociologists frequently study cohorts of people born during different periods, or who experienced some stage of development during or after an important social event, in order to see how their later lives were effected by that historical period, or to compare the developmental outcomes of groups that did and did not experience some important historical event. For example, there have been studies of cohorts of men who were teenagers during the Great Depression (Elder 1976), men who served in the military during World War II, or people who were college students during the peace demonstration era of the late 1960s and early 1970s.

We randomly sampled 1,000 physicians from each of three graduating cohorts of medical students: the 1970, 1980, and 1990 cohorts. These cohorts would represent new physicians, then, who were beginning their professional careers (mostly in residencies following medical school graduation) during different historical periods. For example, the 1970 cohort would have begun their residencies and first medical positions prior to the advent of the Prospective Payment System (PPS) of Medicare hospital reimbursement in 1983. Their early medical careers would have occurred before the push to control costs of care and prior to hospital efforts to drastically reduce the average length of inpatient stays. This cohort of physicians came of age during what has been termed the "good old days" of medical practice. The 1980s cohort of graduating physicians would have been directly effected by the turmoil created by PPS during their residencies and while they were selecting their specialty areas. The 1990s cohort would have been accustomed to the effects of PPS, but they would have been the first group of newly-graduated physicians to see the development and diffusion of managed care organizations and the change in physician–patient relationships engendered by managed care. These three cohorts also differ in the extent to which women are present in their ranks. Recalling figure 7.1, the proportion of all practicing physicians who were women was substantially greater in 1990 than in 1970; we would expect the three graduating cohorts to reflect similar differences in gender representation.

For all of these physicians in each medical school cohort we have extracted career observations on about a five year interval, from 1978 through 1998. Thus, for the 1970 cohort we have five observations for the years 1978, 1983, 1988, 1993, and 1998; we have four observation points for the 1980 cohort, and two for the 1990 cohort. The Masterfile contains information on a number of variables related to career choices and interest diversity, such as choice of specialty, major professional activity, and employment setting. And, since the Masterfile provides the name of the medical school attended and chosen specialty, we have created indicators for the prestige of the medical school attended for each new physician, and the prestige of specialty choice. Our plan is to: (1) examine the overall distribution of physicians on each career decision; (2) examine the distribution on each decision by cohort (to see how these decisions may have changed over time); and (3) examine the distributions on each variable by both cohort and gender (to see how men and women may differ in their choices, over time).

Before we begin our examination of career decisions, let's review the gender breakdown of these cohorts of medical school graduates. Table 7.1 below provides those numbers. As might be expected with simple random samples of medical school graduating cohorts, the representation of women increases over time, from a low of 12.5 percent in the 1970 cohort, to a high of 32.6 percent in the 1990 cohort.

Table 7.1 Medical graduates by cohort and gender (AMA)

Gender	*Cohort*			*Total*
	1970	*1980*	*1990*	
Male	875	767	674	2,316
Female	125	233	326	684
Total	1,000	1,000	1,000	3,000

Prestige of medical school

Many sociological studies have shown that occupational success is influenced by the prestige of the school you attend, whether college or postgraduate. Elite schools, such as the Ivies, and top-ranked professional schools, such as the Harvard Business School or Stanford Law School, tend to produce graduates who are "channeled" to Fortune 500 firms and prestigious law firms. In the field of medicine, graduates from the top medical schools tend to get their preferred residencies and are then courted by successful group practices.

There are 125 accredited medical schools in the United States. In order to rank the prestige of the schools attended by the physicians in our three cohorts, we have used a simple four category schema: high prestige, medium prestige, low prestige, and foreign. The high prestige schools are those ranked by the US News and World Report in 1997 within the top 12 schools in the United States. These rankings are based on four criteria: student selectivity, faculty resources (faculty to student ratios), reputation (based on two surveys of medical school deans and directors of residency programs), and research activity (total NIH research grant funds). The medium prestige schools included all non-top-rank large state university medical schools and well-known private medical schools, which are known reputationally as "solid" schools, and where medical research is regularly federally funded. The low prestige category consisted primarily of very small medical schools, most of them privately owned, and some unaccredited medical schools. The foreign medical schools are unranked, given the great variety in types, quality of programs, and selectivity of admission standards included in this category. Foreign schools include both Canadian and other international medical schools.

Figure 7.3 presents the distribution of our sample of 3000 medical school graduates by prestige of medical school attended. If we ignore the foreign medical school category, the distribution into high, medium, and low prestige forms a very nice standard normal curve: most cases fall into the middle, with about 14 percent at either end of the distribution. This would suggest that our school ranking categories are probably a reasonable way to approximate medical school prestige differences, even though our categories have not been rigorously validated.

Figure 7.4 provides distributions of medical graduates across the prestige categories, organized by cohort, with bars for the youngest cohort in the front of the graph. The same normal distribution is evident in the

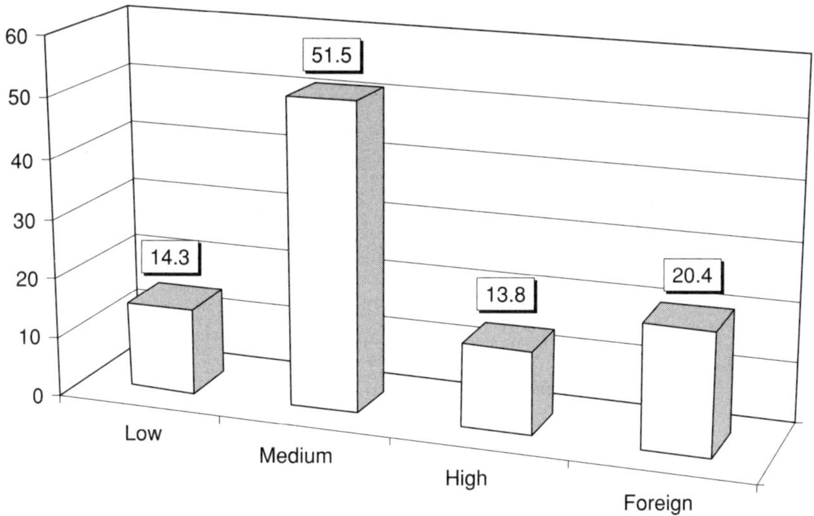

Figure 7.3 Prestige of medical school attended, all cohorts (AMA)

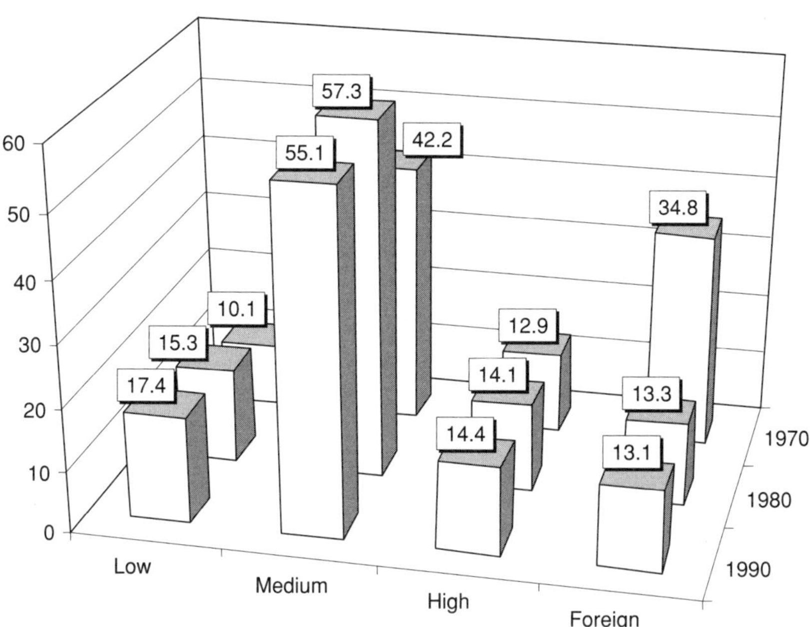

Figure 7.4 Prestige of medical school attended, by cohorts (AMA)

percentage of medical graduates from high, medium, and low prestige schools across the three cohorts, with one major change. The percentage of graduates from foreign medical schools drops dramatically between 1970 and 1980. The percentage of graduates in the 1970 cohort from foreign schools (in our random sample of 1000 physicians) was almost 35 percent; by 1980 that proportion had declined to 13 percent, and remained there into the 1990 cohort. This same drop in the percent of all practicing physicians from international medical schools has been observed in the national statistics of the AMA (physician characteristics and distribution, 1997–8 edition 1997). A large percent of physicians practicing in the US in 1996 who had graduated prior to 1970 came from Canadian and international schools (27.5%). However, following the expansion of US medical schools through the 1970s and early 1980s, the proportion of foreign medical school graduates practicing in the US began to decline.

Those graduating from medical school in 1980 or later are more likely to be graduates of US schools: nationwide, the proportion of active 1996 physicians who had graduated from international schools in 1980 or later had declined to 19 percent. We think this is because of changes in the numbers of US medical school graduates (a much increased denominator) as well as a slight decrease in the rate of more recent international graduates migrating to the US. In 1976 the US enacted federal limitations on the immigration of foreign nationals, and foreign medical graduates were required to take and pass the VISA Qualifying Examination (Physician Characteristics and Distribution 1997–8 edition).

Figure 7.5 further divides our three cohorts by prestige of medical school and by gender (the graph for women is on top). This time we have rearranged the prestige results (medium, low, high), so that taller bars do not block our view of shorter bars. Looking first at the most recent graduating cohort (1990, first row of both graphs) we find that the overwhelming majority of both men and women 1990 graduates were from mid-rank schools: 53 percent (men) and 57 percent (women). Further, the distribution of men and women by prestige of medical school does not differ more than 4 percent in any direction. Men are slightly more likely to have graduated from high prestige US schools, or from international schools; women are slightly more likely to have been graduates from mid and low prestige schools. The same basic distribution was evident in the 1980 cohort (middle bars), with one interesting difference: a larger percent of the males in this cohort were graduates of international schools, compared to the women (15% compared to 7%).

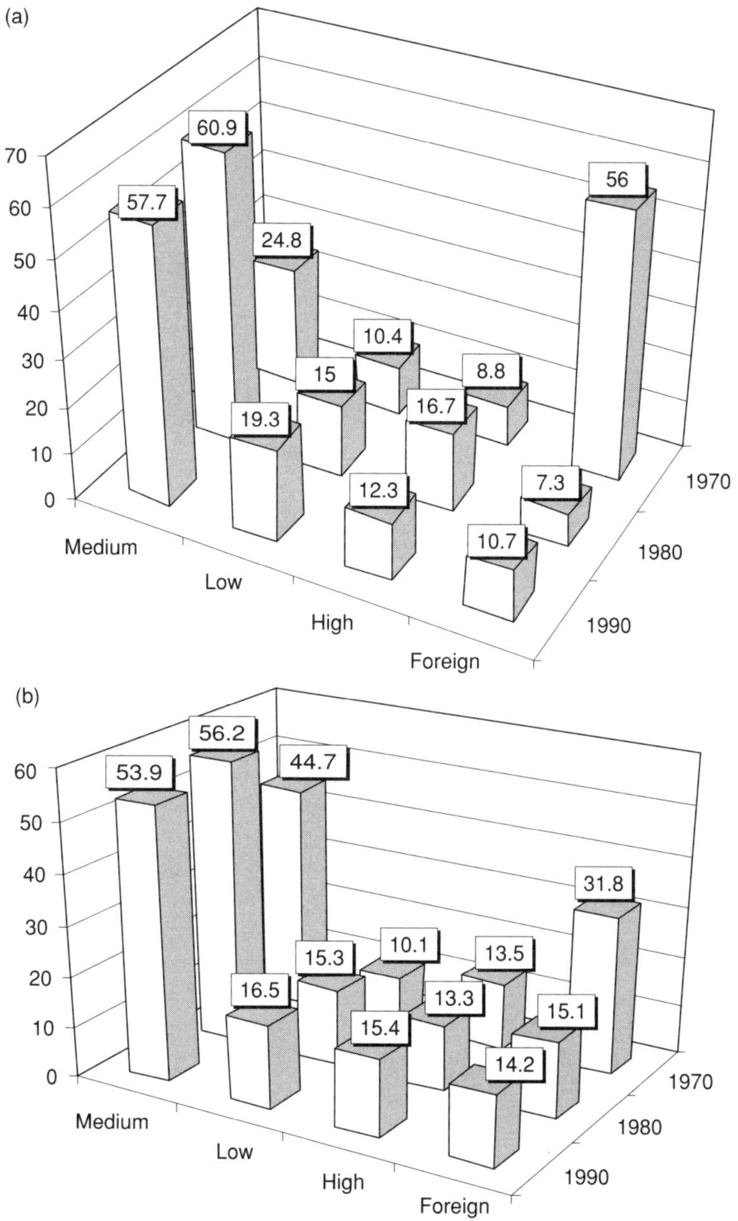

Figure 7.5 Prestige of school attended by cohort: (a) female physicians; (b) male physicians (AMA)

Finally, the 1970 cohort of graduates (two back rows of bars in each graph) was the one with many more graduates from international schools, and the smallest number of women overall (125 women, compared to 875 men). Surprisingly, over half of the 1970 cohort of graduating women were graduates of international schools. Less than 9 percent of the 1970 women graduates had attended high prestige US schools, and about 25 percent had graduated from mid-rank US schools (compared to 13.5 and 44.7% of the men). The same proportion (10%) of men and women had been graduates of low prestige schools. So it would appear that earlier cohorts of women medical school graduates who went on to practice medicine in the US were disproportionately from mid-rank prestige US schools and from non-US medical schools. The subsequent (post-1970 through mid-1980s) expansion of US medical schools probably helped to boost gender representation in higher ranked schools. However, men still have a slight edge in the highest ranked schools.

Choice of medical specialty

For the past decade or more, health policy experts have argued that too many US physicians have chosen to pursue specialty (non-primary-care) practice, and this has artificially created demand for more specialty care and driven healthcare costs ever upward. Primary care is typically defined as "first encounter" or general care, and this includes general practice, family practice, internal medicine, obstetrics and gynecology, and pediatrics. More recent studies have shown that medical students are more likely now than in the recent past to indicate an interest in primary care (about 20% of medical students interviewed in 1995 planned to pursue primary care). But this is still far below the goal of the Association of American Medical Colleges for 50 percent of medical students to select primary care (Grumbach and Lee 1991). In an extraordinary effort to reduce specialty care and re-orient health care delivery toward primary care, Medicare adopted a restructured reimbursement scheme in the late 1980s and early 1990s, the Resource Based Relative Value Scale. RBRVS increased payments to primary care physicians and reduced payments per service to specialists. In addition, the proliferation of health maintenance and managed care organizations has put increased emphasis on primary care physicians as "gatekeepers" or "care managers," in an attempt to reduce the demand for and access to specialty care.

Physician choice of primary vs. specialty care as a career decision has been examined by a number of disciplines, including sociologists, psychologists, health educators, economists, and health policy analysts. The determinants of specialty choice range from income expectations, avoidance of malpractice, personal and demographic traits, to location of practice, medical school attended, expected practice characteristics, and practice prestige. A short list of such studies is included in the additional readings listed in p. 231. In this chapter, however, we are not interested in why physicians choose different specialties, but in whether specialty choice differs by cohort and for men and women.

Other authors have used a number of different schema for categorizing different specialties. There are over 30 different medical specialties, and over 80 different subspecialties; thus, a comparison over all specialties and subspecialties would be tedious. Some categorizations split specialties by primary care vs. specialty care (see Fincher et al. 1992), and then specialty can be split into medical vs. surgical vs. support specialties (see Kiker and Zeh 1998). The AMA uses a list of 39 specialties in its statistical reporting of trends in the supply of physicians, and these are grouped as (1) general/family practice; (2) medical specialties; (3) surgical specialties; and (4) other specialties. The "other" category covers a long list of subspecialized areas, including aerospace medicine, emergency medicine, and psychiatry. The AMA data on specialties are based on self-reported, self-designated physician survey responses from the Physician's Professional Activities (PAA) questionnaire, which has functioned as the AMA's rotating census since 1985. Every year, one-third of all physicians are surveyed.

We have developed our own list of specialty categorizations that is based loosely on both the four-category grouping of the AMA, and the longer list of 39 subspecialties. Based on AMA data on specialty area reporting, our categorization uses ten categories reflecting both the most frequently occurring specialties (like internal medicine, surgery, general practice), as well as an attempt to "clump" many of the "other" subspecialties around identifiable body-systems. The full list of ten specialization categories, and the subspecialties included in each, is provided in Table 7.2 below. Since we are considering specialty choice as a type of interest diversity, our longer list of specialty categories should help us determine more exactly if there are shifts over time or between genders in the medical profession (are interests becoming more diverse, more subdivided, do men and women choose differently?) than if we only used four broad categories.

Table 7.2 Ten groups of medical specialties

Ten Category Grouping	*Specialties*
Brain	Child neurology Clinical neurophysiology Neurology Neurological surgery Neuroradiology Pediatric surgery (neurology)
Heart	Cardiac electrophysiology Cardiothoracic surgery Cardiovascular disease Cardiovascular surgery Pediatric pulmonology (thoracic surgery) Pulmonary disease Thoracic surgery
Cancer	Gynecological oncology Hematology/oncology Medical oncology Pediatric hematology/oncology Radiation oncology Surgical oncology Therapeutic radiology
Surgery	Abdominal surgery Adult reconstructive orthopedics Colon/rectal surgery Facial plastic surgery General surgery Hand surgery (orthopedic surgery) Head and neck surgery Orthopedic surgery Orthopedic surgery of the spine Orthopedic trauma Pediatric orthopedics (orthopedic surgery) Pediatric surgery (general surgery) Plastic surgery Sports medicine (orthopedic surgery) Surgery of the hand (plastic surgery) Surgical critical care Trauma surgery Urological surgery Vascular surgery
Specialty Systems	Allergy Allergy & immunology

Table 7.2 *(cont'd)*

Ten Category Grouping	*Specialties*
	Dermatology Dermatological surgery Gastroenterology Gynecology Immunology Maternal & fetal medicine Neonatal/perinatal medicine Obstetrics Obstetrics & gynecology Ophthalmology Otolaryngology Pediatric ophthalmology (opthalmology) Pediatric otolaryngology (otolaryngology) Reproductive endocrinology
Internal Medicine	Critical care medicine (internal medicine) Diabetes Endocrinology, diabetes & metabolism Geriatric medicine (internal medicine) Hematology (internal medicine) Hepatology Infectious disease Internal medicine Nephrology Nutrition Pulmonary critical care medicine Rheumatology Sports medicine (internal medicine)
General Practice	Family practice General practice General preventive medicine Geriatric medicine (family practice) Public health & general preventive medicine Sports medicine (family practice)
Pediatrics	Adolescent medicine Internal medicine (pediatrics) Pediatrics Pediatric allergy Pediatric cardiology Pediatric critical care medicine Pediatric emergency medicine (pediatrics) Pediatric endocrinology

Table 7.2 *(cont'd)*

Ten Category Grouping	*Specialties*
	Pediatric gastroenterology Pediatric infectious disease Pediatric nephrology
Psychiatry	Child and adolescent psychiatry Forensic psychiatry Pediatric psychiatry Psychiatry Psychoanalysis
Other	Aerospace medicine Anatomical/Clinical pathology Anatomic pathology Anesthesiology Blood banking transfusion medicine Clinical pathology Critical care medicine (anesthesiology) Cytopathology Dermatopathology Diagnostic radiology Emergency medicine Forensic pathology Hematology (pathology) Medical genetics Neuropathology Nuclear medicine Nuclear radiology Occupational medicine Pain management (anesthesiology) Physical medicine & rehabilitation Public health Radiology Selective pathology Vascular and interventional radiology Other specialty Addiction medicine Clinical pharmacology Legal medicine Medical management Other specialty Palliative medicine Pain medicine Sleep medicine

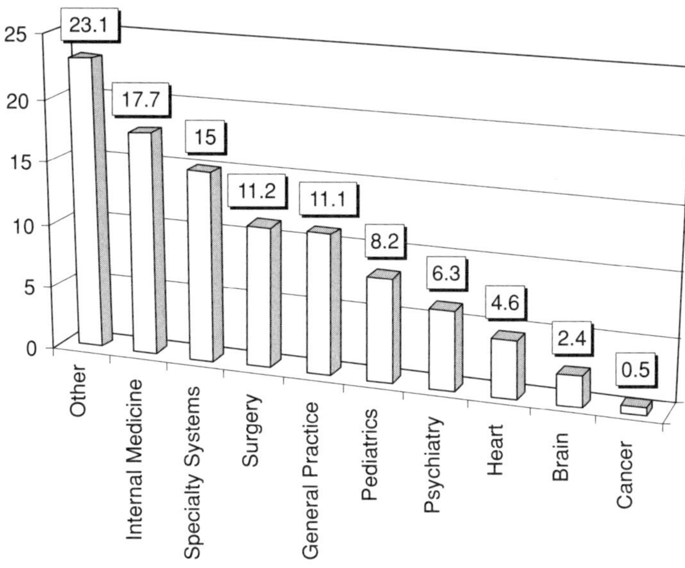

Figure 7.6 Primary medical specialty in 1998, all cohorts (AMA)

Figure 7.6 provides a summary bar graph for our sample of 3000 medical graduates, using each physicians' self-designated primary medical specialization in 1998. The "other" category still contains almost one quarter of our sample, followed by internal medicine (17.7%), specialty systems (like allergy/immunology, dermatology, OB/Gyn, etc.) comprise 15 percent of the total sample, general surgery (11.2%), and general practice (11.1%). The remaining five categories each represented less than 10 percent of the sample (pediatrics, psychiatry, heart, brain, and cancer).

The graph in Figure 7.6 gives us a cross-sectional view of how our sample of 3,000 physicians self-reported their primary specialty in 1998. Older and younger cohorts are combined and examined at the same time point. Another more interesting view is one in which we examine the point in the early career of newly graduated physicians when they are most likely to have chosen their first specialization. This is probably about three to four years after an initial residency has been completed, or about eight years past medical school graduation. Figure 7.7 displays the distribution of each graduating cohort on self-selection of the primary medical specialty, at that early career stage, eight years postgraduation. The 1970 cohort is the top panel, followed by 1980 and 1990 on the

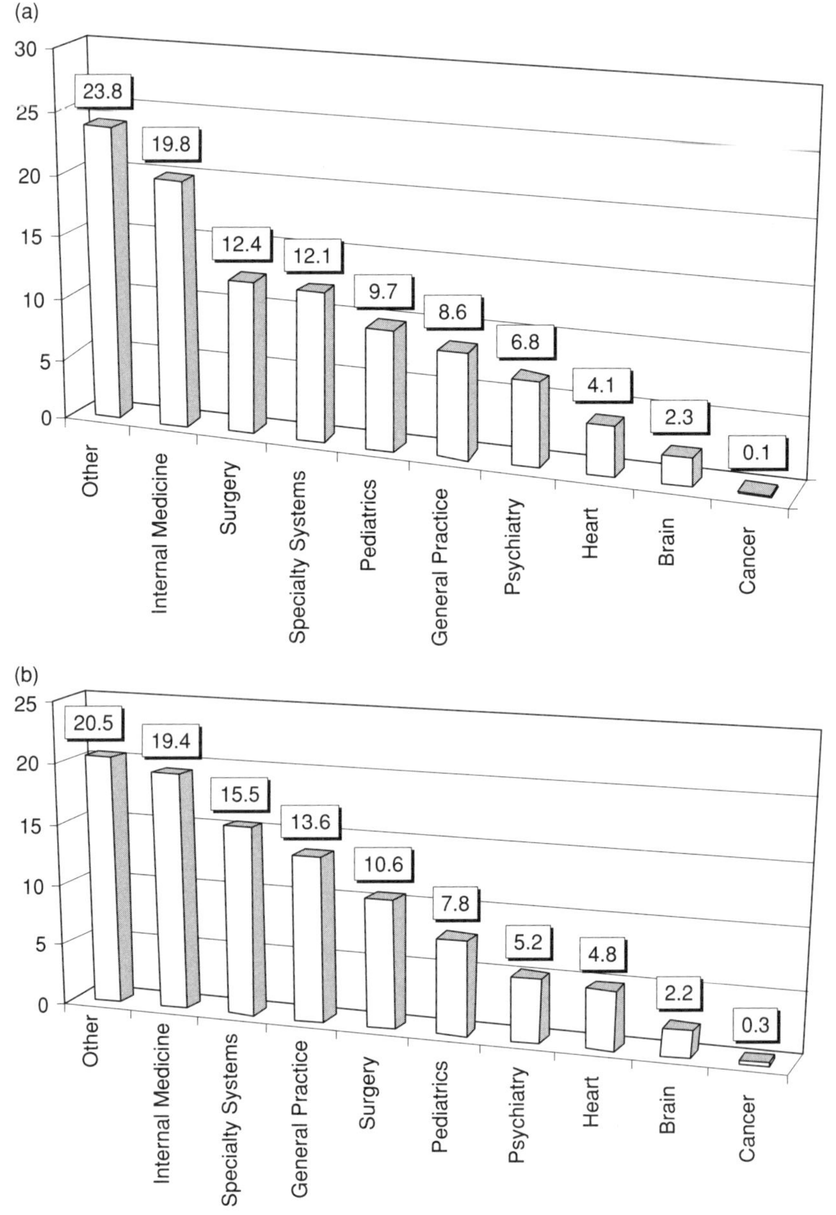

Figure 7.7 Primary medical specialty, eight years after graduation: (a) 1970 cohort; (b) 1980 cohort

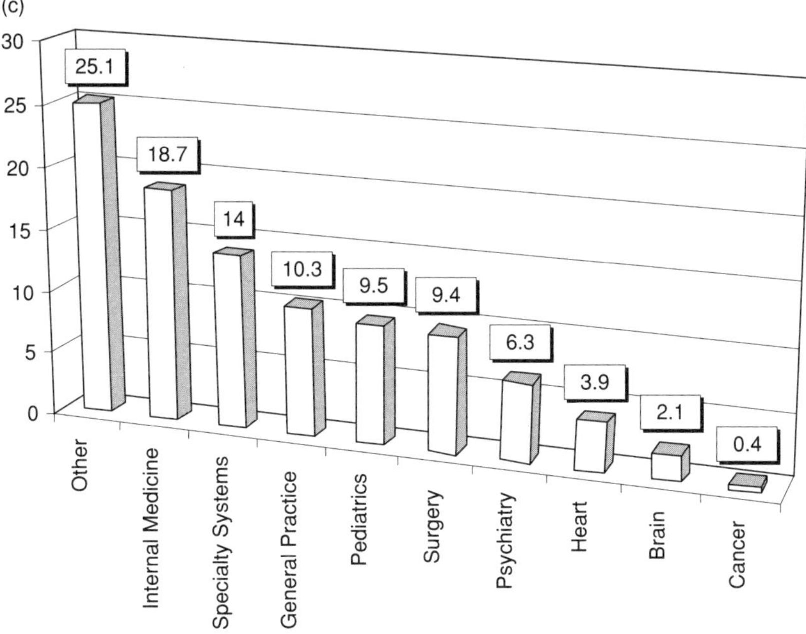

Figure 7.7 (*cont'd*) (c) 1990 cohort (AMA)

bottom. Two things are obvious about this graph: (1) for each cohort, the "other" category is the most frequent choice; (2) except for some shifts by the 1980 cohort that are mostly reversed by the 1990 cohort, there are no really drastic changes in the popularity of these 10 categories of specialization. Surgery as a specialty choice has declined 3 percent in popularity between the 1970 and 1990 cohort (probably related to risks and costs associated with malpractice litigation); and both specialty systems specializations and general practice have increased by about 2 percent.

Figure 7.8 further partitions the frequency of specialty choices by cohort *and by gender*. Once we separate men and women physicians in this graph (women are in the top panel, men are below), it becomes clear that the rank orderings of most frequently chosen specialties are different, and that changes across cohorts are not the same for women and men. Looking first at the women physicians, the most frequently chosen specialties by the 1970 cohort in 1978 were "other," pediatrics, internal medicine, and psychiatry. Those top four were not stable across

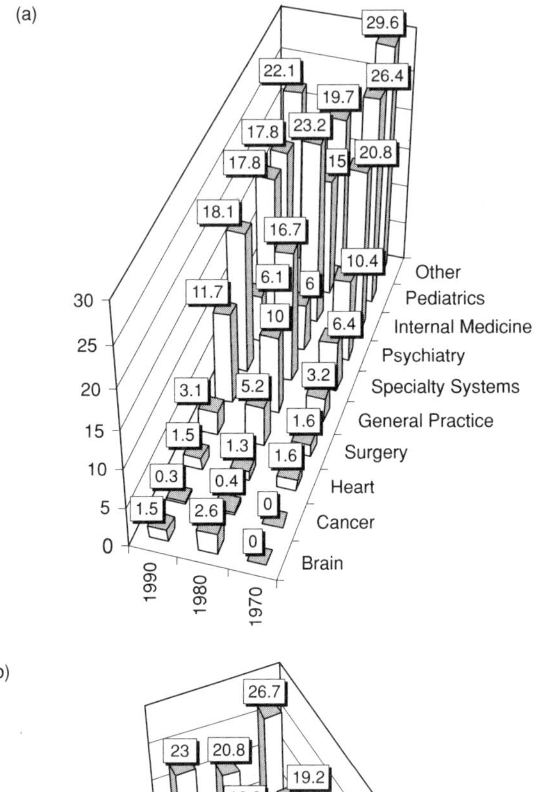

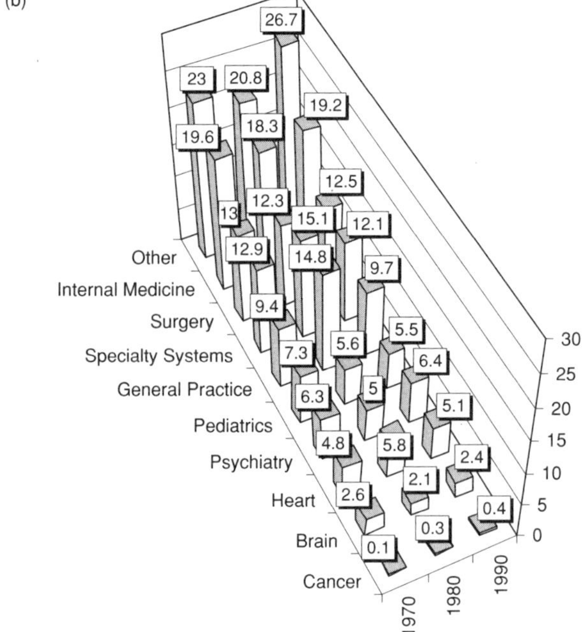

Figure 7.8 Primary specialties eight years after graduation by cohort: (a) female physicians; (b) male physicians (AMA)

either the 1980 or 1990 cohorts. The percentage of women physicians who chose "other" specialties at 8-year-postgraduate mark declined by 7 percent between the 1970 and 1990 cohorts. Also on the decline as a specialty choice among women were pediatrics (loss of 9%!), internal medicine (loss of 3%), and psychiatry (loss of 4%). Large gains in popularity were observed for specialty subsystems (increase of 12% among women), and general practice (increase of 8%). General surgery, brain, and cancer specialties were marginally more popular among women of the 1990 cohort.

Among men of the 1970 cohort, the choice of specialty at the 8-year-mark clustered around the "other" category (23%), internal medicine (19%), surgery (13%), and specialty systems (13%). Twenty-years later, the 1990 cohort of men was still choosing these same four specialties; the "other" category went up about 3 percent and the other three were stable. There were very small increases in the percent of the men choosing psychiatry, heart, and cancer specialties by 1998.

So far what we have uncovered with these detailed bar graphs on medical training and choice of specialty is quite interesting. We know now that the differences in where men and women go to medical school (elite or nonelite schools) have not been that great since the mid-1970s. Increases in women attending US medical schools followed the expansion of medical training in the 1970s and early 1980s, and the reduction in international medical school graduates (especially women) practicing in the US after immigration changes of the mid-1970s. On the other hand, choice of specialty has not been comparable between the sexes since 1970; and, later cohorts of women have changed their set of most preferred specialties, but men have not. Of some note is that our comparison by cohort and gender show that the typical stereotype that all women physicians become pediatricians is simply not true, and has become less true with each successive cohort of medical school graduates. Women in medicine are moving into more areas of medicine in the past two decades, whereas men seem to be stable in their selection of internal medicine, specialty systems, and surgery. The ranking of specialties chosen by men in the 1970s are almost exactly the same in the 1990s. Thus, interest diversity, in terms of type of specialty and variation in choice of specialization, is more marked among women physicians, and those interests are not stable over time. On the other hand, male physicians of the 1990s show a marked resemblance to male physicians of the 1970s.

Our next task is to consider whether these patterns also emerge in an analysis of specialty prestige, comparing across cohorts and between men and women. Prestige or status of medical specialties is an often-cited reason for physicians choosing various specialties, but there is little agreement within the literature on how to define this concept and measure it empirically. Different scholars have emphasized different aspects of occupational prestige, and have focused on different groups' perceptions of what are high prestige jobs and low prestige jobs. Unfortunately, prestige is difficult to define without reference to other important job factors, such as expected income, expected lifestyle postresidency, intellectual content of the specialty, and diagnostic challenge. Some have pointed out that perceptions of prestige may reflect the competitiveness of the specialty, whether in terms of the difficulty of obtaining positions, residencies, becoming certified, or market competition (Fincher et al. 1992). Alternatively, others focus on the lay public's perceptions of ascribed esteem, rather than physician perceptions of prestige (Rosoff and Leone 1991). These authors argue that there is a stable prestige hierarchy among medical specialties, with surgery and cardiology consistently at the top, and dermatology and psychiatry consistently at the bottom.

There are, however, characteristics of the work of physicians themselves – the content and procedures of work – which importantly influence perceptions of status. These work content characteristics may be correlated with higher income and/or the public's perceptions of status, but they are not equivalent. For example, specialty prestige may be partly influenced by whether or not the practitioner comes into contact with stigmatized populations. The medical equivalent of "dirty work" involves treating patients who are dangerous, lacking in resources, and/or socially outcast. Thus, emergency medicine, psychiatry, and infectious diseases are usually always in the low prestige category. Another work content characteristic concerns the level of skill or technological sophistication required in the process of treatment. All other things held constant, medical treatments that are very high-tech and very "dramatic" (i.e., micro-surgery, particularly recent advances in brain surgery and pediatric surgery in various areas) are higher in prestige than dermatology or endocrinology. And finally, the extent to which the specialty's interventions are likely to produce positive results (effectiveness) may influence both physician and public perceptions of prestige. Thus, oncology has probably increased in status over the past two decades due to advances in treatment modalities and increased survival rates for various cancers.

This last example actually brings up an important caveat to this discussion. Status or prestige rankings are not necessarily stable over time. Any of the dimensions of prestige we have mentioned in this section can change over time, especially earnings, technological developments in treatment, or characteristics of the populations treated by a given specialty. This is both a problem (especially for the researcher) as well as a fundamentally interesting aspect of prestige rankings. Very few analysts in any area of social stratification are capable of modeling a status ranking that changes over time. However, it is quite likely that perceptions of those characteristics may take longer to change than the dimensions themselves. This is particularly true within specialties that are very esoteric, or for which general knowledge is fairly limited. We do not claim to have a solution to this complication, but we are aware of the problem and would urge the reader to keep this in mind as well.

For purposes of the descriptive analyses in this chapter, we have adopted a specialty prestige ranking which is: (1) loosely based on the work characteristics described above; (2) assumed to be stable from 1970 through 1998; and (3) fairly compatible with the most accepted rankings in the literature. Again, we use only three levels of prestige: high, medium, and low, and the largest category is the middle rank. High prestige specialties roughly include brain, heart, cancer, and surgical specialties; mid-rank prestige includes specialty systems and internal medicine; low prestige includes general practice, most primary care, pediatrics, and psychiatry. The complete prestige ranking is provided in table 7.3 below.

Figure 7.9 shows the simple distribution of our complete sample of 3,000 doctors by specialty prestige level in 1998. Again, over half our sample falls in the mid-rank category, and 14 percent are in high prestige specialties. Using the same ranking, figure 7.10 shows the specialty prestige level distribution by cohort. Here we again use the eight-years-postgraduation mark as our time frame for specialty choice. Interestingly, in later cohorts a few more physicians have opted for mid-level prestige specialties, but overall, the distribution is very stable.

Finally, figure 7.11 provides the gender by cohort comparisons, again using the 8-year-postgraduation mark for each cohort. The top panel represents women physicians. Recall that in each cohort there are many more men than women. Keeping that in mind, however, the comparisons between genders is very interesting. In each cohort, the percentage of women who opted for high prestige specialties is much lower than the proportion of men. The proportion of each gender in each cohort in the mid-rank specialties is fairly comparable: around 50–55 percent. However, the gender comparison on low prestige specialties also shows differences. In this case, the percent of men in each cohort found in low-prestige specialties is much lower than the percent of women, and this is true for each cohort.

Table 7.3 Medical specialty prestige ranking

Low	*Medium*	*High*
Aerospace medicine	Allergy	Abdominal surgery
Adolescent medicine	Allergy & immunology	Adult reconstructive orthopedics
Child and adolescent psychiatry	Anatomical/clinical pathology	Cardiothoracic surgery
Dermatology	Anatomic pathology	Cardiovascular disease
Dermatological surgery	Anesthesiology	Cardiovascular surgery
Emergency medicine	Blood banking transfusion medicine	Colon/rectal surgery
Family practice	Cardiac electrophysiology	General surgery
Forensic pathology	Child neurology (neurology)	Gynecological oncology
Forensic psychiatry	Clinical neurophysiology	Hand surgery (orthopedic surgery)
General practice	Clinical pathology	Head and neck surgery
General preventive medicine	Critical care medicine (anesthesiology)	Hematology/oncology (internal medicine)
Geriatric medicine (family practice)	Critical care medicine (internal medicine)	Medical oncology
Internal medicine (pediatrics)	Cytopathology	Neurological surgery
Occupational medicine	Dermatopathology	Orthopedic surgery of the spine
Pediatrics	Diabetes	Orthopedic trauma
Pediatric allergy	Diagnostic radiology	Pediatric orthopedics (orthopedic surgery)
Pediatric critical care medicine	Endocrinology, diabetes & metabolism	Pediatric surgery (general surgery)
Pediatric endocrinology	Facial plastic surgery	Pediatric surgery (neurological surgery)
Pediatric emergency medicine (pediatrics)	Gastroenterology	Pulmonary critical care medicine
Pediatric gastroenterology	Geriatric medicine (internal medicine)	Radiation oncology
Pediatric hematology/oncology	Gynecology	Surgical critical care
Pediatric infectious disease	Hematology (internal medicine)	Surgical oncology
Pediatric nephrology	Hematology (pathology)	Thoracic surgery
Pediatric psychiatry	Hepatology	Trauma surgery
Pediatric pulmonology	Immunology	Vascular surgery
Physical medicine & rehabilitation	Infectious disease (internal medicine)	
	Internal medicine	

Psychiatry	Maternal & fetal medicine
Psychoanalysis	Medical genetics
Public health	Neonatal perinatal medicine
Public health & general preventive medicine	Nephrology
Sports medicine (family practice)	Neurology
Other specialty	Neuropathology
Addiction medicine	Neuroradiology
Legal medicine	Nutrition
Medical management	Nuclear medicine
Other specialty	Nuclear radiology
Clinical pharmacology	Obstetrics
Palliative medicine	Obstetrics & gynecology
Pain medicine	Ophthalmology
Sleep medicine	Otolaryngology
	Pain management (anesthesiology)
	Pediatric cardiology
	Pediatric ophthalmology (opthalmology)
	Pediatric otolaryngology (otolaryngology)
	Pediatric radiology (radiology)
	Plastic surgery
	Pulmonary disease
	Radiology
	Reproductive endocrinology
	Rheumatology
	Selective pathology
	Sports medicine (internal medicine)
	Sports medicine (orthopedic surgery)
	Surgery of the hand (plastic surgery)
	Urological surgery
	Therapeutic radiology
	Vascular and interventional radiology

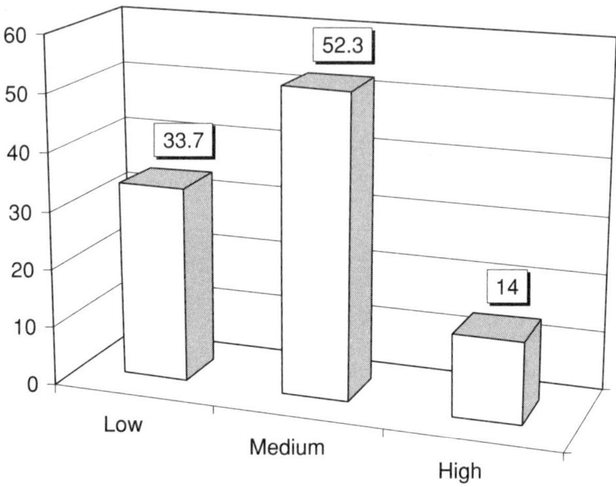

Figure 7.9 Prestige of primary medical specialty eight years after graduation, all cohorts (AMA)

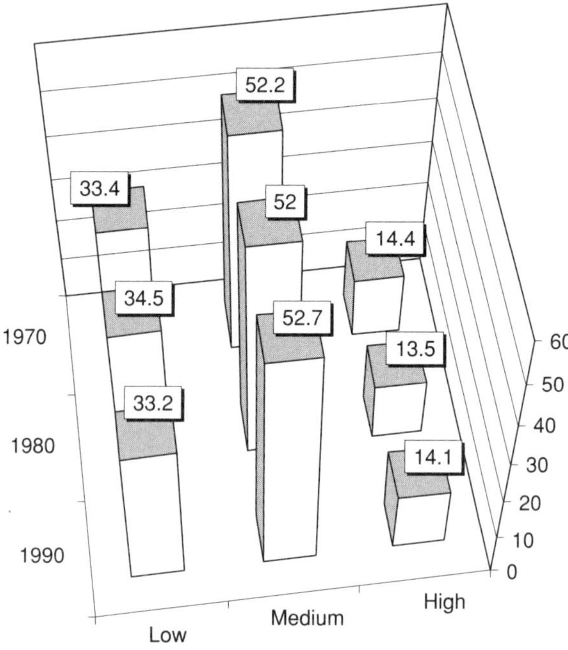

Figure 7.10 Prestige of primary medical specialty eight years after graduation, by cohorts (AMA)

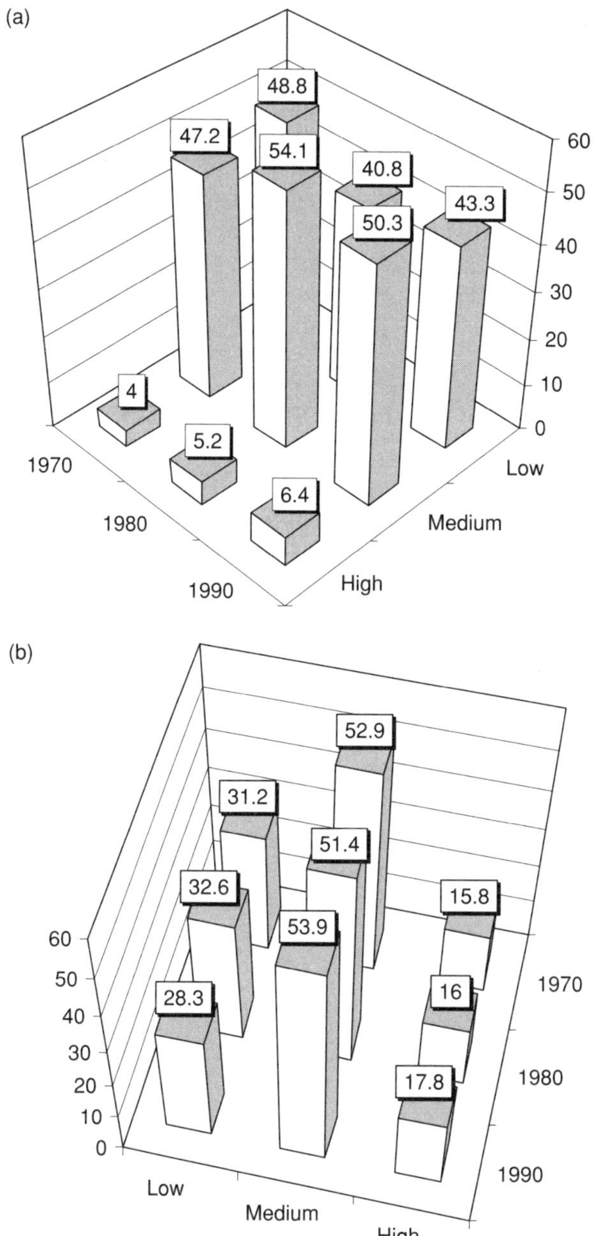

Figure 7.11 Prestige of primary specialty eight years after graduation by cohort: (a) female physicians; (b) male physicians (AMA)

Once again, the cohort by gender comparisons reveal a different picture, one that is typically masked by an examination of the entire population of physicians at one time point. Clearly, not all women become pediatricians, and not all men become brain surgeons. Similarly, women in medicine do not automatically opt for the "safe," routine, 9–5 specialties. Male medical graduates are more likely to opt for high prestige specialties than women, and a larger proportion of women medical graduates go into low prestige specialties than men. The intercohort comparisons do not show distinct changes in prestige of medical specialty: the patterns of the 1970 cohort are fairly similar to those of the 1990 cohort.

Major professional activity

Another way to examine interest diversity within the profession of medicine is to consider variation in how physicians self-define their major professional activity. The AMA Masterfile provides data from the PPS questionnaire on two categories of medical work: patient care and nonpatient care. Patient care work includes both office-based and hospital-based practice; hospital-based practice subsumes physicians in residency training and full-time members of hospital staffs. Nonpatient care activity is broken down into administration, medical teaching, medical research, other activity (MDs employed by insurance carriers, pharmaceutical firms, corporations, medical societies, etc.), and inactive (retired physicians, semi-retired, part-time, and temporarily not in practice). A final category, "no classification," is used to code physicians who did not provide information on their major activity. In the graphs below we show the distributions for direct patient care (combining hospital-staff and office-based practice), residents, medical research, medical training, administration, other nonpatient care, inactive, and no classification.

Figure 7.12 provides the 1998 snapshot of all cohorts combined, with the most frequently reported type of professional activity arrayed from left to right. Not surprisingly, the overwhelming majority (80%) of our sample of 3,000 physicians self-categorized as involved in direct patient care. Although not shown in this graph, most of those indicated office-based practice (71%), and 10 percent indicated direct patient care as hospital staff. The next most frequently encountered activity was that of work as residents: 7 percent of the total sample. Almost as many physicians reported other non-patient care as their major activity (6.2%),

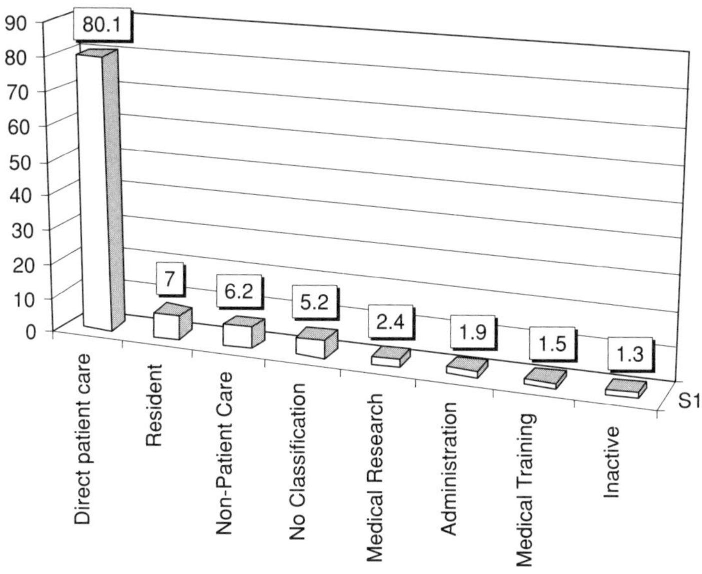

Figure 7.12 Major professional activity of physicians in 1998, all cohorts (AMA)

and over 5 percent declined to report their major professional activity. The remaining four categories each accounted for less than 3 percent of the total sample.

Figure 7.13 provides the cross-cohort comparison, using the early career stage of 8-year-postgraduation as the observation point. The 1970 cohort is shown by the first row of bars, and the array of activities presents the rank ordering of most frequently occurring categories for the 1970 cohort. This cohort reported 59 percent of its graduates were involved in direct patient care at the 8 year mark, followed by almost 18 percent in the no classification category, 11 percent in residencies, and 6.6 percent in medical research. The 1980 cohort shows a different pattern: almost 80 percent in direct patient care, followed by 11.6 percent in residencies, and three percent in medical research. The 1990 cohort shows yet another pattern at the 8 year mark: about 67 percent in direct patient care, almost 20 percent in residencies, and over 11 percent refusing to report.

How do we interpret these confusing patterns? First, the categories themselves have not changed in the AMA reporting system since 1967, so we know that all of these categories have been on the yearly survey

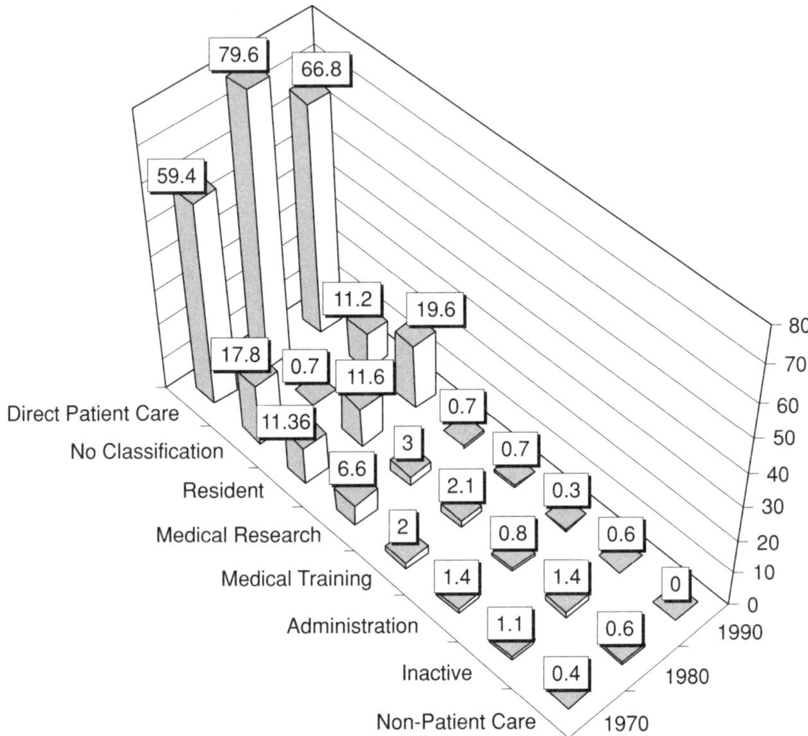

Figure 7.13 Major professional activity of physicians eight years after graduation, by cohort (AMA)

since that time. Further, physicians are asked to report average hours worked per typical week in each activity, and the categorization of their major professional activity is done through computer programs based on hours per week in each category. The categorization should have some degree of validity (Physician Characteristics and Distribution 1997–8 edition). Further, the "not classified" category is only assigned if no additional follow-up information can be obtained from the physician to allow categorization. So this category is not a typical "missing data" or residual/NA category.

The cross-cohort comparison is clear on at least three results. First, for each cohort, direct patient care is the major activity reported at the 8-year-postgraduation mark, although the proportion in this category varies by as much as 20 percent across cohorts. Second, the proportion of the 1990 cohort still in residency training eight years after graduation represents a definite increase over previous cohorts; this bears continued observation in future years. It may be the case that residencies are increasing in average length, or that it is more common for new physicians to opt for a second residency after graduation. Third, the "not classified" category seems to lose or gain cohort members as a trade-off with other categories. This suggests that the meaning of the professional activity categories is not completely stable over time. For whatever reason, each cohort varies in the proportion of its members who do not provide information on their major professional activity.[1]

Figure 7.14 further breaks down major professional activity by cohort and gender. Women physicians are displayed in the top panel, men in the bottom panel. Once again, there are substantial proportional differences between men and women within each cohort. Beginning with the 1970 cohort, the proportion of men who are involved in direct patient care at the 8-year mark is substantially larger than proportion of women; a difference of 22 percent. Women in this cohort are more likely to be categorized as "no classification" (24.8% compared to 16.8% of the men), or to be medical residents at the 8 year mark (18% compared to 10% of the men). The only other notable difference is in the "inactive" category; 5.6 percent of the women are inactive compared to less than one percent of the men.

The 1980 cohort shows no gender difference in either the proportions in direct patient care (about 80% of each gender) or the proportion with "no classification" (less than 1% each). There are, however, a larger proportion of men reporting resident work at the eight-years mark than women (13% compared to 6%), and more women in the "inactive" category (4.3% compared to less than 1% of men). There are slightly larger proportions of women in medical research and medical teaching, but the percentages are very small (less than 5%).

Finally, the 1990 cohort changes the profile once again. The different proportions of men and women in direct patient care reverse the 1970 difference, and both proportions are much smaller than the 1980 proportions (almost 74% of women, and 63% of men in direct patient care). The percent of each gender in the "no classification" category is equal and back up to 11 percent. The proportion of men in residencies at the 8 year mark increased to 23 percent, and is much larger than the proportion for women (12%). There are very small proportions of all other categories of activity (1% or less).

Where does that leave us? First, direct patient care is consistently the "nine hundred pound gorilla" with which all cohorts dance, both

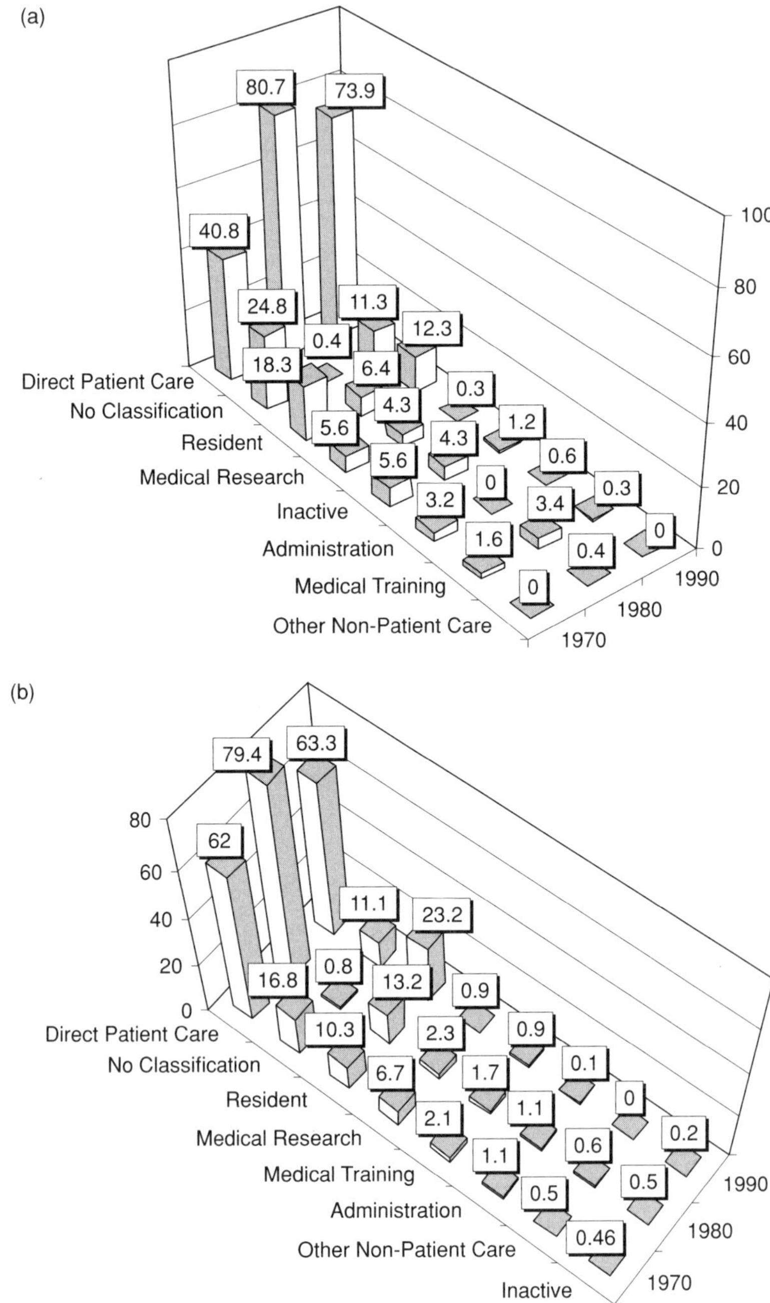

Figure 7.14 Type of medical practice eight years after graduation by cohort: (a) female physicians; (b) male physicians (AMA)

men and women. Second, there's something unusual about the 1980 cohort; it doesn't behave as an intermediate step between what we see in 1970 and what we see in the 1990 cohort. Third, there are gender differences in every cohort, but they aren't consistent in direction. This may be a function of the initial very small numbers of women in the 1970 cohort, and the problem with unstable or shifting meanings attached to the categories of professional activity. The gender difference in "not classified" disappears by 1980, but then the proportions for both genders jump from zero in 1980 to 11 percent in 1990. Fourth, more newly graduated physicians of both genders are prolonging their time in residencies. This may be due to the need for more intense training in many newer subspecialties, and due to the increased instability in the medical sector in general (post-PPS and managed care). Young physicians may find it preferable to extend their training period in order to delay decision-making and thus outlast the uncertainty in the industry.

Type of employment setting

The last indicator of professional diversity we will examine concerns type of employment. We have data for our sample on each physician's self-designated employment setting, whether self-employed/solo practice, two-physician practice, group practice, HMOs, medical schools, nongovernmental hospitals, government hospitals of various sorts, VA, military and other federal institutions, and other patient care and non-patient care settings. We would argue that the profession of medicine is becoming more interest-diverse as a wider range of employment settings become more common.

Figure 7.15 provides our last 1998 "snapshot" of our entire sample by employment setting. The largest category of employment in 1998 was group practice, at 25.7 percent. An almost equal number of physicians from this sample fell into the "no classification" category, meaning that the data are missing for 25.2 percent of the sample. A similar proportion of the total population of physicians also are listed under "no classification" (Table A-23 of the Physician Characteristics and Distribution 1997–8 edition).[2] The next largest category of employment in 1998 was solo practice, at 17.8 percent, and non-governmental hospitals at almost 12 percent. An additional 6.3 percent of this sample were employed by military hospitals, and just under 5 percent in each of the categories of medical schools and two-physician practices. According to national

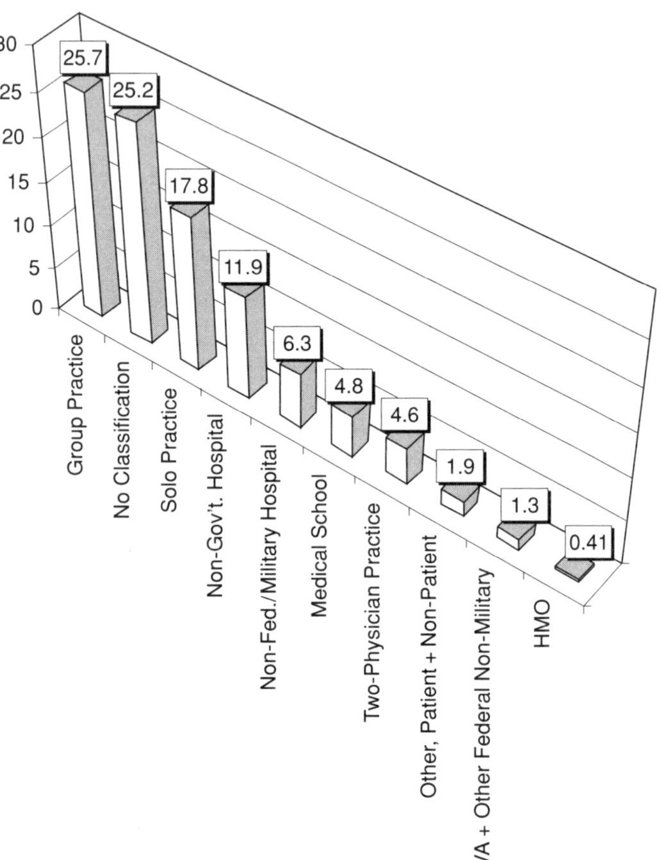

Figure 7.15 Employment setting in 1998, all cohorts (AMA)

statistics, the largest growing categories of physician employment through the 1990s have been group practice and nongovernmental hospitals (PC and D 1997–8 edition).

Figure 7.16 provides the 8-year-postgraduation data for each of our three cohorts on employment setting with the 1970 cohort displayed in the rows to the far right. In 1978 this cohort was primarily unclassified (36.8%). Useable categories ranged from 13.9 percent in nongovernmental hospitals, 11.3 percent in solo practice, 11.1 percent in group practice, and 10.2 percent in military or state/local government hospitals. The 1980 cohort only had 23.5 percent in the unclassified

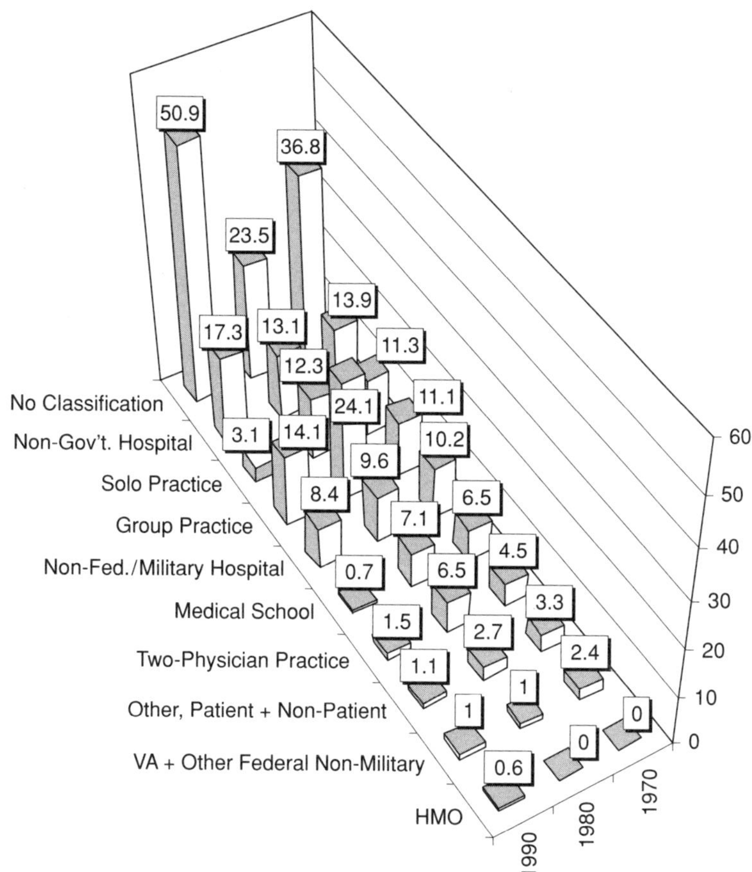

Figure 7.16 Employment settings eight years after graduation, by cohort (AMA)

category in 1988, with 24.5 percent in group practice (a big increase), 13.1 percent in non-governmental hospitals, 12.3 percent in solo practice, and 9.6 percent in military or state/local hospitals. Data for the 1990 cohort is almost unusable, with 50.9 percent unclassified. The rest of this cohort sample distributed across nongovernmental hospitals (17%), group practice (14%), military or state/county hospitals (8.4%), and solo practice (3.1%). Of some note in this cohort is the very small percent indicating employment within an HMO in 1998 – less than one percent – when we know from all other scholarly and public

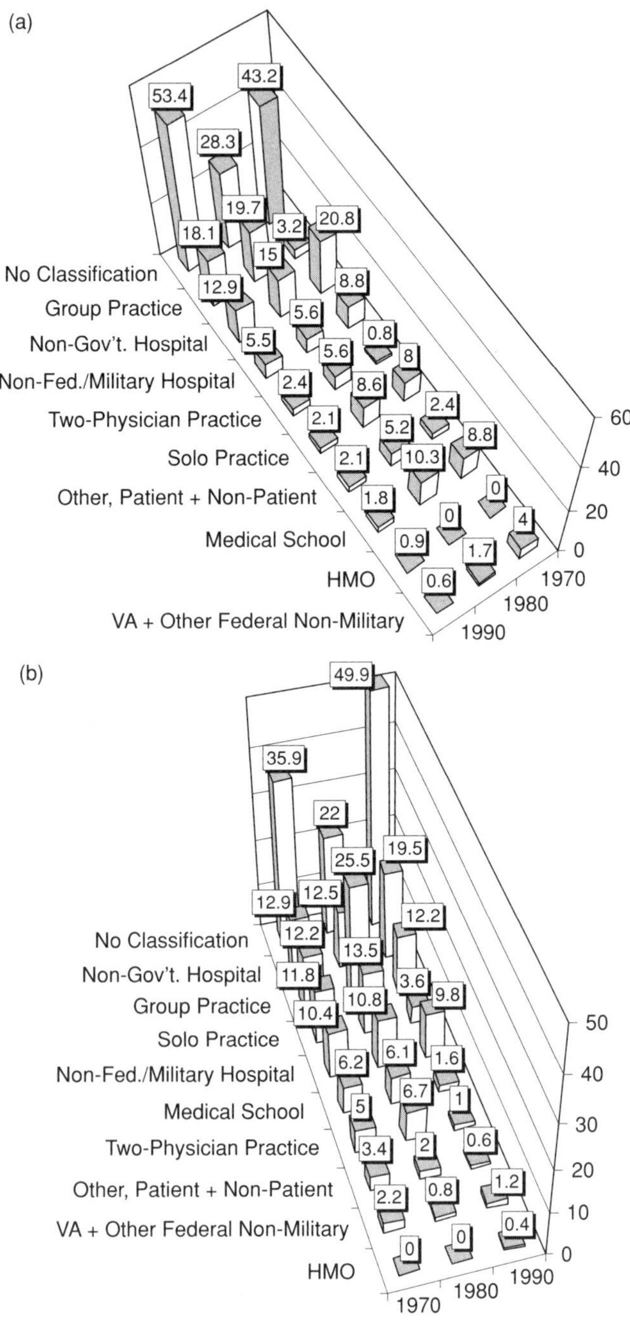

Figure 7.17 Employment setting eight years after graduation by cohort: (a) female physicians; (b) male physicians (AMA)

media outlets that that proportion should be about 15–20 percent. Other data sources report that 54 percent of all physicians currently contract with HMOs, and 64 percent contract with preferred provider organizations (PPOs), and what might operate like an employment relationship within such contracts would be disguised in the AMA data as "group practice."

Finally, the cohort by gender comparisons appear in Figure 7.17, again using the time point of eight-years-postgraduation for each cohort. In every cohort, the proportion of women with "no classification" for employment setting is greater than proportion of men in that cohort, from a seven percent difference in 1970 to a 3.5 percent difference in 1990. Gender differences are also found within cohorts for group practice, but in 1978 and 1988 there were larger proportions of men in group practice, and in 1998 there are more women (as a proportion of 1990 graduates) in group practice. There are consistently larger proportions of women in the 1970 and 1980 cohorts in non-governmental hospital employment, but in 1998 the proportion of men in this setting far outnumbers the proportion of women (19.5% compared to 12.9%).

Given the large percentage of each cohort with members in the "no classification" category, we must revisit the issue of changing interpretations of the employment categories provided on the AMA survey. There appear to be both cross-cohort differences in the proportions of unclassified doctors, and gender differences. The categories may be perceived differently in each decade, or men and women may define them more or less inclusively, with more or less excess meaning or applicability to their individual situations. There is no way to determine that with this set of data. However, the issues of interest diversity cannot be completely addressed unless more complete data is available, over time, for men and women, and ideally for various ethnic and racial groups as well.

Summary

Even though our data are not perfectly suited to definitely answer the question we asked at the outset of this chapter (i.e., are the professions becoming more diverse, and if so, on what dimensions – demographic or interest diversity, or both?) we are certainly closer to a more comprehensive answer. Yes, the professions are in general becoming more demographically diverse, but that diversity has been slow to develop and is not anywhere near parity in any elite profession. The most diverse professions, medicine and law, are still both predominantly white male.

Second, the process of "diversification" within one profession – medicine – has occurred over several decades marked by other significant changes, including technological changes in medical work, cost-control regimes aiming to curtail physician autonomy, and changes in immigration patterns. Women are moving into medicine, but other under-represented groups are not. Women are not equally likely to begin their careers by training in the top elite schools; men still have a proportionate edge on that. Women tend to move into a wider variety of specializations. Men still predominately move into a few. Women are more likely to move into low and mid-prestige specialties in their early careers, but their numbers are still so small that men predominate in all specializations.

We know from observation, case studies, and anecdote that there are many more types of professional activities and employment settings within medicine now than 20 years ago, but the data available on physician careers are not structured to provide useful information on those issues, thus it is difficult to demonstrate how employment diversity is related to interest diversity. We do know that on almost all career choice indicators there are differences over time between successive cohorts of graduating physicians, and differences between male and female physicians in the choices they make. Some of those choices are circumscribed by other structural constraints or ascribed characteristics (race, SES, personal resources), such as access to elite medical schools. However, other career choices are not, such as specialization and type of employment setting. Our limited data suggests that medical career structures are changing, often because of decisions made by women. As more women enter the profession, perhaps those alternative career paths will become more observable than they are now.

NOTES

1 We suspect there may be some slippage in either understanding or definitions of the categories of hospital-based and office-based patient care categories. Through a process of elimination, we were able to compare numbers from each cohort on the nonpatient care activities indicated for both this question, as well as a similar item on "type of practice." Most of the nonpatient care categories report comparable numbers for either item. However, the summation of office-based and hospital-based patient care under "major professional activity," and the category of "direct patient care" under the item

on type of practice do not always sum. For the 1980 cohort, that difference seems to be equivalent to the difference between 80 percent in direct patient care and the almost zero percent in "No classification" category. Unfortunately, no similar explanation falls out for the 1970 and 1990 cohorts.

2 This amount of missing data is troublesome, but given that lack of any alternative nationally-based data, we will proceed with caution.

8

Organizations as Vehicles for Producing Stratification among Professionals

So far we have focused on describing changes affecting professional and managerial work over the past 20 years. The classic "free professions" have experienced profound changes in the past two decades, change that has altered the content and the terms of professional work. Professionals increasingly are employed by organizations where traditional professional powers are constrained. Like other writers, we would argue that these enormous changes in professional work call for a multilevel examination of professional careers, organizational change, and industry-level change.

We've already discussed the diversification of professional interests, changes in the shape and structure of professional and managerial careers, the increased diversity of professional work settings, and the convergence of control structures over professional and managerial work. However, the professions as occupational groups do not represent a unified constituency. There always have been discussions of the divisions created within professions through the development of subfields of specialization, particularly in medicine and science. Newer cohorts of professionals in medicine, science, engineering, and law are increasingly diversifying by gender, race, and ethnicity. We also see cleavages within professions over preferred professional identities and preferences for governance structures. Friedson and others (see Haferty and Light 1995) have discussed the fragmentation of medicine into knowledge elites, administrative elites, and of course, rank-and-file practitioners. In law, divisions exist between those who practice criminal law, corporate law, consumer law, and more (see Nelson 1988). Unfortunately, the evidence we have on growing professional diversity is fragmentary at best, and often confuses demographic diversity with interest and workplace diversity (see Brint 1994 for an excellent discussion of interest diversity among "new class" professionals).

As an example of the demographic diversification of professional work, we examine the changing diversity of the labor market for corporate in-house attorneys. We present a theoretical overview of ways to understand change among organizations that employ professionals. We present a description of the increased gender diversity in corporate in-house counsel in the 1980s and 1990s, and document the types of firms most likely to diversify while addressing the problem of "tokenism."

The Legal Profession as an Example of Demographic Diversification

The legal profession presents a particularly interesting case for further scrutiny, and that's what we do in the rest of this chapter. While women increased their representation in the legal profession considerably in the past 20 years, legal practice has moved toward an increasingly diverse set of organizational arrangements. Historically, lawyers have enjoyed autonomy from employing organizations. Law is now practiced in environments that vary in the level of bureaucratic control over professionals – solo practitioners, joint practices and partnerships, non-profit organizations, and legal departments within corporations and government agencies. While a majority of lawyers continue to work in private practice (see Halliday 1987; Nelsen 1988), the practice of law increasingly takes place in a bureaucratic employment setting where traditional professional prerogatives are constrained. Others have reported that an increased number of women are working in highly bureaucratic legal settings, such as the in-house legal departments of large corporations (Halliday 1987; Hagan 1990; Roach 1990). In spite of these trends we know very little about the structure of some of these work settings, and in particular corporate legal departments.

In this chapter we provide an analysis of the increasing gender diversity in corporate legal departments. Corporate legal departments represent the fastest growing employment setting for lawyers (see Leicht and Fennell 1997). Like any discussion of professional work, we have a particular perspective or lens that we use to examine increasing demographic diversity. This perspective is strongly identified with the *neoinstitutional approach.*

A neoinstitutional view of demographic diversity

The neoinstitutional perspective in organizational analysis focuses our attention on change in organizational activity that are responses to change in the social, political, and cultural environments of organizations. *Institutional isomorphism* is a process whereby groups of organizations move toward similar organizational forms and practices over time as they compete for political power and institutional legitimacy.

What, exactly, does institutional isomorphism look like in everyday life? Colleges and universities are classic examples of organizations that have faced similar pressures for so long that their organizational structures and practices are all remarkably similar. Chances are, if we transferred most of our readers to different colleges and universities throughout the country, it wouldn't take long for you to find where to go to register for classes, where to pay tuition, how to apply for job openings, how to find housing, and a myriad of other decisions that are involved with enrolling at a university. The fact that universities all have a registrar, a bursar, a Dean of Students, and a personnel office is the result of common sets of pressures that have produced common solutions to the typical problems universities face.

Or take an example that is closer to our interests in diversity among professionals. Large and visible organizations of all kinds have equal employment opportunity offices that work to assure that the organization is in compliance with current regulations and "good practices." The definition of what constitutes a good practice comes from a combination of other stakeholders including the professions themselves, governments interested in enforcing equal opportunity statutes, and organizations attempting to persuade stakeholders and the public that they are "good citizens" worthy of public trust. Those who work for equal employment opportunity offices are responsible for determining what these "good practices" are. One of the ways they do this is by consulting other equal employment opportunity officers about what they think good practices look like.

But institutional pressures extend far beyond universities and equal employment opportunity offices. Behind professional practices of all kinds are strongly institutionalized norms regarding how professional practice will "look" and "feel." These institutionalized norms (until very recently) have been honored, understood, and taken for granted by professionals and other stakeholders.

What were some of these institutionalized norms and how do they affect professional working life? First, professional work traditionally has involved considerable *autonomy*. The professional expects to make decisions according to the needs of clients and patients without interference from other professionals or stakeholders. Obviously, there are cases where professional decision-making is questioned and judgment is interfered with, but to highlight such instances (where lawyers are "disbarred"; doctors lose their licenses; psychotherapists are accused of malpractice) is to show that professionals are assumed to be competently and ethnically using their professional autonomy. This assumption will drive the normal behavior of professionals and those around them, except in unusual circumstances. Even in unusual circumstances, the burden of proof lies with those who wish to interfere with the professional's right to make an autonomous judgment on behalf of their clients.

A second strongly institutionalized norm of professional practice is *independence*. Professionals are expected to make their own judgments and act on them. While there may be consultation about the appropriate actions to take in specific circumstances, professionals expect and are expected to act on the basis of their own judgments about what is best. In practice, younger, less experienced practitioners often defer to older colleagues or ask their advice concerning especially difficult cases, but professional training normally leads older practitioners, mentors, and others in senior positions to act as if the young professional will eventually make decisions on their own without mentoring help.

Professional practice also involves the assertion of *prerogatives* over professional decision-making. At most, decisions periodically are reviewed by other professionals for competence in execution and clarity of judgment. But this oversight promptly stops at the boundaries of professional practice. Consumers, insurance companies, and funding agencies are supposed to exercise (at most) nominal oversight over professional decisions and (in effect) "leave things to professionals."

Finally, traditional professional practice involves interaction in an occupational *community of equals*. All those with the appropriate training and certifications are treated as members of the profession, part of the "in" group that can ask competent questions, evaluate the answers given, and otherwise interact as part of an intellectual community in a common universe of professional knowledge. These norms are informally bent to allow for differences in age and experience, but the overriding norm is that professionals will treat each other with respect due to their membership in the professional group.

The historical result of these norms is that most professional practice settings "look alike." But how do they come to be this way? How can walking into a doctor's office in Boston, Los Angeles, Dallas, or Cedar Rapids, Iowa lead to an experience that is similar in almost all details?

DiMaggio and Powell (1983; Powell and DiMaggio 1991) outline three mechanisms that pressure organizations to appear alike. *Coercive pressure* comes from governing bodies or the state. The requirement that some employers comply with equal employment opportunity laws is an example of coercive pressure. Requiring physicians to be licensed and pass a board exam is another example of coercive pressure. In practice, coercive pressures rarely dictate how professional work will actually be performed, but reactions to coercive pressures tend to become institutionalized so that specific sets of actions and activities are defined as "showing compliance" with the rules of governing bodies or the state.

Mimetic pressure results from the push for common responses to specific types of uncertainty. When organizations are under pressure from environments that are unstable, there is an overwhelming temptation to borrow existing adaptations from other organizations in similar circumstances. These at least serve as a starting point for evaluating the options available and may act as a source of comfort and relief to decision-makers ("It worked for them, so why won't it work for us?").

Finally, organizations face *normative pressures* that reflect the expectations of powerful professional groups. These are probably most salient for the definition of professional practice norms. Professional practice, traditionally, has "looked" a certain way because practitioners have had considerable power and autonomy to define their working conditions. The cumulative result of these decisions by prior generations of practitioners is that new practitioners are socialized to expect professional work to look and feel a certain way. Employers who violate these professional practice norms usually face (at minimum) informal social opprobrium, difficulty in finding competent professionals who are willing to work under "unprofessional" conditions, and sanctions from professional governing bodies.

Our presentation looks at the effects of different types of institutional pressures on diversification in corporate legal departments. We focus on gender diversification because there have been large increases in the number of women in law. Women have made greater inroads into the legal profession than any of the professions we examine here (see Abel 1986; Epstein 1993; Chiu and Leicht 2000). The rise in employment in corporate legal departments is a good venue for studying the interface of a traditional professional group (lawyers) with a new and different employment setting that is rapidly growing (see Spangler 1993). On the one hand, corporate employment usually involves extensive commitments to bureaucratic norms that are contrary to traditional professional prerogatives. But the profession of law also has faced increasing pressure from a wide variety of groups seeking to reform and diversify the profession (see Halliday 1987).

At the very time when there seem to be pressures to change the profession from within there also are changes in the organization of the client base for legal work. Corporate clients used to retain law firms for long periods of time to do all types of legal work from routine deeds, trusts, and real estate transactions to litigation and copyright infringement. The client/firm relationship often would last decades. Clients would pay retainers to law firms monthly and there would be extensive social interactions and ties between clients and law firms as well (see Nelson 1988).

Beginning in the late 1970s, this relationship began to change. Large corporate clients began to question legal fees, shop around for specialized legal work, and hire in-house attorneys to do routine legal transactions (see Nelson 1988). This change resulted, in part, from the same crises that we discussed when we examined economic restructuring, corporate downsizing, and the severing of the social pact between the classes in chapter 4. Corporate clients represent a major portion of the legal work available. Changes in their relationship with traditional law firms led to changes in the stratification system for the profession as a whole.

Within more traditionally structured law firms and partnerships, women often have been segregated into junior ranks and nonsupervisory positions. This gender stratification within traditional law firms has been labeled the "mommy track" by the popular press, referring to the proliferation of part-time female associates, usually with small children at home. Women consistently have been overrepresented at the rank of associate in large private law firms, and women face considerable barriers as they seek promotion to partner (see Curran 1986; Morello 1986; Nelson 1988; Menkel-Meadow 1989; Epstein 1993). In the largest and most prestigious private firms, women were hired as associates long before any women were promoted to partnership (see Morello 1986). The inequalities between men and women lawyers has been justified on the economic grounds that partners need to bring in clients and capital to the firm (sometimes referred to as "rainmaking," see Nelson 1988). Women (because of domestic responsibilities) cannot devote the time and energy to finding prosperous new corporate clients.

In contrast, in-house legal departments of corporations serve only one client – the firm – that eliminates the need to search for clients and capital. However, in-house legal departments introduce the complexity of hierarchical job ladders and finely distinguished job titles, characteristics identified with persistent gender inequality in bureaucratic organizations (see Baron and Bielby 1984, 1986; Bridges and Nelson 1989; Baron et al. 1991). This makes the study of this rapidly growing segment of the legal profession all the more interesting.

A description of the data we will use to examine the growing gender diversity of corporate legal departments is presented in the Appendix to this chapter, as are the technical details of the analysis we present. We follow a representative sample of 960 corporate legal departments selected in 1979 through 1995. We have a maximum of seven observations for each department selected. Some legal departments ceased to exist during the timeframe of our study, so we have only as much information as each department produced during the years we examine. Overall, there are 6,507 different legal departments spread over the 15 years we examine. These are the most comprehensive and far-reaching data yet collected on the work environments of corporate in-house attorneys in the United States (see Leicht and Fennell 1993).

We argue that gender representation can be analyzed as an important characteristic of corporate legal departments, and that departmental diversity represents the middle level of analysis where individual careers and organizational structures and institutions meet. We examine the ability of women to make inroads into corporate legal departments and we compare the settings where these inroads are extensive to corporate settings where women's inroads into corporate legal departments appear to be blocked.

Trends in women's representation in corporate legal departments

Figure 8.1 examines the trend in women's representation in corporate legal departments from 1980 to 1995. There is a slow but steady increase in the number of corporate legal departments that have at least one female lawyer. The percentage rises steadily from just under 30 percent of all departments to 47 percent of all departments. In spite of the big gains that women are making in admission and graduation from law school, there are still many corporate legal departments that are all male. We think that this pattern has something to do with differences

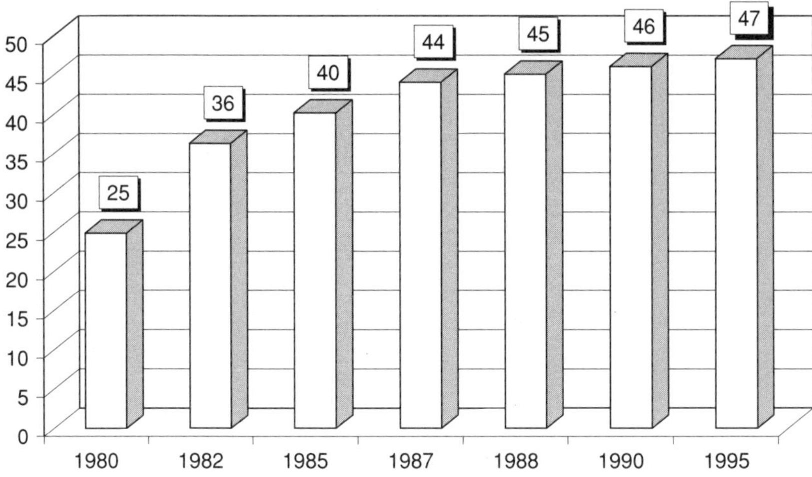

Figure 8.1 The percentage of corporate legal departments with female attorneys, 1980–1995

in overall hiring across firms, an issue we will return to later in the analysis.

While these results get at the representation of women across corporate legal departments, they don't assess whether there are small numbers of token women in a large number of departments or high concentrations in specific locations. To see the types of inroads women have made, figure 8.2 looks at the average percentage of female attorneys in the subset of our firms that have a least one woman on their legal staff. The percentage of women in corporate legal departments rises about 9 percent over the 15 years we examined. In 1980, women worked in corporate legal departments where an average of 32 percent of all legal staff were female. By 1995, this average had risen to 41 percent. In a nationally representative sample of private corporations from a wide variety of circumstances, this is a substantial shift in the direction of greater representation of women. Still, there are many firms that hire their first female attorney during our study period, and few firms have more than one or two female attorneys on their legal staffs.

We suspect that there are substantial differences across industries in the institutional pressures to diversify high-visibility professional staffs. Generally, older, established industries should have fewer incentives to hire different types of people because they already have a well-established

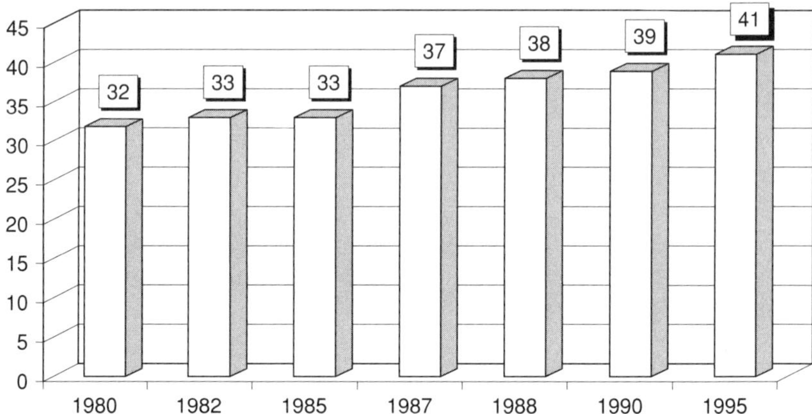

Figure 8.2 The percentage of female attorneys in corporate legal departments in firms with at least one female attorney, 1980–1995

routine that they use. This routine often reflects the conditions that existed at the time the industry or firm was established (see Stinchcombe 1997). Younger industries with less entrenched ways of doing things should be more susceptible to institutional pressure to diversify their professional staffs. These also are industries with clients and stakeholders that expect greater sensitivity to "doing the right thing." Our analysis looks at seven broadly-defined industry groups.[1] Manufacturing and transportation represent older, well-established industries in our analysis. High-technology, finance, insurance, and communications reflect newer service industries that have grown considerably in importance since the early 1980s. Utilities firms represent a unique industry, one that is older and well-established but often extensively regulated as a "natural monopoly." Consequently utilities firms should face pressures to diversify their professional staffs that are similar to those faced by governments. These differences should lead to differences in the representation of women on corporate legal staffs.

The percentage of firms with female attorneys in each industry group is presented in figure 8.3. Our results match our expectations on some dimensions but not on others. Manufacturing firms have the lowest percentage of firms with female attorneys on their staffs, and utilities firms have the highest percentage. The percentage of women in legal departments also is higher in insurance, high-technology, and communications relative to manufacturing. But the results for transportation and

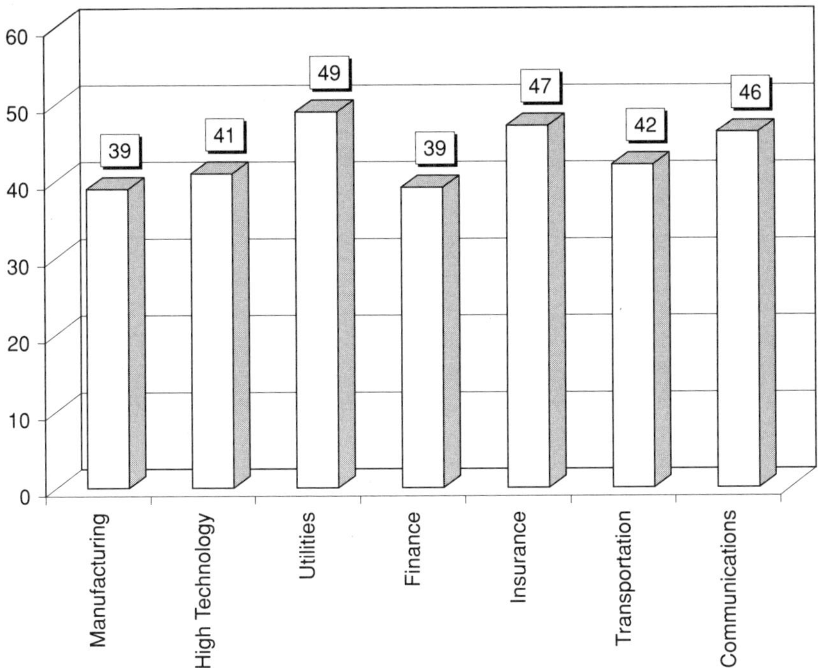

Figure 8.3 The percentage of corporate legal departments with female attorneys, by industry

finance firms are directly contrary to what we would expect. Transportation firms rank with high-technology firms in their representation of women, and finance firms rank with manufacturing firms. These results suggest that environmental pressures are more complex than simply accounting for the activities of the broad industry where the firm and legal department do business.

Ironically, the probability that firms will hire women in their legal departments does not translate into greater overall representation of women in each industry. Figure 8.4 suggests that firms in finance have the greatest representation of women even though the percentage of firms with women on their staffs is the lowest among our industry groups. The only set of firms whose rankings correspond are high-technology firms. Insurance and utilities firms are no more likely to employ large numbers of female attorneys than manufacturing firms. These results point to the limits to environmental pressures to diversify professional positions. That pressure is greatest on firms to hire one or a

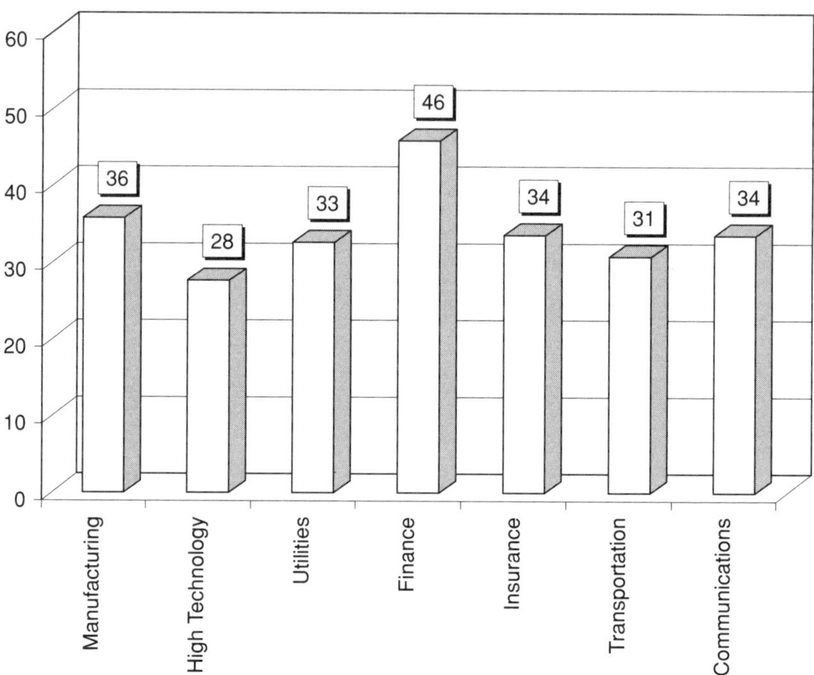

Figure 8.4 The percentage of female attorneys in departments with at least one female attorney, by major industry

few attorneys from underrepresented groups. But there is still considerable inertia involved that prevents the actual percentage of female attorneys from increasing rapidly.

Figure 8.5 presents a year-by-year account of the presence of female attorneys for four industries at the extremes of the distributions presented in figure 8.4; manufacturing, finance, high-technology, and utilities. These also are industries with enough firms represented in each year to get stable estimates of year-by-year change. The patterns across these environments is interesting and sheds insight on the relative growth in the representation of women on legal staffs. Manufacturing firms start from a relatively low level and women's representation slowly rises over 15 years. Utilities and high-technology firms fit this pattern as well, though they experience slight downturns from 1990 to 1995 and their overall representation of women ends up higher in 1995 than in manufacturing firms. Financial firms start from the highest overall representation of any industry in 1980, but women's representation fails to grow at

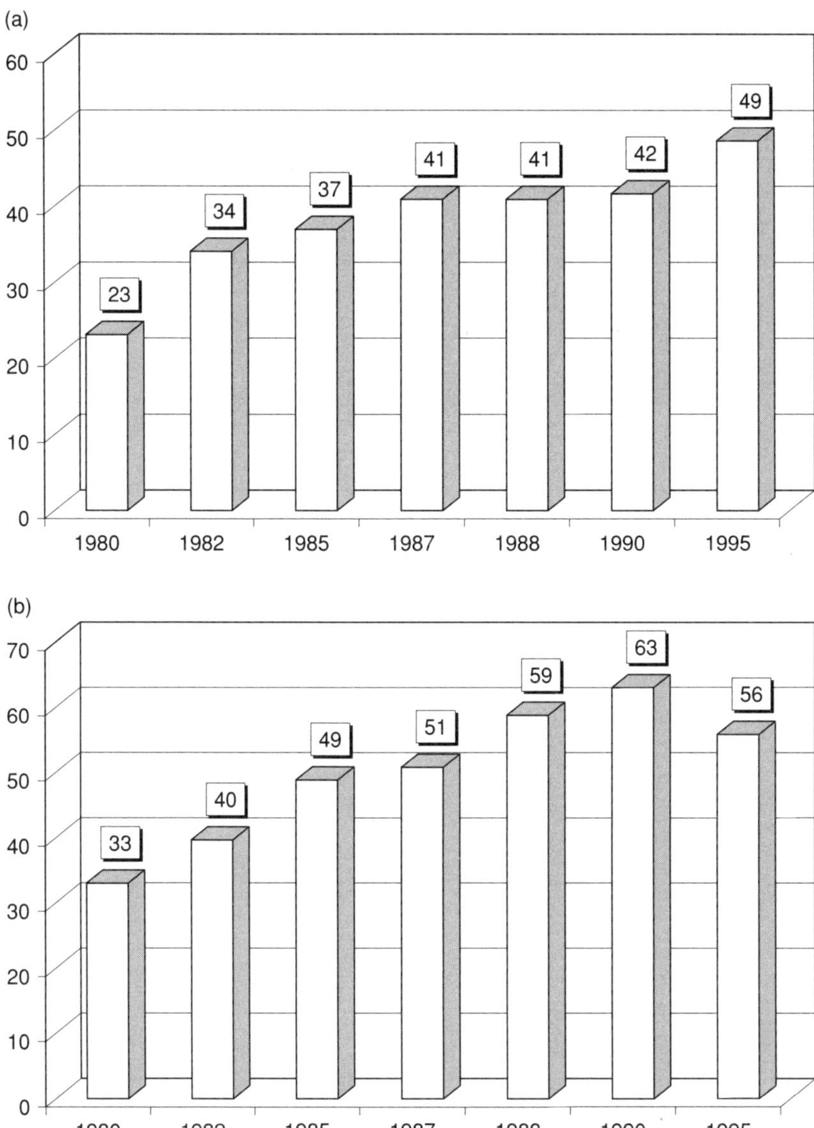

Figure 8.5 (a) The percentage of manufacturing firms with female attorneys by year; (b) the percentage of utilities firms with female attorneys by year

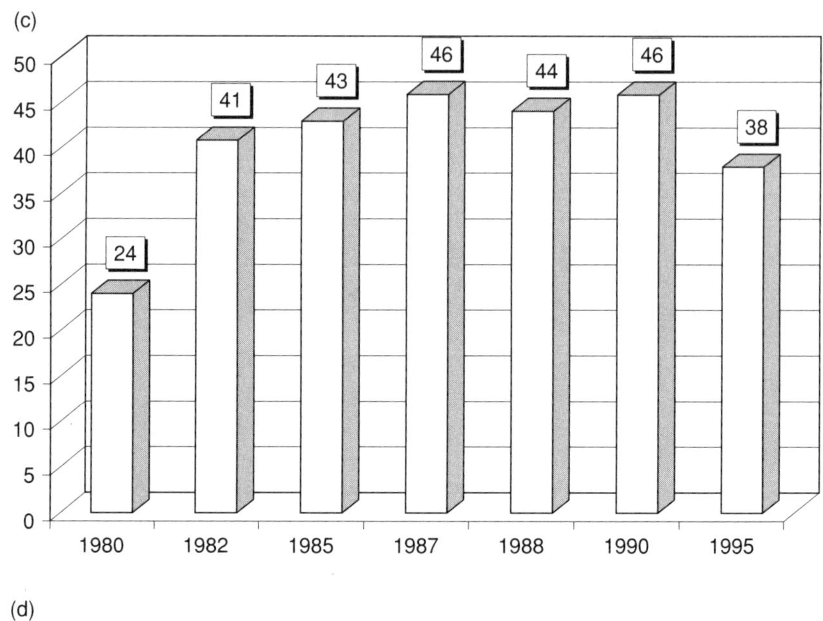

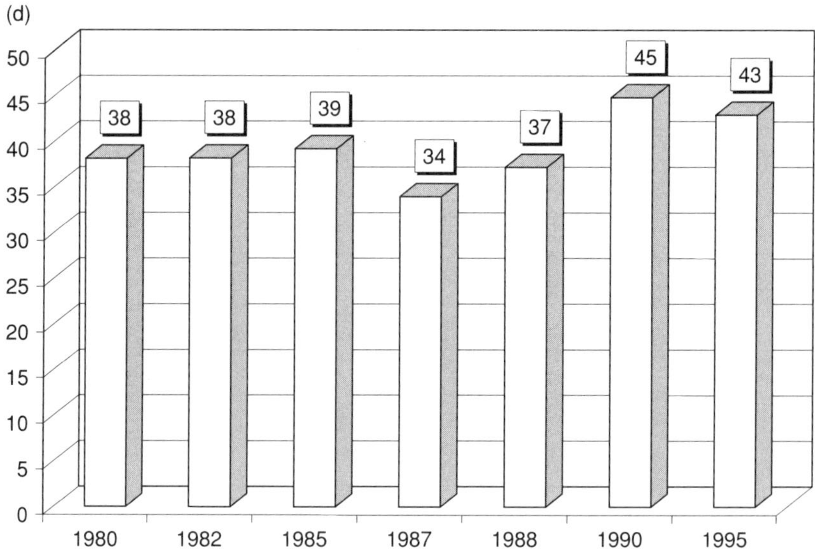

Figure 8.5 (*cont'd*) (c) the percentage of high technology firms with female attorneys by year; (d) the percentage of financial firms with female attorneys by year

the pace that it grows elsewhere. Overall, the surge in women's representation in manufacturing comes later and brings manufacturing closer to the representation of women in other industries. Representation in industries that we think would be more receptive either begins at a higher level in 1980 and stays there or peaks before 1995. This suggests that manufacturing firms were beginning to modify their hiring practices in the mid-1990s to conform to activities carried out in other industries that had already moved to diversify their legal staffs.

These results are reflected in the slow but steady advancement in the percentage of female attorneys in each of these industries over time. These results are presented in figure 8.6. The average percentage of women on the legal staffs of manufacturing, high-technology, utilities, and financial service firms rises steadily during the 1980–95 period. In addition to the differences across industries in the representation of women across firms, there has been a slow and steady increase in women's representation in firms that already have female attorneys as well. This is a separate dimension of the diversification of the professions. Women have moved into firms where they traditionally have been excluded, but they also have increased their representation in firms where they were already making inroads.

These findings tell us what industries women are making inroads into and when they began making those inroads. They don't tell us much about the characteristics of organizational environments and corporations themselves that promote diversity among professionals. Our next analysis is designed to answer this question.

Figure 8.7 presents some of the key corporate characteristics that affect which firms have women attorneys and which do not. These results are reported as odds, with average odds being those closest to "1" and odds above "1" reflecting a greater chance of having a female attorney on staff and odds below "1" reflecting a lesser than average chance of having a female attorney on staff. Details of the methods used to produce these findings are presented in the Appendix to this chapter (p. 205). What do these results tell us?:

1 *Women's representation is more likely in departments of companies that have engaged in acquisition activity.* Clearly one way to expand your pool of lawyers on staff is to merge legal departments with others that you take over.

2 *Fortune 500 firms are more likely to have women attorneys.* This effect reflects both normative and coercive pressures we discussed. Fortune 500 firms are scrutinized widely for changes in and compliance with

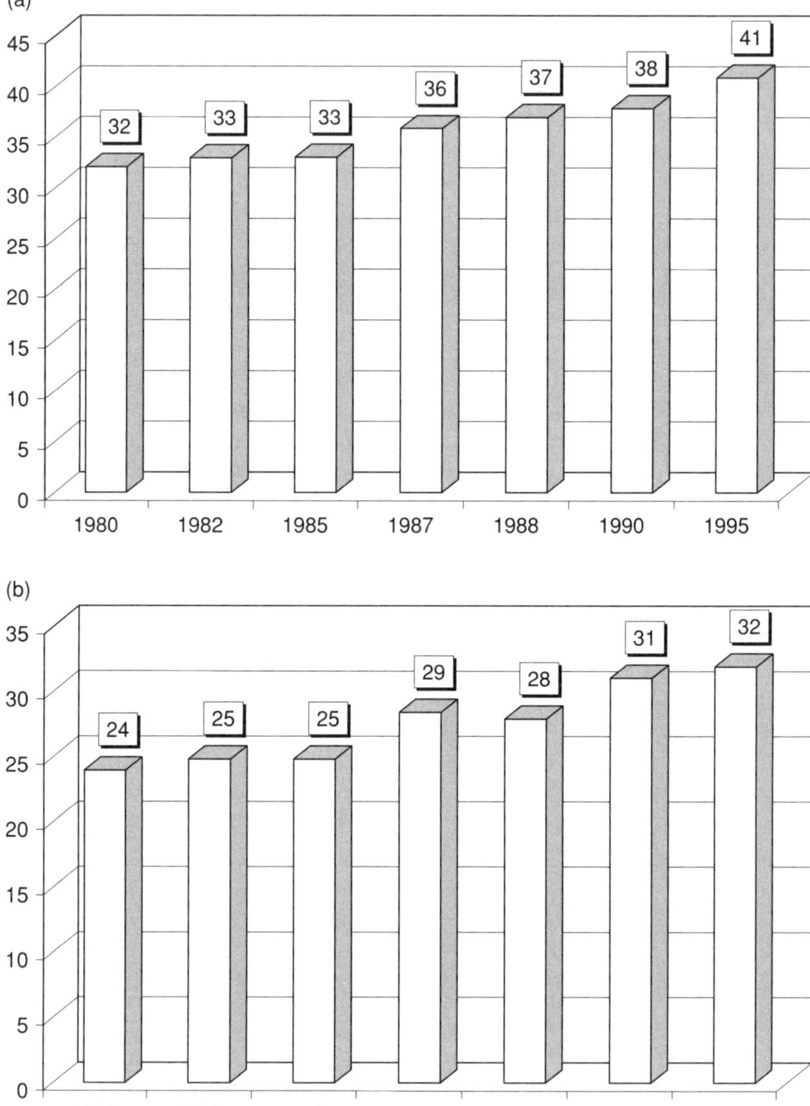

Figure 8.6 (a) The percentage of female attorneys in manufacturing flrms that have female attorneys, by year; (b) the percentage of female attorneys in high technology firms that have female attorneys, by year

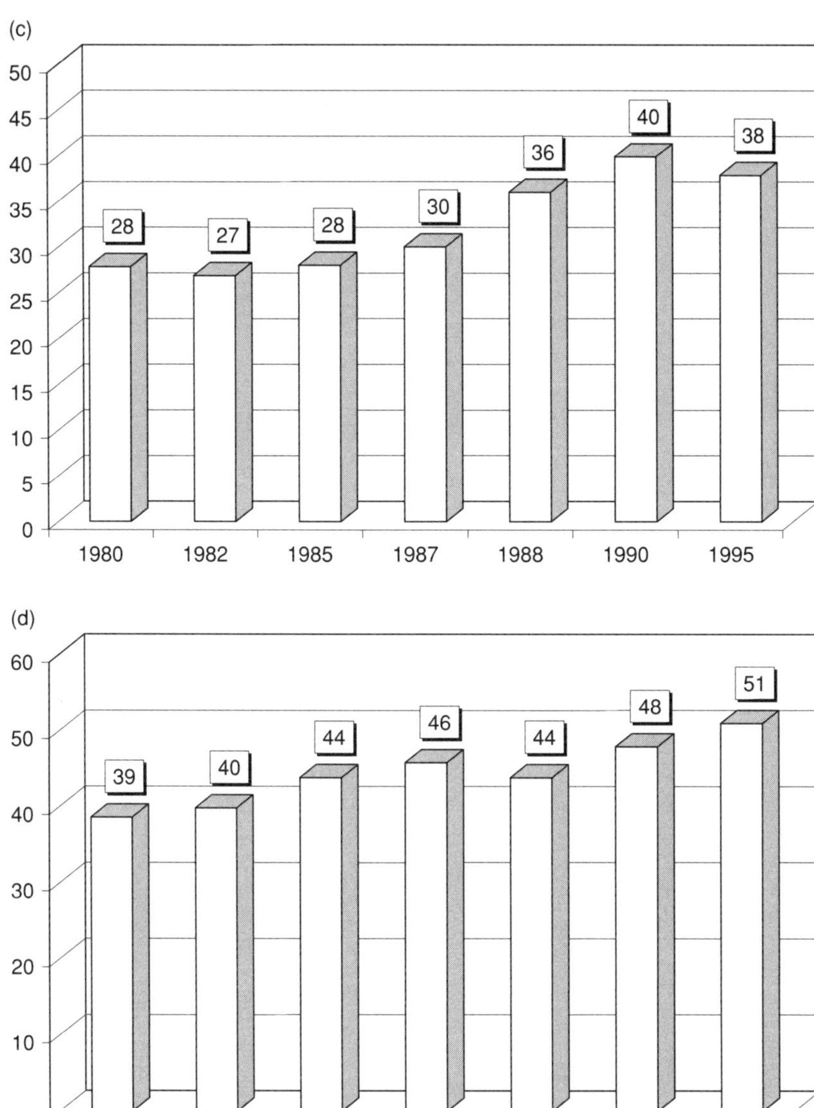

Figure 8.6 (*cont'd*) (c) the percentage of female attorneys in utilities firms that have female attorneys, by year; (d) the percentage of female attorneys in finance firms that have female attorneys, by year

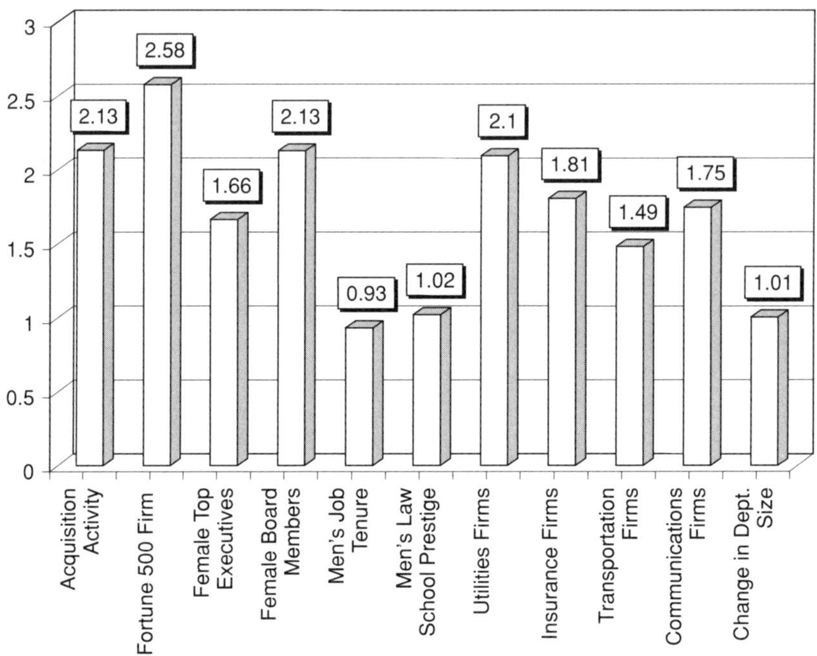

Figure 8.7 Effects of measures of corporate, department, and environmental attributes on the odds of having female attorneys in corporate legal departments, 1980–1995

good personnel practices, not the least of which is expressing commitments to a diverse workforce. The growing diversity of law school graduates available represents an ideal opportunity for Fortune 500 firms to diversify their legal staffs.

3 *Women's representation in law rises with women's representation on corporate boards and as corporate officers.* Clearly the prior experience of women in high-level, visible, executive positions puts normative and coercive pressure on legal departments to diversify their staffs. This effect is quite strong and suggests that the diversification of key executive positions in large corporate firms helps to diversify other levels of professional work in these organizations as well.

4 *Women's representation rises as the number of young male attorneys rises.* This probably reflects two related trends, one of which we will address

later in the chapter. Younger attorneys are more likely to be socialized into the idea that they will be working with diverse colleagues in their professional practice settings. Newly-minted women attorneys may realize this as well and shun corporate legal departments with (what appears to be) an "old boys network." This effect may also reflect the existence of recent hiring by corporate legal departments. New attorneys from different demographic groups can't move into legal departments that aren't hiring anybody. Departments that do hire a lot of new attorneys are likely to have numerous younger attorneys on their staffs. The relative increase in the chances of hiring women in these types of settings may reflect this.

5 *The odds of having women attorneys increases as the number of men who graduate from prestigious law schools rises.* This is an unexpected but very interesting result. This suggests that certain types of legal departments are under strong normative pressure to hire women attorneys. Those pressures are likely to be acute in places that are most connected to national prestige networks in the profession. Departments with relatively high percentages of graduates from prestigious law schools fit this description.

6 *Gender representation varies considerably across industries.* Given our expectations, one would expect "new" industries to have the least institutionalized norms against increasing professional diversity, and "old, established" industries to have the most institutionalized and entrenched norms. Almost all industries in the "new service" economy have greater women's representation in corporate legal departments, as do industries with considerable public service dimensions to their corporate mission or that function as natural monopolies (utilities). Manufacturing, high-technology, and finance seem to be areas of corporate legal governance that remain least susceptible to the hiring of women attorneys.

7 *Gender representation increases as the size of the legal department grows.* Legal departments that hired extensively in the 1980s and 1990s increased their chances of hiring women attorneys considerably. This result makes sense. One can't hire attorneys from underrepresented groups if your department doesn't have any open slots to fill. Increasing the number of open slots increases the probability that firms will hire female attorneys.

8 Finally, *the odds of gender representation increase every year*, net of controls for the other significant determinants in our analysis. These odds are not presented in figure 8.7 (but see table A8.1 in the appendix p. 208). These odds seem to peak around 1990, but even the odds of

having women in legal department staffs is far higher in 1995 than it was in 1980.

When do firms hire their first female attorney?

The previous analysis helped us to identify which firm and environmental conditions promote the hiring of female attorneys. But this doesn't answer a different question that is more important given the context of recent demographic changes in the legal profession; of the legal departments in our sample that had no women attorneys in 1980, where are women eventually hired? This question is important because the composition of many corporate legal departments is a product of current decisions that take into account many of the changes we've been discussing, and decisions made years ago in much different contexts. Our next analysis looks at the characteristics that promote the hiring of female attorneys among firms that hadn't hired any female attorneys. The details of this analysis are discussed in the Appendix to this chapter (p. 205). The results, summarized in figure 8.8, look a lot like those for all of our legal departments (see figure 8.7). There are a few significant differences that we will highlight. All of them say something important about the effects of current contexts on changes in legal departments that have no women attorneys in 1980:

1 *The presence of female corporate officers does not affect the hiring of the first female attorney.* A diverse set of corporate executives does not necessarily help with the hiring of the first female attorney in corporate legal departments in the 1980s or 1990s. Placing women on corporate boards of directors still has the same effect that it has in our prior analysis. Apparently, the institutional dynamics that affect the late hiring of women attorneys do not necessarily affect the early hiring of women attorneys. This suggests that firms diversified their legal staffs in the 1970s for different reasons than firms in the 1980s.

2 *Women's employment in legal departments in the 1980s is not affected by the relative ranking of the law schools male attorneys graduate from.* Interestingly, these rankings seem to matter for firms that are "first movers" in the hiring of women attorneys, but not for late movers. The effects of firm tenure for male attorneys are the same as that found in the analysis of the total sample.

3 *Otherwise, the same institutional characteristics that affect the presence of women attorneys also affect the hiring of the first woman attorney among firms*

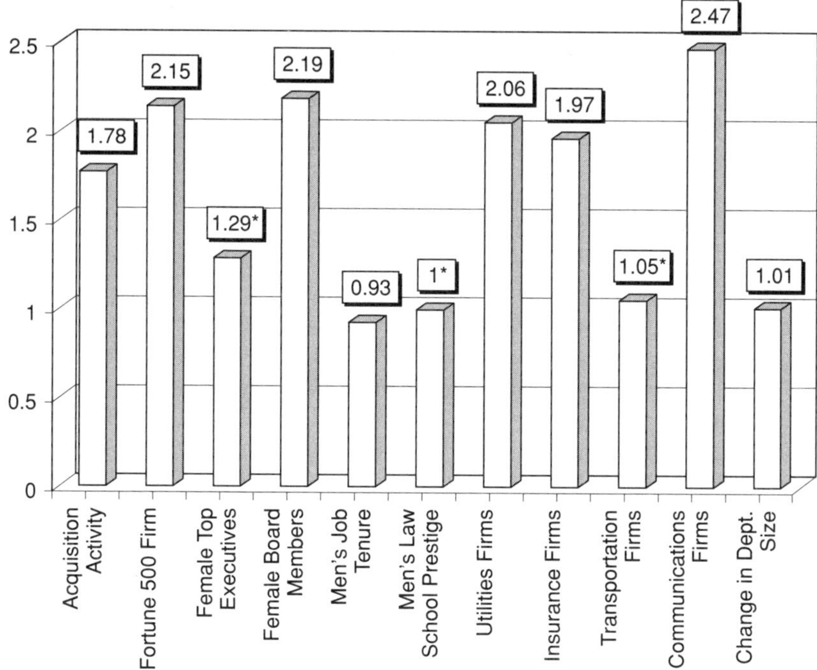

Figure 8.8 Effects of measure of corporate, department, and environmental attributes on the odds of hiring female attorneys in corporations that had no female attorneys in 1980

Note: * = not statistically significant, $p \leq .05$

that don't have one. Growing departments are especially likely to hire women attorneys in both analyses.

Together, these results suggest that legal departments of major corporations are highly sensitive the larger the institutional environment and the prevailing definitions of the situation that significant stakeholders define as important. Generally, firms that are visible, nationally connected into elite legal networks, firms in newer industries with fewer established routines, and firms that are growing and changing rapidly, all hire women attorneys with greater frequency. The hiring of attorneys from underrepresented groups depends on having open slots, but in addition it depends on the institutional pressures that corporate legal departments face.

Which firms have women on corporate boards and hire women as top corporate executives?

Clearly, the presence of women in other top corporate positions facilitates the hiring of women as corporate attorneys. These high-visibility positions probably are subject to the same institutional pressures from organizational environments as the hiring of a diverse set of corporate attorneys, maybe even more so. To examine this we present some results for the representation of women on corporate boards of directors and as top executives in our sample of firms.

Figure 8.9 suggests that the representation of women as top corporate executives and on corporate boards is by no means universal, though the percentages do rise from 1980–95. The distribution across firms that have women in their legal department staffs versus those that don't suggests that women's presence in all three venues rises and falls together (see figures 8.10 and 8.11).

Our next set of findings suggests that there are differences across industries in the presence of women as top executives and corporate

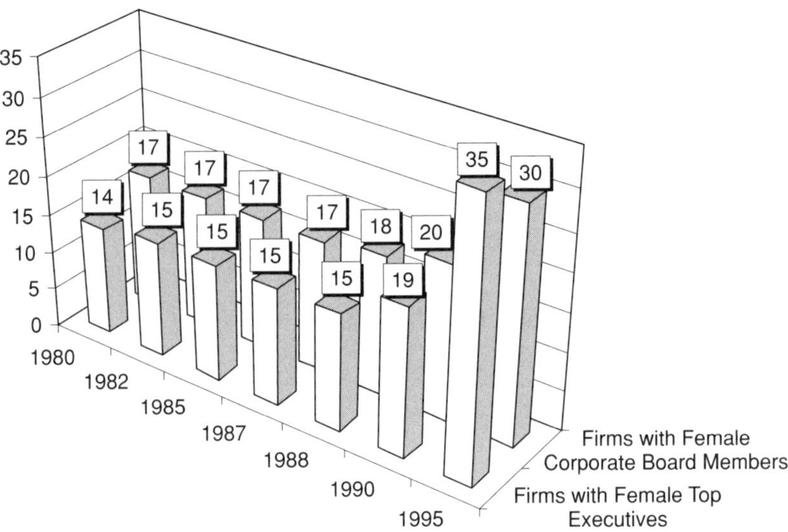

Figure 8.9 Percentage of firms with female top executives and corporate board members, by year

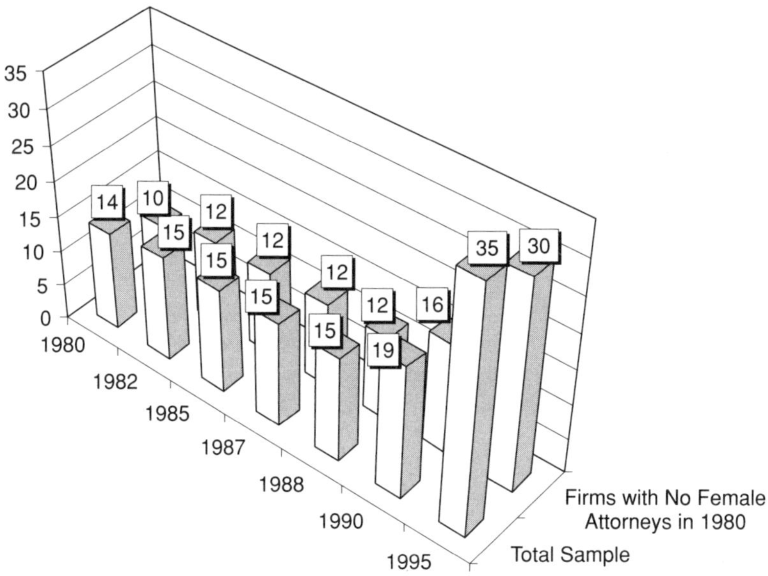

Figure 8.10 Percentage of firms with female top executives, by year, total sample and subsample of firms with no female attorneys in 1980

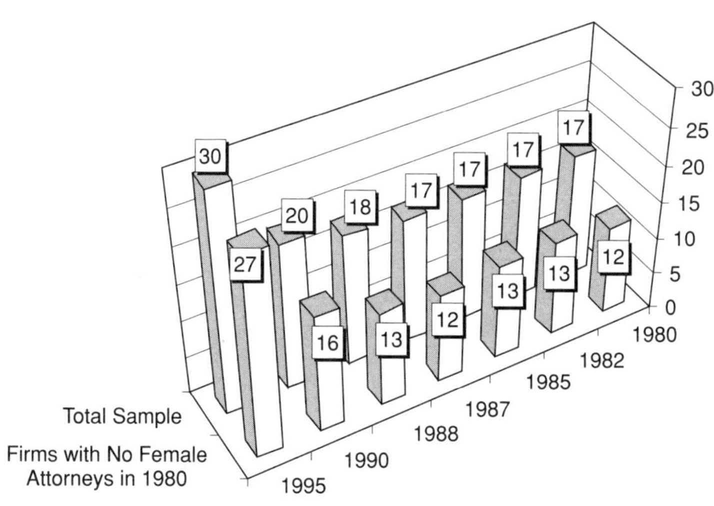

Figure 8.11 Percentage of firms with female corporate board members, by year, total sample and subsample of firms with no female attorneys in 1980

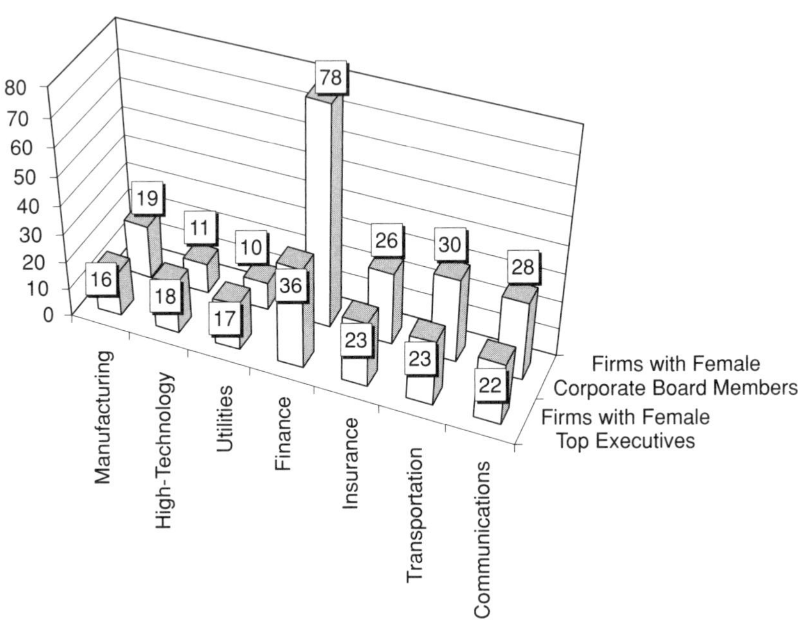

Figure 8.12 Percentage of firms with female top executives and corporate board members, by industry

board members (see figure 8.12). In this analysis the position of financial firms stands out; 78 percent of all financial firms have women on their corporate boards, far surpassing the representation found anywhere else. Women also have the greatest representation as corporate executives in financial firms as well.

Which of our indicators of firm environments affects the probability of having women in top executive posts? Figure 8.13 examines these results (the analysis details are presented in the Appendix to this chapter, pp. 210–11). *Far and away the most important determinant of women's presence in executive positions is working in the financial industry.* Women are more likely to be found in executive positions of Fortune 500 firms, insurance firms, and (surprisingly) firms with headquarters in the Southern United States. The remaining significant effects result in decreased chances that women will be found in top executive positions. High-technology, Utilities, Transportation, and Communications firms are less likely than manufacturing firms to have women in top corporate executive positions. This general pattern of results also applies to

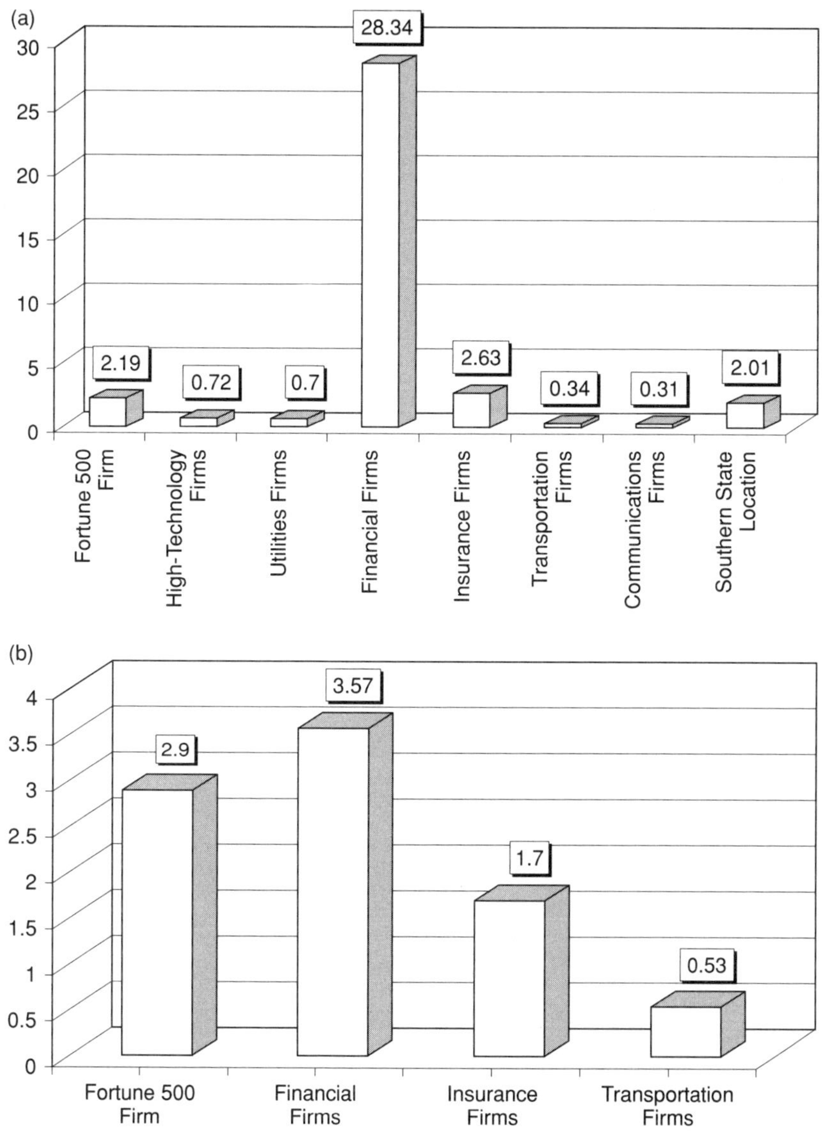

Figure 8.13 (a) Effects of measures of corporate and environmental attributes on the odds of having female top executives, total sample, 1980–1995; (b) Effects of measures of corporate and environmental attributes on the odds of having female corporate board members, total sample, 1980–1995

women's presence on corporate governing boards, though the effects of industry location are less pronounced and the overall strength of the effects is lower.

These results suggest that some of the same characteristics that affect the hiring of women in corporate legal departments also affect the representation of women in other top executive posts. We conducted an additional analysis to determine whether the effects of women on corporate boards and as top executives reduced the effects of the other environmental and corporate characteristics we highlighted earlier (in figure 8.9). The size of the effects and pattern of results was largely unchanged, which suggests that the institutional pressures of corporate environments exert important and independent pressures on firms to diversify their corporate legal departments. These results also mean that women's presence in top corporate positions acts as an important, and independent, force for change in the representation of women in visible professional positions in corporations.

How many available slots are there, and how many of these slots are filled by women?

So far, we've examined the presence and movement of women into corporate legal departments in large corporations in the United States. We've looked at the firms where women are present, we've looked at the average percentage of corporate attorneys who are women, and we've looked at the prominent features of corporations and their environments that increase the chances that they will hire women as corporate attorneys and appoint women to top corporate positions.

While much of our analysis so far has answered important questions, we have been avoiding two critical issues that almost everyone would want to know. *How many new legal positions were available in the 1980s and 1990s and, of those, how many were filled by women?* These questions are critical for assessing the overall advancement of women into new positions that open up just as the number of women graduating from law schools is increasing rapidly. They are also critical because new entrants into a labor market can't move into jobs that aren't vacant. A substantial percentage of the attorneys in the corporate legal departments we study have occupied their current positions for years. These positions aren't available for a new attorney to fill, regardless of who they are.

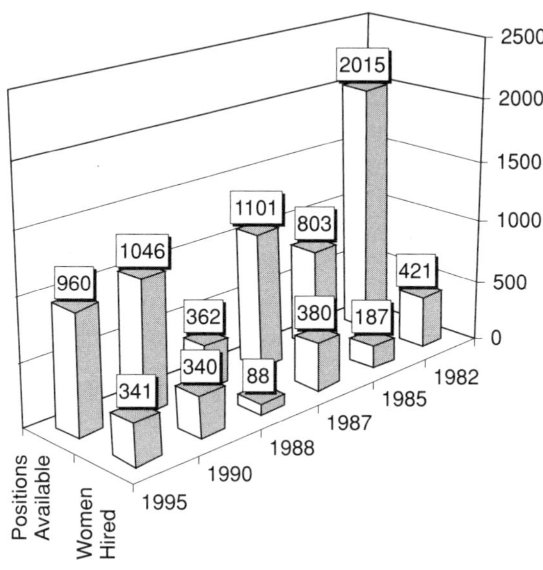

Figure 8.14 Positions available and number of women filling slots in corporate legal departments, 1980–1995

Our analysis now shifts to these questions. The analysis is presented in figures 8.14, 8.15, and 8.16.[2] The figures reveal that there is considerable cyclical variation in the growth of employment in corporate legal departments. This variation is reflected in the hiring of women as well. Women's representation in new legal department positions ranges from 20 to 35 percent (figure 8.14). These numbers do not include existing jobs where a replacement is hired for someone who has retired or quit. The same results are reflected in analyses of those legal departments that had no women on staff in 1980 (figure 8.15). Of 1,134 new jobs in corporate legal departments in 1982, women were hired in 197 cases (17%). Of the 417 new jobs in corporate legal departments in 1995, women were hired in 148 cases (35%).

Our last look at this issue attempts to get at the overall ability to hire women under different circumstances of growth and decline in the size of the legal department. Figure 8.16 looks at the percentage of legal departments with female attorneys under three separate conditions; growth in department employment, declines in department employment, and stability in employment.[3]

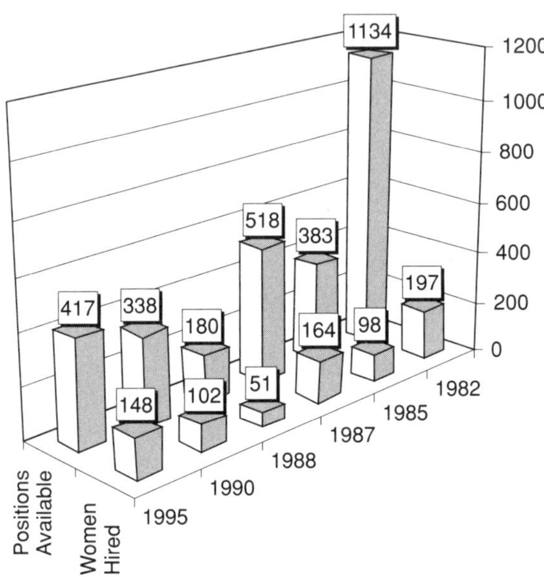

Figure 8.15 Positions available and number of women filling slots in corporate legal departments with no female attorneys in 1980

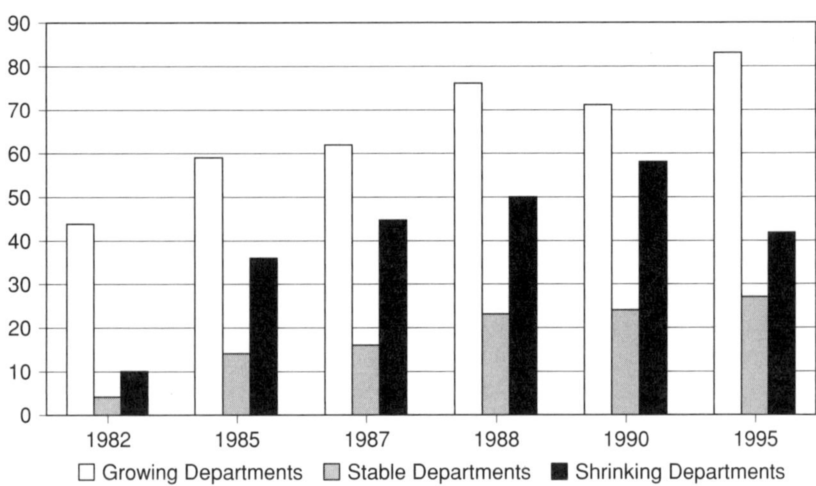

Figure 8.16 The percentage of legal departments with female attorneys in firms that had no female attorneys in 1980, for growing, stable, and declining departments, 1982–1995

The results here are interesting and mirror the results for organizational growth and decline that we found in chapter 6. More interesting perhaps is that our analysis in chapter 6 dealt with the relative mix of different groups of health care professionals in hospitals, an analysis with a totally different focus from this one. Firms that are growing are by far more likely to have women on the corporate legal staffs than the others. This result was what we expected. But (interestingly) firms that are *shrinking* in size are more likely to hire women than firms that stay the same size. These results point to the role that environmental turbulence plays in changing employment patterns. Just as hospitals in turbulent environments change the relative usage of nurses, physicians, and hospital administrators, corporations change their employment practices during turbulent times. These results suggest that organizational decline is a threat to legitimacy, and the resulting turmoil leads to attempts to conform to pressures from outside the firm.

Which firms have the most women attorneys?

It is one thing to examine the contexts where women are most likely to be hired and look at variations in when this change occurs. It is quite another to examine what the relative representation of women attorneys is and to see what larger institutional characteristics affect the proportion of attorneys that are women. We turn to this task now and present the results in figure 8.17. Details of the results are discussed in the Appendix to this chapter (p. 212). These results can be summarized easily:

1 *Fortune 500 firms have the highest percentage of women attorneys.* These effects are the largest "pull factors" in favor of hiring women attorneys. Clearly Fortune 500 firms spend a lot of effort diversifying their corporate staffs, and this includes corporate legal departments.
2 *Corporate acquisition activity increases the percentage of women attorneys.* This result dovetails nicely with our look at which companies have any women attorneys on their staffs at all. Companies that engage in acquisition activity are doing a lot of legal work and they are also changing their corporate structures (in all likelihood). This impetus for change clearly affects the context of the corporate legal department.
3 *Women in prominent executive positions and corporate board positions increase the proportion of women in corporate legal departments.* The

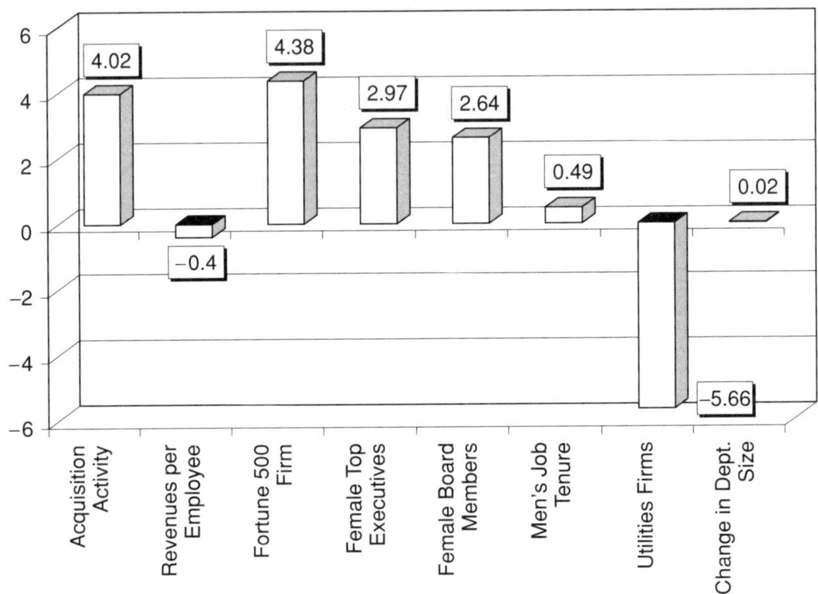

Figure 8.17 Effects of measures of corporate, department, and environmental attributes on the percentage of female attorneys in corporate legal departments, 1980–1995

average increase in women's representation is about 3 percent given the presence of women in high-visibility, corporate slots. Since the mean percentage of women in legal departments that have any women at all is around 33 percent, and the effects of top executives and board members are independent from each other (since the other corporate characteristics in the figure act as controls) the cumulative difference between firms with women in visible corporate governance positions and firms without this representation is about 6 percent, a 17 percent change in the representation of women produced by these characteristics alone.

4 *Women's representation is driven by growth in legal department size.* As was true in he analysis of hiring the first female attorney and the overall presence of female attorneys, regardless of when they were hired. The independent effect of growth in department size is important because it reflects changes in the number of openings for new labor force entrants to fill. The substantive size of the net effect is not very large because there is also a smaller effect of

declines in department size on the growing representation of women (see figure 8.16). The net effect of department size growth would leave the average firm with four more female attorneys in 1995 than they had in 1980.

5 *There are relatively few industry effects*; only utilities (firms) have significantly fewer women attorneys. This suggests that industry context affects the initial hiring of women attorneys, but that effects as distant as the industry can't pressure individual firms to go much further beyond the initial first hire.

Are there mimetic effects? Evidence that firms within industries "copy" each other

We have compiled extensive evidence that there are independent effects of women in top corporate positions and environmental characteristics on the diversification of corporate legal departments. These effects correspond (roughly) to normative and coercive pressure to conform to a larger institutional and professional environment that is promoting workplace diversity. The question we haven't answered is whether there are mimetic pressures to hire female attorneys. As a preliminary attempt to assess this question, we present figure 8.18. The details of the analysis are presented in the Appendix to this chapter (p. 214).

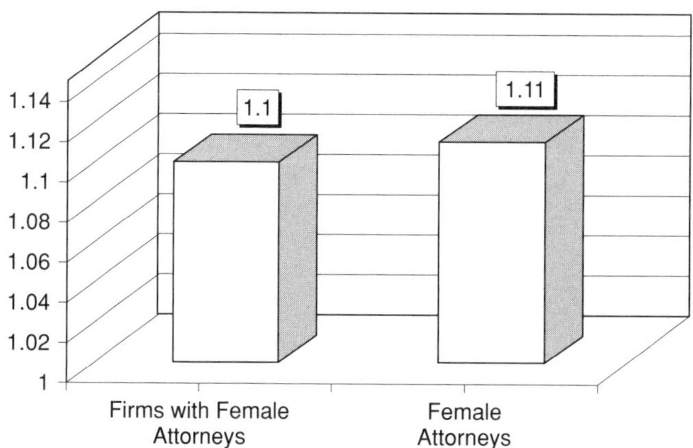

Figure 8.18 Effects of women's representation in corporate legal departments on the probability of hiring the first female attorney and the percentage of women in each legal department, 1980–1995

The key result revealed in figure 8.18 is that, net of all of the other controls in our analysis, firms in industries with a growing representation of women in their legal departments will more than likely start hiring female attorneys themselves if they haven't done so already. In other words, there is considerable evidence that corporations start to diversify their legal departments because other firms in their industry are doing it. Since we control for the presence of women in other top corporate positions, industry location, and other characteristics of the firm, these results come closest to gauging mimetic effects. The chances that firms will hire their first female attorney rises about 10 percent with each 10 percentage point change in women's representation elsewhere in the firm's industry.

Taken together, our results provide support for all three types of institutional pressure on corporate legal departments. Large and visible corporations, corporations in newer and publicly regulated industries, corporations with women in visible top executive positions, and corporations in environments with strong upward trends in hiring women hire women themselves and employ them in larger numbers. This trend is all the more important because it is occurring in a profession whose work environment, professional interests, and demographic makeup is changing rapidly. We discuss the implications of our results in our conclusions.

SUMMARY

We need to put these results in a larger context representing the overall thesis of our book. Our results look a lot like those you would find in an analysis of gender representation in other bureaucratic workplaces (see Baron and Bielby 1984, 1986; Ospina 1996; Bielby 1999). Firms in visible, public positions, publicly regulated and "new" service industries, in firms experiencing growth and decline in demand for professionals, in firms with women already represented in highly-visible corporate positions, and firms in industries that are rapidly diversifying their professional staffs are most likely to hire female attorneys for their in-house staffs. These results provide considerable support for our neoinstitutional approach to change in professional and managerial work settings.

While all professional groups are diversifying demographically, this doesn't imply that there are other changes besides those involving the movement of underrepresented groups into professional labor markets. Other researchers (most notably Brint 1994) caution against the inference that demographic diversity translates into identifiable change in interests and political outlooks. There isn't a straightforward connection between the movement of women and minorities into professional and managerial work and other changes in professional work settings, but the coincidence of these changes makes the study of changes in professional work all the more interesting and challenging.

What our results suggest is that many of the same institutional pressures that affect the hiring of women in large bureaucratic settings also influence the hiring of professionals as well. The combination of demographic diversification in the legal profession and the movement of legal practice away from traditional law firms to corporate work settings produces patterns of inclusion and exclusion that mirror patterns found in large organizations elsewhere. Our final chapter examines the implications of changes in work settings for professionals and managers on the future of professional work.

Appendix: Details of Analysis Using Data from the Law and Business Directory of Corporate Counsel (1980–1995)

Data on corporate legal departments and in-house attorneys are taken from the *Law and Business Directory of Corporate Counsel* for the years 1980, 1982, 1985, 1987, 1988, 1990, and 1995. These data are organized by corporation and list every attorney in every legal department for over 4,000 US firms. The *Directory* attempts to provide a comprehensive listing of all companies (without charge) that maintain legal departments staffed by full-time employees, and has been available on a biannual basis since 1979. In addition to the name and location of the corporate legal department, the *Directory* provides comprehensive information on the names, specialty areas, present job titles, and length of time in present position for all attorneys in each legal department. Information is also provided on previous positions with the company (including job title and job tenure), previous positions outside the company (including employer name, job title, and tenure in each job), and educational backgrounds of attorneys.

In our analysis we look at the changing composition of legal departments from 1980 through 1995. To do this, we constructed a random sample of firms from the 1979 *Directory* (N = 930), with observations in the years listed above through 1995. Because of the variable availability of back issues of the *Directory* it was not possible to code information from all of the directories in existence from

This appendix is taken from Mary L. Fennell and Kevin T. Leicht. 1998. "The Changing Organizational Context of Professional Work: Implications for Gender Representation in Corporate Law." Presented at the 1998 meetings of the American Sociological Association, Toronto, Ontario, Canada and National Science Foundation SBR#9310557.

1980–95. However, our sample provides reasonable coverage and our analysis techniques attempt to account for the variability in time lags between data points. The sample was stratified by size and primary industry (industry listings came from Moody's investor service and Standard and Poor's *Directory of Corporate Directors and Officers*). Industry sampling was based on the one-digit SIC level, and firms were stratified into eight groups; high-technology (using industry definitions taken from Riche et al. 1983), utilities, service, finance, insurance, transportation, communications, and manufacturing. We also used Fortune 500 lists to stratify the sample into Fortune 500 and non-Fortune 500 firms, which leads to an oversampling of larger and better-performing firms.

In each observation year, all of the firm-level data were collected along with data on the composition of attorneys in each legal department. Individuals were added to the firm data and remain as long as those new lawyers stay with the firm. The goal of this sampling technique was to follow a fixed set of firms over time to document the changing characteristics of sampled firms, the changing composition of lawyers in each firm, and the characteristics of lawyers within firms (such as the firm tenure of male attorneys). In addition to *Directory* data, firm-level data were collected from Moody's *Investor Service*, Standard and Poor's, *Dunn and Bradstreet*, Ward's Business Directories, *Fortune*, and *Mergers and Acquisitions Monthly*, allowing us to add data on the composition of boards of directors, composition of top management teams, firm performance, and merger and acquisition activity.

Additional supplementary information on college and law school ranking was provided from the Gourman Report, which ranks universities and law schools on fourteen different criteria; Both undergraduate colleges and law schools are partitioned into two separate groups; those falling into the top quintile of rankings (those with scale scores between four and five) and total rankings of all colleges and law schools. Information on the educational composition of attorneys was created by aggregating the information taken from the Gourman report to the department level.

These data were analyzed using four dependent variables; (1) the presence or absence of women attorneys, analyzed using logistic regression, (2) the presence or absence of women on corporate boards of directors (using logistic regression), (3) the presence or absence of women as top corporate officers (using logistic regression), and (4) the percentage of women attorneys in each legal department that has women attorneys (using two-way fixed effects models and corrections for sample selection bias).

Measures used in the analysis of women's representation in corporate legal departments

The specific measures we used to predict which firms will have female corporate attorneys and when they will hire them include measures of *firm performance*, *normative pressure*, *male networks*, *industry*, *region*, *change in department size*, and *year*. Details of specific indicators are discussed below:

1 firm performance is measured using an indicator of *Fortune 500 firm* listing (= 1; non-Fortune 500 firms = 0), and *sales/revenues per worker* for each survey year. Sales/revenues per worker standardizes our performance measures across service and production industries, and controls for firm size (number of employees).
2 Normative pressure is measured using measures of *women on corporate boards* of directors (= 1; no women present = 0), and *women as corporate officers* (= 1; no women present = 0). These data are taken from Standard and Poor's *Directory of Corporate Directors and Officers.*
3 Male networks are assessed using the *average ranking of men's law schools* in each legal department and the *average tenure of male attorneys* in each legal department. The law school rankings are reversed so that large values represent higher-ranked law schools.
4 Industry is measured using a series of categorical variables for *high technology* (= 1), *utilities* (= 1), *finance* (= 1), *insurance* (= 1), *transportation* (= 1), and *communications* (= 1). Manufacturing firms are the omitted category.
5 Region measures whether the corporate headquarters is in a *southern state* (= 1, all others = 0). Southern states are defined as all of the states of the former confederacy.
6 *Change in legal department size* is a measure of the percentage change in department size between the data panels.
7 Year variables index each year of data collection after 1980 (1982 = 1; 1985 = 1; 1987 = 1; 1988 = 1; 1990 = 1; and 1995 = 1).

Missing data were dealt with using mean values from other firms for the same industry and year. In some cases, we knew that a firm and legal department were still in existence but the information provided in the *Directory* was fragmentary or partial. In these cases we took data from the first prior year that provided complete *Directory* information for a given firm. Both instances of data substitution are flagged in the analysis to control for design effects resulting from our substitutions for missing data.

The analysis of odds of hiring the first attorney for firms with no female attorneys in 1980 uses an event-history design. Firms are followed until they hire their first female attorney, then they drop out of the sample. All firms that hired attorneys in 1980 or earlier drop out immediately after the first wave. The total number of cases for this analysis is 4,213.

The analysis of the odds of having women on corporate boards of directors and as top corporate officers uses the entire sample (N = 6,507) and predicts the presence or absence of women in these corporate positions.

The complete analysis used to construct figures 8.7, 8.8, 8.13, 8.14, 8.17, and 8.18 are provided below. The analysis predicting the percentage of women attorneys among firms that have female attorneys corrects for sample selection bias and also uses two-way fixed effects estimation to control for unobserved heterogeneity over time and across firms.

The complete data set and further documentation are available from the authors (*kevin-leicht@uiowa.edu; mary_fennell@brown.edu*).

Table A.8.1 Logistic regression predicting the presence of women lawyers, total sample (N = 6,507)[c]

Independent Variables	*Log Odds Coefficient*	*Odds*
Firm Performance:		
Fortune 500 Firm	.95★★★	2.58
Sales/revenues per worker	–.010	.99
Acquisitions (= 1)	.76★★★	2.13
Normative Pressure:		
Women on corp. board	.75★★★	2.13
Women corp. officers	.51★★★	1.66
Male Networks:		
Avg. ranking of men's law schools	.01★★	1.02
Avg. firm tenure of male attorneys	–.067★★★	–.93
Industry:[a]		
High technology	–.01	.99
Utilities	.74★★★	2.10
Finance	–.27	.76
Insurance	.59★★★	1.81
Transportation	.40★	1.49
Communication	.56★	1.75
Southern State (= 1)	–.03	.97
Change in legal dept. size	.01★★★	1.01
1982[b]	.40★★★	1.49
1985	.74★★★	2.09
1987	.75★★★	2.11
1988	.86★★★	2.36
1990	.80★★★	2.22
1995	.56★★★	1.76
Missing data (= 1)	–.32★★★	.73
Intercept	–6.38★★★	–
Chi-Square	1,110.4★★★	
Percentage concordant	72.9%	

★ $p \leq .05$; ★★ $p \leq .01$; ★★★ $p \leq .001$

[a] Manufacturing industry is the reference category.

[b] 1980 is the reference year.

[c] This analysis is used to produce figure 8.7.

Table A.8.2 Logistic regression predicting the presence of women lawyers, event-history sample (N = 4,213)[c]

Independent Variables	*Log Odds Coefficient*	*Odds*
Firm Performance:		
Fortune 500 Firm	.76***	2.15
Sales/revenues per worker	–.04	.96
Acquisitions (= 1)	.58*	1.78
Normative Pressure:		
Women on corp. board	.78***	2.19
Women corp. officers	.26	1.30
Male Networks:		
Avg. ranking of men's law schools	.01	1.00
Avg. firm tenure of male attorneys	–.07***	–.93
Industry:[a]		
High technology	–.02	.98
Utilities	.72**	2.06
Finance	–.02	.98
Insurance	.68***	1.97
Transportation	.04	1.05
Communication	.90*	2.47
Southern State (= 1)	–.04	.96
Change in legal dept. size	.01***	1.01
1982[b]	–.97***	.38
1985	–1.22***	.30
1987	–1.38***	.25
1988	–1.91***	.14
1990	–1.79***	.17
1995	–1.94***	.14
Missing data (= 1)	–.75***	.47
Intercept	–6.07***	–
Chi-Square	737.17***	
Percentage concordant	82.3%	

* $p \leq .05$; ** $p \leq .01$; *** $p \leq .001$

[a] Manufacturing industry is the reference category.

[b] 1980 is the reference year.

[c] This analysis is used to produce figure 8.8.

Table A.8.3 Logistic regression predicting the presence of women top executives (N = 6,507)[d]

Independent Variables	*Log Odds Coefficient*	*Odds*
Firm Performance:		
Fortune 500 Firm	.78★★★	2.19
Sales/revenues per worker	–.01	1.00
Acquisitions (= 1)	.05	1.06
Industry:[a]		
High technology	–.33★★	.72
Utilities	–.35	.70
Finance	3.34★★★	28.34
Insurance	.97★★★	2.64
Transportation	–1.07★★	.34
Communication	–1.18★	.31
Southern State (= 1)	.69★★★	2.01
Change in legal dept. size	–.01[c]	1.00
1982[b]	.28★	1.33
1985	.37★	1.45
1987	.19	1.20
1988	.28★	1.33
1990	.47★★★	1.60
1995	1.35★★★	3.87
Missing data (= 1)	–.96★★★	.38
Intercept	–1.66★★★	
Chi-Square	1,005.05★★★	
Percentage concordant	73.9%	

★ $p \leq .05$; ★★ $p \leq .01$; ★★★ $p \leq .001$

[a] Manufacturing industry is the reference category.

[b] 1980 is the reference year.

[c] Coefficient × 100.

[d] This analysis is used to produce figure 8.13.

Table A.8.4 Logistic regression predicting the presence of women on corporate boards of directors (N = 6,507)[d]

Independent Variables	*Log Odds Coefficient*	*Odds*
Firm Performance:		
Fortune 500 Firm	1.07★★★	2.90
Sales/revenues per worker	−.01	1.00
Acquisitions (= 1)	.27	1.31
Industry:[a]		
High technology	−.13	.88
Utilities	.14	1.15
Finance	1.27★★★	3.57
Insurance	.53★★★	1.70
Transportation	−.63★	.53
Communication	−.71	.49
Southern State (= 1)	.27★★	1.32
Change in legal dept. size	.01[c]	1.00
1982[b]	.16	1.17
1985	.26★	1.30
1987	.08	1.09
1988	.23	1.25
1990	.16	1.18
1995	.70★★★	2.01
Missing data (= 1)	−1.08★★★	.34
Intercept	−1.18★★★	–
Chi-Square	598.11★★★	
Percentage concordant	69.0%	

★ $p \leq .05$; ★★ $p \leq .01$; ★★★ $p \leq .001$

[a] Manufacturing industry is the reference category.

[b] 1980 is the reference year.

[c] Coefficient × 100.

[d] This analysis is used to produce figure 8.13.

Table A.8.5 Two-way fixed effects models predicting percentage of women attorneys, total sample with sample selection correction (lambda) ($N = 6{,}507$)[b]

Independent Variables	*(1)*
Firm Performance:	
Fortune 500 Firm	4.38***
Sales/revenues per worker	–.04*
Acquisitions (= 1)	4.02**
Normative Pressure:	
Women on corp. board	2.64*
Women corp. officers	2.97***
Male Networks:	
Avg. ranking of men's law schools	–.001
Avg. firm tenure of male attorneys	.491***
Industry:[a]	
High technology	–1.97
Utilities	–5.66*
Finance	.48
Insurance	.30
Transportation	1.22
Communication	4.08
Southern State (= 1)	4.74
Change in legal dept. size	.02**
Lambda (no female attorneys = 1)	–3.04**
Missing data (= 1)	–962.70**
Intercept	–21.6*
R-Square	.68

* $p \leq .05$; ** $p \leq .01$; *** $p \leq .001$

[a] Manufacturing industry is the reference category.

[b] This analysis is used to produce figure 8.17.

Measuring positions available and number of women filling available slots in corporate legal departments

With the data from the *Directory*, there are two ways to assess the relative availability of open slots and the identity of those who fill them. First, we could follow the individual names of those who are employed in each department and count a position as "open" when names disappeared and were replaced by others. The new incumbent could then be classified as male or female and we could follow the gender composition of people who fill open slots in corporate legal departments during the 1980s and 1990s. The second strategy we could use would be to plot changes in the size of corporate legal departments and follow the incumbents who fill new slots in each department as they are hired. Ideally, both strategies should be used, but both are quite labor intensive.

In place of these methods, we use a much simpler method to gauge open slots and the gender composition of attorneys that fill them. We calculate the raw change in legal department size for each firm, and sum that total. This method allows growth and detraction to cancel each other out, giving us a measure of the net increase/decrease in the number of positions that are available in the legal departments in our sample. This number constitutes the *positions available* listings in figure 8.15.

We use a similar method to calculate the number of women filling these available slots. We calculate changes in the number of women in each legal department, and sum these across the entire sample for each year of our data collection. This yields the number of *women hired* listed in figure 8.15.

This method does have some trade-offs relative to the more complicated measures listed above. Measuring new positions using changes in legal department size does not count positions where an incumbent quits or retires and is replaced by a new lawyer. However, our measure of changes in women's representation in each department does count women (and men) who are hired to replace others who retire or are replaced. So our measure probably underestimates the number of open slots available for new job incumbents to fill and more accurately estimates the number of women who fill slots as they become available.

Assessing mimetic effects

In assessing mimetic effects we are interested in the relationship between what other firms in a given firm's "reference group" is doing, and whether that directly affects the chances that a given firm will do the same thing.

To measure the hiring of women attorneys in the reference group, we look at the effects of hiring female attorneys in the industry that each firm is in. We look at the effects that prior hiring of women in specific industries has on the probability that a firm with no female attorneys will hire their first female attorney. We examine two measures of women's presence in each industry; (1) the percentage

Table A.8.6 Logistic regression predicting the hiring of the first female attorney in legal departments with no female attorneys, including the percentage of firms in each industry with female attorneys and the percentage of female attorneys in each industry (with sample selection correction, N = 4,863)

Independent Variables	*Log Odds Coefficient*	*Odds*	*Log Odds Coefficient*	*Odds*
Firm Performance:				
Fortune 500 Firm	.89***	2.44	.89***	2.44
Sales/revenues per worker	–.01**	.98	–.01	.99
Acquisitions (= 1)	1.12***	3.07	1.12***	3.07
Normative Pressure:				
Women on corp. board	.85***	2.34	.85***	2.34
Women corp. officers	.30*	1.35	.30*	1.35
Male Networks:				
Avg. ranking of men's law schools	.01***	1.01	.01***	1.01
Avg. firm tenure of male attorneys	–.12***	.88	–.12***	.88
Southern State (= 1)	–.14	.86	–.14	.87
Change in legal dept. size	.01***	1.01	.01***	1.01
Missing data (= 1)	–.24*	.78	–.24*	.79
Lambda (sample selection correction)	–.42**	.66	.01***	1.01
Mimetic Effects:				
Percentage of firms with female attorneys in industry	.01***	1.10	–	–
Percentage of female attorneys in industry	–	–	.01***	1.11
Intercept	–11.6***	–	–11.6***	–
Chi-Square	657.8***		657.8***	
Percentage concordant	72.1%		72.1%	

* $p \leq .05$; ** $p \leq .01$; *** $p \leq .001$

[a] This analysis is used to produce figure 8.18.

of firms in each industry with at least one female attorney in their legal department (which produces the left bar in figure 8.18), and (2) the average percentage of women in each legal department (which produces the right bar in figure 8.18). We use a subsample of firms with no female attorneys in 1980, since our purpose is to assess whether mimetic pressure exerted from other actors in the industry persuades others to follow the actions of leading firms. We control for normative pressure, male networks, region, and a sample selection correction indexing cases who were excluded from the sample because they had hired female attorneys by 1980. We don't control for industry or year because these are components of the mimetic effects measure we use (see table A.8.6).

NOTES

1 These industries are defined at the one-digit SIC level, with the exception of high-technology, which uses the definition provided by Riche et al. (1983).
2 Note that growth is assessed after 1980, and the year 1980 is taken as a baseline to begin the calculation of new openings and new hires.
3 Unlike our measures of stability, growth, and decline in chapter 5, these measures use change in legal department employment and assess changing employment patterns in departments that remain the same size, those that employ more people over time, and those that employ fewer people over time.

9

Conclusion: The Rise of the Postorganizational Workplace

This book has attempted to get you to think about the organization of work in a different way. Specifically, we have argued that the world of professionals and managers are "changing places," and that the elite division of labor is changing rapidly. These changes defy easy categorization. Elite managers now enjoy much of the autonomy and prerogatives that professionals once enjoyed. Instead of describing professionals as proletarianized, we think it is better to say that professional work is gradually changing and, in some cases, is becoming more accountable to other stakeholders who have an interest in the performance of professional work. What this accountability means varies drastically depending not only on the profession but also on the specific organizational setting where professional work is performed.

Let's review the highlights of our argument before we turn to the conclusions that follow for the study of workplace change and for understanding the future direction of professional work. In chapter 1, we argued that professional and managerial workers were "changing places" as each adapted and responded to changes in the larger work environment caused by the growing use of information technology and changes in the markets for professional services. We highlighted what we think is a convergence in organizational forms that defines the elite division of labor, an organizational form we label "neoentrepreneurialism." This organizational form encompasses the aspirations of the managerial project, the increasing diversity of professional work settings, the convergence of control structures among professionals, and the diversification of interests among professional workers. We provided a graphic display of the neoentrepreneurial market for professional services, which highlights the subcontracted and outsourced relationships between elite workers and those that purchase their labor.

In chapters 2 and 3 we discuss prior conceptions of professional and managerial work. Chapter 2 focused on different definitions of professional work and definitions of systems of professional work. Chapter 3 provided an abbreviated historical description of the managerial project, which we define as the long-term attempt to expand the autonomy and freedom of action of managers *vis-à-vis* investors and nonsupervisory workers. We trace the development of managerial thinking from entrepreneurialism to scientific management, the human relations approach of the 1940s, and to human resource management in recent years. In both of these chapters we attempt to highlight the extensive work that has been done in an attempt to understand professionals and managers, in part by defining what it is that is distinctive about those who occupy these relatively elite occupational positions. Both groups, in different ways, are engaged in professional projects to expand their decision-making authority and professional prerogatives, though they go about it in different ways from drastically different starting points and historical circumstances.

Chapter 4 lays out our case for the development of the neoentrepreneurial workplace. We claim that long-term declines in unionization, the globalization of communications and supply networks, employment downsizing, and the rising use of temporary, part-time, and subcontracted workers constitutes a fundamental change in the organization of work that has broad implications for the elite division of labor in addition to the well-documented changes that have occurred to middle managers and nonsupervisory workers. Rather than predicting the end of work, the neoentrepreneurial workplace looks a lot like a professional, collaborative workplace where a premium is paid on teamwork, flexibility, broad training, and drastic reshuffling as people with different competencies are assembled into groups that exist only for the length of specific projects.

Chapter 5 looks at the implications of different theories of professionalization for the new roles that professionals play in the elite division of labor. This chapter introduces the neoinstitutional perspective for understanding workplace change among professionals. Professional work is driven by a series of norms that are legal, normative, and cultural, leading to coercive, normative, and mimetic pressures for relative conformity in professional life. A neoinstitutional perspective helps us to understand how professionals act as active agents in the creation of workplace norms, and how these norms translate educational credentials and technical skills into prestige, relatively high incomes, power, and prerogatives.

Chapter 6 then returns to the workplace of the 1990s and asks what sets of changes are driving professional and managerial work toward common sets of experiences, albeit from different starting points. Deindustrialization and the power that disinvestments, capital flight, and the globalization of capital markets place in managers' hands helped to expand managerial prerogatives at the same time as workers, nonsupervisory employees, and middle managers were facing an uncertain future in drastically downsized workplaces. These changes ended the postwar social contract between the classes and enhanced the development of managerial projects. At the same time, professionals were facing new calls for greater accountability from clients, compromised skills as a result of new technologies, tight labor markets, and the rise of competing paraprofessional groups that were attacking traditional professional task domains. Professionals were maintaining their status and much of their technical skills, but the stakeholders around professional actors were demanding more, paying less, and paying much more attention to what professionals did and said they were going to do.

The last part of chapter 6 looked at the responses hospitals make to radical organizational change and the implications that these changes have for the elite division of labor between physicians, administrators, and nurses. Our results suggest that there are only a few circumstances that lead to greater administrative control over the work of physicians. However, virtually any organizational change that tightens resources hurts nurses in comparison to physicians and administrators. These results highlight the ability of professional groups to weather organizational storms even in organizations that attempt to control their activities.

Chapter 7 takes a specific look at interest diversity and demographic diversity among professionals, focusing on physicians. There is very little evidence that the rise of managed care, preferred provider organizations, and greater attempts by the US federal government and health insurers to control costs has substantially changed the specialties that young physicians choose to enter. Men are still concentrated in high prestige, high cost, dramatic intervention activities and women are still concentrated in relatively low prestige, low cost, and undramatic physician specialties. If anything, women are moving toward parity with men in some high visibility, high prestige areas. But there is only a small amount of evidence (as of 1997) that female physicians are moving toward primary care specialties because of changes in the organization of payment plans in the health care industry.

Chapter 8 documents that larger organizational changes, even changes outside of the portion of an organization that is "professionalized," can affect the division of labor among professional workers. In the case of corporate, in-house attorneys, larger institutional forces within and outside of corporate legal departments affect the representation and hiring of women. Many of the same processes that lead to the hiring of women as elite managers and corporate board members also spawn the hiring of female corporate attorneys in corporate legal departments. Further, we showed that there was considerable mimetic pressure within industries to hire and promote female attorneys during the 1980s and 1990s.

Our results don't suggest that professionals are being deskilled, or that managers are going to be downsized out of existence. Instead, we see the roles of managers and professionals evolving toward a common set of themes that the neoentrepreneurial workplace model is designed to highlight; greater teamwork, accountability, and prerogatives exercised in contexts where there are unprecedented abilities to monitor and sanction performance. In the rest of our concluding chapter, we speculate on some implications of the consequences of this type of workplace for those we have described as members of the working elite.

The Labor Market Implications of the Neoentrepreneurial Workplace

The growth of a debureaucratized workplace for professionals and managers produces a set of interesting implications for policy-makers and researchers. Social networks will become more important for securing new assignments and staying active in your profession. Internal labor markets will cease to exist for many people. Some employees will find further increases in professional prerogatives. Others will find decreasing rewards and increased routinization. These changes have political and social implications that go beyond those involved in the new elite division of labor. We touch on each of these implications briefly and recommend them as avenues for future research.

The rising importance of social networks

A debureaucratized, neoentrepreneurial workplace for professionals and managers is a workplace where people will rely on social networks across long distances to secure and maintain professional contacts and employment. Researchers in sociology, in particular, have always been ambivalent about bureaucracies and their role in producing social inequality (see Kanter 1977; Ospina 1996; Nelson and Bridges 1999). Bureaucracies seemed to provide protections to elite employees; employment stability, reliable retirement plans, extensive sets of fringe benefits, and regular promotions and pay raises. Further, bureaucracies were usually credited with creating procedural guarantees against arbitrary dismissal and other forms of workplace injustice (see Edwards 1979; Burawoy 1985).

But bureaucracies are also blamed for producing and perpetuating gender and racial inequality through the proliferation of job titles, the creation of relatively closed job ladders that "propel" certain employees toward the top of organizations, and for producing "glass ceilings" that allow for promotions to accumulate early in the career only to stall out as one nears the top of the organization (see Baron et al. 1986, 1991). The segregation and ghettoization of underrepresented groups in bureaucratic organizations has led some to question whether discriminatory practices are inherently part of the bureaucratic organizational form (see Wallace 1998).

But the case for eliminating bureaucracy as a way of reducing inequality is by no means clear-cut. Networks of professional contacts are (as of now) quite segregated by race and gender. Ibarra and others (1995) report that elite workers from underrepresented groups usually have two sets of personal network contacts; instrumental contacts (those who are viewed as sources of job tips, workplace advice, mentoring, and potential promotions and new jobs) and expressive contacts (similar others with whom one shares "war stories" and provides emotional support). The growing use of networks in the workplace leads one to wonder whether minority groups will be excluded from professional and managerial work entirely, or whether the growing recognition of personal competence will free people from traditional gender and racial stereotypes through broadening and diversifying network contacts.

The decline of internal labor markets

The growing use of networks and the decline of bureaucracy as an organizing principle in the elite division of labor is in the process of eliminating a regular feature of many managerial workplaces; the internal labor market. Internal labor markets are orderly job progressions that are accompanied by a progressive development of skill and knowledge (Wallace and Kalleberg 1981). In the neoentrepreneurial workplace, there are few, if any, formally organized internal labor markets, either within firms or occupations. The closest thing that will exist is a common set of institutionalized experiences that all incumbents in an occupation will be expected to go through. In medicine, the internship is one such well-entrenched institution that is unlikely to disappear anytime soon. Whether similar norms will develop among managers remains to be seen. However, the orderly and steady career that internal labor markets produced seems to be going the way of domed stadiums and mainframe computers.

If this type of orderly career is all but over, what will replace it? People need some semblance of order and stability in their lives, and this applies for employees in the elite division of professional work as much as anyone else. What we believe will follow is a set of individualized, personalized, business and professional networks that tie people to significant professional contacts not only in their home communities, but (increasingly) around the world as well. These contacts will become increasingly important and the growing use of computers and internet technologies will make experts of various kinds accessible from anywhere. The well-positioned professional will have a web of such contacts and move from job to job, mostly from the privacy of his/her own office in a consulting business. For professionals, this change will be less drastic because many professional tasks still require personalized service in the physical presence of clients with whom they must maintain extensive contact.

But this change has important meaning for students of the workplace as well. Traditional economic models of competitive markets might end up explaining more labor market activity rather than less. As with transaction-cost economics (see Williamson 1985, cited in chapter 5) many of the claims against traditional economic models of employer and firm behavior rest on the premise that information is not costless, cannot be gathered quickly, and can be systematically misinterpreted or used in opportunistic ways. The world of the neoentrepreneurial workplace is one of almost costless information that is frictionlessly produced and relatively easy to act on. Further, the traditional impediments to employment relationships that follow from problems in information gathering are disappearing. These problems were one of the major reasons for the development of bureaucracies in the first place. When individual entrepreneurs couldn't watch all of the activity relevant to their operations, bureaucracies (complete with armies of managers, lots of paperwork, and bureaucratic employment relationships) were created as a proxy for the "eyes and ears" of business owners. Instead of overwhelming top managers with random pieces of information on workplace performance coming from everywhere, bureaucracies produced ordered chains of command and responsibility hierarchies that produced limited, but clear, systems of accountability.

Much of this information-gathering role of middle managers is now automated, and the bureaucracy that accompanies it is disappearing for many, to be replaced by automated networks of interaction, and freelance employment relationships. What isn't clear is whether old impediments for economic action will be replaced by new impediments, misattributions, and other human foibles that will prevent relatively free, costless, and accurate economic information from spawning purposeful action. Studying the adoption of new technologies and focusing on the paper trails they produce will be a fruitful avenue for new research in the workplace.

Professionalization for some; Proletarianization for others

The neoentrepreneurial workplace will certainly increase the status of some jobs at the expense of others. Highly-personalized professional activities will still be in high demand; who will want to have brain surgery done by just any random person an HMO chooses? But many of the important changes will come among those whose status is presently just below the elite managers and professionals that we've been focusing on throughout this book.

Some jobs and occupational groups in the elite division of labor will probably not fare as well. Looking at our examples in chapter 1 it is not hard to see where some big changes will take place. John was our bank manager for a trust department of a local branch bank. Whether branch banking has a future, and what type of future it will have, depends greatly on financial regulations controlling the creation of banks, branch banks, local ownership laws, and community reinvestment statutes. Not all of these rules and regulations come from the US federal government. Individual states and other jurisdictions also have a say in the organizational forms that banking takes.

However, it isn't difficult to see jobs like John's disappearing or radically changing, especially if current trends toward consolidation in the banking and financial service industry continue. A home office dictates much of the activity that John presently does. In the absence of any reason to physically locate banks in specific spots, there is no particular reason for John's branch bank to exist in Grand Rapids rather than Minneapolis, Seattle, Omaha, or any other specific location where skilled labor is available. One thing is for sure. The elite manager who controls the activity of John and others like him at other branch banks within the corporation has amassed a great deal of power and professional prerogative at the expense of branch bank managers. To a considerable degree this is a classic example of the process we've been describing for managers throughout this book.

The same could be said of Mark's position as a nonpracticing lawyer working for an insurance company. It isn't difficult to see the increasing struggles that many young lawyers will have as routine and lucrative forms of corporate legal work either dry up or are taken over by large, consolidated law firms and corporate legal departments. Since the production of new lawyers from certified law schools shows no signs of decreasing, this problem is likely to get worse.

A more interesting question, perhaps, is what will happen to Mark's job at the insurance company he currently works for. The insurance industry is, slowly but surely, becoming automated, especially at the level of the initial purchase of insurance. It is possible to shop for almost any type of insurance on-line and to get quotes from an unprecedented number of insurance companies, each of which is anxious for your business. Will automated quotes replace people like Mark? Not completely, but we see little reason for assuming that jobs like Mark's will increase in number.

Julie (the adjunct professor of English in the Boston area) is a classic example of a professional who has been captured by a tight labor market. Much like Mark, Julie's future (professionally at least) is not bright. The same chronic oversupply of professionals plagues Julie's chosen field as it does Mark's. Further, universities and colleges are taking advantage of this oversupply and hiring more and more instructors like Julie on a temporary, class-by-class basis. The results of doing this goes far beyond the loss of steady income and occupational prestige for Julie herself. The growing number of instructors like Julie make life much more difficult for the full-time, tenure track professors that remain. The prospect of being replaced by labor that is (superficially) a "perfect substitute" for the skills you bring to the labor market is an ever-present danger for many academics below a small number of elite researchers and writers.

Finally, it would seem that, of all of our examples, Mary's case as a newly-minted MD looking for a slot in a pediatrics practice is the brightest, and this is probably true. The chance that Mary will find a pediatrics practice to her liking is probably pretty good, and (in any event) she will be able to practice medicine and be more than adequately compensated. The real question, for her, is what kind of work setting this will be. In an era where managed care is growing at a rapid rate, people should turn to pediatricians and other primary care physicians as the new "gatekeepers" in HMOs and Preferred Provider Plans. The part of working life that will change the most for Mary is that there will be no interacting with patients. What will change for her is the entire environment surrounding patient treatment as more stakeholders demand that she account for (and justify) the treatments she proscribes and as more groups from outside the doctor/patient relationship question the proper course of treatment and define "health" for each of us.

Can everyone be a subcontractor?

One could look at many of the changes we've described in this book and view them as an unremitting disaster producing massive social dislocation. But the changes surrounding the move toward a globalized, downsized, "postbureaucratic," neoentrepreneurial workplace have allowed some people to re-evaluate their situation and (for the first time) voluntarily opt out of corporate employment. For all of it's economic and social security, corporate employment always had an impersonal, faceless quality to it that participants and analysts alike viewed as profoundly alienating (see Jackall 1988). One could leave our book convinced that subcontracting, outsourcing, and the other changes that have accompanied the reorganization of the elite division of labor have been thrust, kicking and screaming, on an unwilling and unmoving group of professionals and managers. Undoubtedly, some economic opportunities and traditional prerogatives have been lost. But, especially for managers, there certainly are large numbers of written-off and tuned out members of the corporate hierarchy that were never enamored with the whole corporate world in the first place. New research on the lives and workplace arrangements of the relatively skilled who decide to end formal corporate affiliations is at least as important as studying those who are permanently disadvantaged by job loss. If nothing else, they can provide us with useful templates for adapting to new situations.

What about the "new class" and the "old middle class"? The political and social implications of changes in the elite division of labor

One of the more interesting characteristics of the US political system is that there has been a clear division of labor between the political parties in the United States. The Democratic Party has generally favored wage earners at the expense of those with investments and nonearnings income, and the Republican Party has generally favored investors over wage earners in developing social and economic policies. But what happens to the political and social identification of elite workers who derive their incomes from a growing mix of earnings, deferred compensation, stock options, bonuses, and profit-sharing plans? Such compensation doesn't fit easily into the traditional dichotomy between wages and investment income. Further, our political parties have assumed that one or the other forms of compensation were the "dominant" income producing mechanism for most people.

If this is becoming less true, and especially if it is becoming less true for occupants of the elite division of labor, then the conventional party system in the US must change to meet those demands. These people are the people that most political parties want to appeal to. The Republicans could reap substantial gains from a new middle class whose income was derived from a mix of earnings, investment income, bonuses, and stock options. The current Republican Party doesn't seem interested in doing much for this group except taxing most of its spending power away, and otherwise turning the tax system into a regressive labyrinth of user fees, sales taxes, and social security taxes, while running up huge budget deficits that shift monetary policy in favor of big investors (see Phillips 1990). However, the current Democratic Party has yet to expand its base of support to this group either. Both parties, in fact, seem to have opportunities to build new coalitions that would end much of the political apathy afflicting the United States while broadening and sharpening their differences and appeals. Republicans could focus on income and investments of smaller investors and limit their favoritism of the rich and superrich. The Democrats could turn their traditional emphasis on wage earners into a renewed focus on developing a regime of general workplace rights with new methods of enforcement. At present, neither party seems to be willing to do this.

Of course, equivalent attention should be devoted to the political and social expression of the economically alienated, those who have been left behind by the development of the neoentrepreneurial workplace. One suspects that the plethora of hate groups, growing racial unrest, and the growth and visibility of militia and other quasi-revolutionary protest organizations (many with millenarian predictions of a grim future) are outgrowths of massive changes in the social meanings surrounding the workplace and the cultural uncertainty that follows from interacting in an increasingly diverse and immediate world.

Changing Places: Are There Limits?

Our general argument in this book is that managers and professionals are changing places in an increasingly unified, elite division of labor. Elite, collaborative, managerial work that accompanies a downsized, outsourced, internationally networked, and debureaucratized workplace is starting to "look like" traditional professional work on many important dimensions, and the prerogatives that elite managers have amassed for themselves since the late 1970s have placed them in positions with unprecedented decision-making authority and flexibility. Professional workers, by contrast, face an increasing set of organized stakeholders who question the content, quality, and cost of professional work, increasingly "shop around" for the professional services they want, and otherwise act to control professional activity in ways that were unheard of as late as 20 years ago.

By themselves, none of the information we present "proves" that this new arrangement of the elite division of labor is taking place. In some sense, we are simply connecting the dots that others have spent considerable effort laying out. If you accept our argument, then what (if any) are the potential limits to the trends we have been discussing throughout this book?

There are a number of limits we can think of, most of which result from the activities of other stakeholders in the division of labor. These stakeholders include, (1) other white collar and nonelite employees and former employers in the labor market, and (2) consumers and clients of elite managers and professionals. We address each of these briefly before we offer our closing remarks.

First, as numerous newspaper and journalistic accounts have made clear, there are large numbers of people (formerly comfortable members of the middle class) who have not fared well as a result of the changes that are producing the neoentrepreneurial workplace. The political and cultural implications of downsizing, layoffs, and the growing installment credit debt that confronts many members of the middle class is not a pretty sight. If the ranks of the disenchanted grow large and vocal, there could be unanticipated consequences of the creation of the neoentrepreneurial workplace, including growing resistance to globalization and increasing calls for economic nationalism. The contrasting scenes of massive protests in Seattle against the World Bank, combined with the rising political coverage of American political candidates like Pat Buchanan and Ross Perot, are examples of this trend. The changes in the elite division of labor that we've focused on are not meant to downgrade or push aside the real, wrenching social changes that have accompanied workplace upheavals for large numbers of people in the United States and other parts of the developed and developing world.

Second, clients and consumers of professional services continue to demand personalized service from professionals that they know and trust. One of the biggest complaints about Preferred Provider Plans is the fear that one's favorite physician is "preferred" by you alone, and not your insurance company. At key and stressful moments in people's lives, when facing life-threatening decisions about medical treatment options, when deciding how to defend yourself against traumatic lawsuits, when deciding in which mutual fund to invest your life savings, or when initiating psychiatric treatment for depression, there is still no substitute for the services of a professional that we know, trust, and that we meet with face-to-face on a regular basis. Corporatization, accountability, and efficiency are things we collectively need but individually (when we need key professional services) don't want. In this respect, the drive to rationalize professional life by making professionals accountable to other stakeholders in the system of professional services can only go as far as clients and consumers want it to.

However, the prospect of "putting on the brakes" with regard to elite managers and their relationship to the increasingly globalized economy shows few signs of changing. We can stop companies from laying-off massive numbers of employees. We can penalize them for engaging in short-term, opportunistic investments that do little but shuffle money into specific pockets and do nothing to increase the size of the economic pie. But as long as we are committed to some semblance of free trade (and the United States shows no signs of turning away from free trade, widespread discontent about the NAFTA and GATT agreements notwithstanding) and as long as finance capital can move around the world looking for the highest short-term gains, groups of elite managers will find ways to evade new regulations or penalize those that attempt to control their actions. This is the one key dimension of the neoentrepreneurial workplace that separates professionals from managers.

Finally, we close with a reflexive thought. In spite of the changes we've described here, elite managerial and professional work is still exciting, desirable, relatively prestigious, and relatively well-compensated. Your authors are relatively elite college professors who love their jobs (based on your evaluation of this book, you can make your own judgment about whether we're any good at it!). Young people will still aspire to have these positions, and many of the occupants of these jobs will find new sets of joys and frustrations that will accompany their day-to-day work lives. These are exciting times for people who do these jobs, and not all of the excitement is undesirable. We argue that the neoentrepreneurial workplace has placed professionals and managers in new places in the elite division of labor, but these new places still have much to recommend them, and people will still find meaning and make sense of their lives while doing them. Ours is just a preliminary attempt to make sense of their lives as professionals and managers come together and their work worlds converge.

Additional Readings on Professions

Engineering

Evetts, Julia. 1996. *Gender and Career in Science and Engineering*. Bristol, PA: Taylor & Francis.

Frankel, Ernst G. 1993. *In Pursuit of Technological Excellence*. Westport, CT: Praeger.

Kemper, John D. 1990. *Engineers and Their Profession*. Philadelphia, PA: Saunders College Publishing.

McIlwee, Judith S., and J. Gregg Robinson. 1992. *Women in Engineering: Gender, Power, and Workplace Culture*. Albany: State University of New York Press.

Morgan, Laurie A. 1998. "Glass-Ceiling Effect or Cohort Effect? A Longitudinal Study of the Gender Earnings Gap for Engineers, 1982–1989," *American Sociological Review* 63(August): 479–83.

National Research Council. 1994. *Women Scientists and Engineers Employed in Industry: Why So Few?* Washington, D.C: National Academy Press.

Reynolds, Terry S. (ed.). 1991. *The Engineer in America: A Historical Anthology From Technology and Culture*. Chicago, IL: The University of Chicago Press.

Whalley, Peter. 1986. *The Social Production of Technical Work: The Case of British Engineers*. Albany, New York: State University of New York Press.

Zussman, Robert. 1985. *Mechanics of the Middle Class: Work and Politics Among American Engineers*. Berkeley, CA: University of California Press.

Lawyers

Abel, Richard L., and Philip S. C. Lewis (eds.). 1995. *Lawyers in Society: An Overview*. Berkeley, CA: University of California Press.

Abel, Richard L. (ed.). 1997. *Lawyers: A Critical Reader*. New York: New Press.

Curran, Barbara A. 1985. *The Lawyer Statistical Report: A Statistical Profile of the U.S. Legal Profession in the 1980s*. Chicago, IL: American Bar Foundation.

Epstein, Cynthia Fuchs. 1993. *Women in Law*, 2nd edn. Urbana, IL: University of Illinois Press.

Epstein, Cynthia Fuchs, Carroll Seron, Bonnie Oglensky, and Robert Saute. 1999. *The Part-Time Paradox: Time Norms, Professional Lives, Family, and Gender.* New York: Routledge.

Gerber, Rudolph J. 1989. *Lawyers, Courts, and Professionalism: The Agenda for Reform.* New York: Greenwood Publishing Group.

Hagan, John, and Fiona Kay. 1995. *Gender in Practice: A Study of Lawyers' Lives.* New York: Oxford University Press.

Heinz, John P., and Edward O. Laumann. 1994. *Chicago Lawyers: The Social Structure of the Bar.* Evanston, IL: Northwestern University Press.

Kay, Fiona M., and John Hagan. 1998. "Raising the Bar: The Gender Stratification of Law-Firm Capital," *American Sociological Review* 63(October): 728–43.

Kelly, Michael J. 1994. *Lives of Lawyers: Journeys in the Organizations of Practice.* Ann Arbor, MI: University of Michigan Press.

Lentz, Bernard F., and David N. Laband. 1995. *Sex Discrimination in the Legal Profession.* Westport, CT: Quorum Books.

Martin, Susan Ehrlich, and Nancy C. Jurik. 1996. *Doing Justice, Doing Gender: Women in Law and Criminal Justice Occupations.* Thousand Oaks, CA: Sage Publications.

Nelson, Robert L., David M. Trubek, and Rayman L. Solomon. 1992. *Lawyers' Ideals/Lawyers' Practices: Transformation in the American Legal Profession.* Ithaca, NY: Cornell University Press.

Scott, Joan Norman. 1996. "Watching the Changes: Women in Law," chapter 2 in *Women and Minorities in American Professions*, Joyce Tang and Earl Smith (eds.). Albany: State University of New York Press.

Sommerlad, Hilary, and Peter Sanderson. 1998. *Gender, Choice, and Commitment: Women Solicitors in England and Wales and the Struggle for Equal Status.* Aldershot: Ashgate Publishing Company.

Thornton, Margaret. 1996. *Dissonance and Distrust: Women in the Legal Profession.* New York: Oxford University Press.

Pharmacy

Gambardella, Alfonso. 1995. *Science and Innovation: The U.S. Pharmaceutical Industry During the 1980s.* Cambridge: Cambridge University Press.

Fincham, Jack E., and Albert I. Wertheimer (eds.). 1997. *Pharmacy and the U.S. Health Care System*, 2nd edn. New York: Pharmaceutical Products Press.

Knowlton, Calvin H., and Richard P. Penna (eds.). 1996. *Pharmaceutical Care.* New York: Chapman & Hall.

Phipps, Polly A. 1990. "Industrial and Occupational Change in Pharmacy: Prescription for Feminization," chapter 5 in *Job Queues, Gender Queues: Explaining Women's Inroads into Male Occupations*, Barbara F. Reskin and Patricia A. Roos (eds.). Philadelphia, PA: Temple University Press.

Spivey, Richard N., Albert I. Wertheimer, and T. Dona Rucker (eds.). 1996. *International Pharmaceutical Services: The Drug Industry and Pharmacy Practice in*

Twenty-Three Major Countries of the World. New York: Pharmaceutical Products Press.

Doctors

American Medical Association. 1994. *The Future of Medical Practice*. Chicago, IL: American Medical Association.

Gonzalez, Martin L., and Puling Zhang (eds.). 1998. *Socioeconomic Characteristics of Medical Practice 1997/98*. Chicago, IL: American Medical Association.

Halpern, Sydney A. 1988. *American Pediatrics: The Social Dynamics of Professionalization, 1880–1980*. Berkeley, CA: University of California Press.

Hafferty, Fredric W., and John B. McKinlay. 1993. *The Changing Medical Profession: An International Perspective*. New York: Oxford University Press.

Hafferty, Frederic W., and Donald W. Light. 1995. "Professional Dynamics and the Changing Nature of Medical Work," *Journal of Health and Social Behavior* (extra issue): pp. 132–53.

Harrison, Michael I. 1993. "Medical Dominance or Proletarianization? Evidence From Israel," *Research in the Sociology of Health Care* 10:73–96.

Havlicek, Penny L. 1998. *Medical Groups in the U.S.: A Survey of Practice Characteristics, 1999*. Chicago, IL: American Medical Association.

Leicht, Kevin T., Mary L. Fennell, and Kristine M. Witkowski. 1995. "The Effects of Hospital Characteristics and Radical Organizational Change on the Relative Standing of Health Care Professions," *Journal of Health and Social Behavior* 36(2): 151–67.

Lorber, Judith. 1984. *Women Physicians: Careers, Status, and Power*. New York: Tavistock Publications.

Starr, Paul. 1982. *The Social Transformation of American Medicine*. New York: Basic Books.

Stevens, Rosemary. 1998. *American Medicine and the Public Interest*. Berkeley, CA: University of California Press.

Walsh, Diana Chapman. 1987. *Corporate Physicians: Between Medicine and Management*. New Haven, CO: Yale University Press.

Watson, Wilbur H. 1999. *Against the Odds: Blacks in the Profession of Medicine in the United States*. New Brunswick, NJ: Transaction Publishers.

Specialty groups

Babbott, David, Dewitt C. Baldwin, Jr., Charles D. Killiam, and Sheila O'Leary Weaver. 1989. "Racial-Ethnic Background and Specialty Choice: A Study of U.S. Medical School Graduates in 1987," *Academic Medicine* October: 595–9.

Bazzoli, Gloria J. 1985. "Medical Education Indebtedness: Does It Affect Physician Specialty Choice?," *Journal of Health Economics* 4: 1–19.

Bobula, Joel D. 1980. "Work Patterns, Practice Characteristics, and Incomes of Male and Female Physicians," *Journal of Medical Education* 55 (October): 826–33.

Coffin, Susan E., and David Babbott. 1989. "Early and Final Preferences for Pediatrics as a Specialty: A Study of U.S. Medical School Graduates in 1983," *Academic Medicine* (October): 600–5.

Colquitt, Wendy L., Michael C. Zeh, Charles D. Killian, and James M. Cultice. 1996. "Effect of Debt on U.S. Medical School Graduates' Preferences for Family Medicine, General Internal Medicine, and General Pediatrics," *Academic Medicine* 71(4): 400–11.

Hsiao, William C., Peter Braun, Douwe Yntema, and Edmund R. Becker. 1988. "Estimating Physicians' Work For a Resource-Based Relative-Value Scale," *New England Journal of Medicine* 319(13): 835–41.

Kassebaum, Donald G., and Philip L. Szenas. 1994. "Factors Influencing the Specialty Choices of 1993 Medical School Graduates," *Academic Medicine* 62(2): 164–70.

Kiker, B. F., and Michael Zeh. 1998. "Relative Income Expectations, Expected Malpractice Premium Costs, and Other Determinants of Physician Specialty Choice," *Journal of Health and Social Behavior* 39: 152–67.

Montgomery, Kathleen. 1990. "A Prospective Look at the Specialty of Medical Management," *Work and Occupations* 17(2): 178–98.

Rogers, Laura Q., Ruth-Marie E. Fisher, and Lloyd A. Lewis. 1990. "Factors Influencing Medical Students to Choose Primary Care or Non-Primary Care Specialties," *Academic Medicine* 65(9): S47–S48.

Schwarz, Richard W., Roy K. Jarecky, William E. Strodel, John V. Halley, Byron Young, and Ward O. Griffen, Jr. 1989. "Controllable Lifestyle: A New Factor in Career Choice by Medical Students," *Academic Medicine* (October): 606–9.

Weisman, Carol S., David M. Levine, Donald M. Steinwachs, and Gary A. Chase. 1980. "Male and Female Physicians Career Patterns: Specialty Choices and Career Patterns," *Journal of Medical Education* 55(October): 813–25.

References

Abbott, A. D. 1991. "The Future of Professions: Occupation and expertise in the Age of Organization." *Research in the Sociology of Organizations* 8: 17–42.

——. *The System of Professions: An Essay on the Division of Expert Labor.* Chicago: University of Chicago Press; 1988.

Abel, R. 1986. "The Transformation of the American Legal Profession." *Law and Society Review* 20: 7–18.

——. 1989. *American Lawyers.* New York: Oxford University Press.

Academy of Management Journal. 1998. *Special Research Forum on Managerial Compensation and Firm Performance* 41: 135–99.

Agency for Health Care Policy and Research. Using Clinical Practice Guidelines to Evaluate Quality of Care. AHCPR Publ. No. 95-0045. Washington, D.C.: US Department of Health and Human Services, 1995.

Alexander, J. and T. L. Amburgey. 1987. "The Dynamics of Change in the American Hospital Industry: Transformation or Selection?" *Medical Care Review* 44: 279–321.

Alexander, J. and T. D'Aunno. 1990. "Transformations of Institutional Environments: Perspectives on the Corporation of U.S. Health Care." Pp. 53–85 in *Innovations in Health Care Delivery: New Insights into Organizational Theory.* Edited by S. Mick and Associates. San Francisco: Jossey-Bass.

Alexander, J., M. Fennell, and M. Halpern. 1993. "Leadership Instability in Hospitals: The Influence of Board – CED Relations on Organizational Growth and Decline." *Administrative Science Quarterly* 38: 74–99.

Althauser, R. P. and A. L. Kalleberg. 1981. "Firms, Occupations, and the Structure of Labor Markets: A Conceptual Analysis." Pp. 119–52 in *Sociological Perspectives on Labor Markets*, edited by Ivar Berg. New York: Academic Press.

American Medical Association. Physician Characteristics and Distribution, 1997–1998 edition. Chicago, IL: American Medical Association.

Arthur, Michael B., Douglas T., Hall, and Barbara S., Lawrence. 1989. *Handbook of Career Theory.* New York: Cambridge University Press.

Association of Adademic Health Centers. 1996. *The US Health Workforce: Power, Politics, and Policy.* Neal A., Vanselow. New Health Workforce Responsibilities and Dilemmas. Association of Academic Health Centers.

Baird, C. W. 1990. "Labor Law Reform: Lessons From History." *Cato Journal* 10: 175–208.

Bakke, E. W. 1958. *The Human Resources Function.* New Haven: Yale Labor-Management Center.

Banta, T. W. and Associates, eds. 1993. *Making a Difference: Outcomes of a Decade of Assessment in Higher Education.* San Fransisco: Jossey-Bass.

Barley, S. R. and G. Kunda. 1992. "Design and Devotion: Surges of Rational and Normative Ideologies of Control in Managerial Discourse." *Administrative Science Quarterly* 37.

Baron, J. N. and W. T. Bielby. 1984. "The Organization of Work in a Segmented Economy." *American Sociological Review* 49: 454–73.

——. 1986. "The Proliferation of Job Titles in Organizations." *Adminstrative Science Quarterly* 52: 524–57.

Baron, J. N., F. R. Dobbin, and P. D. Jennings. 1986. "War and Peace: The Evolution of Modern Personnel Administration in U.S. Industry." *American Journal of Sociology* 92: 350–83.

Baron, J. N., B. S. Mittman, and A. E. Neuman. 1991. "Targets of Opportunity: Organizational and Environmental Determinants of Gender Integration within the California Civil Service, 1979–1985." *American Journal of Sociology* 96: 1362–401.

Baumol, W. J. 1967. *Business Behavior, Value and Growth, Revised Edition.* New York: Harcourt, Brace, and World.

Becker, H. S. et al. 1961. *Boys in White: Student Culture in Medical School.* New Brunswick, NJ: Transaction Publishers.

Bell, D. 1976. *The Coming of Postindustrial Society.* New York: Basic Books.

Bendix, R. 1956. *Work and Authority in Industry: Ideologies of Management in the Course of Industrialization.* New York: Wiley.

Berle, A. A. Jr. and G. C. Means. 1932. *The Modern Corporation and Private Property.* New York: Macmillan.

Blauner, Robert. 1964. *Alienation and Freedom: The Factory Worker and His Industry.* Chicago, IL: University of Chicago Press.

Bluestone, B. and B. Harrison. 1982. *The Deindustrialization of America: Plant Closings, Community Abandonment, and the Dismantling of Basic Industry.* New York: Basic Books.

Bogue, D. J. 1959. *The Population of the United States.* Glencoe, IL: Free Press.

Bok, D. 1993. *The Cost of Talent: How Executives and Professionals are Paid and How It Affects America.* New York: Free Press.

Bonner, T. N. 1992. *To the Ends of the Earth: Women's Search for Education in Medicine.* Cambridge, MA: Harvard University Press.

Boyett, J. H. and H. P. Conn. 1992. *Workplace 2000: The Revolution Reshaping American Business.* New York: Plume.

Bradshaw, Y. and M. Wallace. 1996. *Global Inequalities.* Thousand Oaks, CA: Pine Forge Press.

Braverman, Harry. 1974. *Labor and Monopoly Capital.* New York: Monthly Review Press.

Bridges, W. and R. L. Nelson. 1989. "Markets and Hierarchies: Organizational and Market Influences on Gender Inequality in a State Pay System." *American Journal of Sociology* 95: 616–58.

Brint, S. 1994. *In an Age of Experts: The Changing Role of Professionals in Politics and Public Life*. Princeton, NJ: Princeton University Press.

Broom, L. and P. Selznick. 1973. *Sociology: A Text with Adapted Readings*, fifth edition. New York: Harper and Row.

Burawoy, M. 1979. *Manufacturing Consent*. Chicago: University of Chicago Press.

——. 1985. *The Politics of Production*. Thetford, Norfolk: Thetford Press Ltd.

Burns, L. R., M. Denton, S. Goldfein, L. Warrick, B. Morenz, and B. Sales. 1992. "The Use of Continuous Quality Improvement Methods in the Development and Dissemination of Medical Practice Guidelines." *Quality Review Bulletin* 18: 434–39.

Carr-Sanders, A. P. and P. A. Wilson. 1933. *The Professions*. Oxford: Oxford University Press.

Carroll, G. R. 1984. "Organizational Ecology." *Annual Review of Sociology* 10: 71–93.

Carroll, G. R. and J. R. Harrison. 1994. "On the Historical Efficacy of Competition Between Organizational Populations." *American Journal of Sociology* 100: 720–49.

Castells, M. 1996. *The Rise of the Network Society*. Oxford: Blackwell Publishers.

Castells, M. 1998. *End of Millenium*. Oxford: Blackwell Publishers.

Chamberlain, M. K., ed. 1988. *Women in Academe: Progress and Prospects*. New York: Russell Sage.

Chandler, Alfred D. Jr. 1977. *The Visible Hand: The Managerial Revolution in American Business*. Cambridge, MA: The Belknap Press of Harvard University Press.

——. 1990. *Scale and Scope: The Dynamics of Industrial Capitalism*. Cambridge, MA: The Belknap Press of Harvard University Press.

Chiu, C. and K. T. Leicht. 2000. "When Does Feminization Increase Equality? The Case of Lawyers." *Law and Society Review* 33: 557–94.

Christianson, J. B., S. M. Sanchez, D. R. Wholey, and M. Shadle. 1991. "The HMO Industry: Evolution in Population Demographics and Market Structures." *Medical Care Review* 48: 3–46.

Cihon, P. J. and J. O. Castagnera. 1988. *Labor and Employment Law*. Boston: PWS-Kent.

Clark, L. and C. L. Estes. 1992. "Sociological and Economic Theories of Markets and Nonprofits: Evidence from Home Health Organizations." *American Journal of Sociology* 97: 945–69.

Clogg, C. C. 1979. *Measuring Underemployment*. New York: Academic Press.

Colwill, J. M., G. T. Perkoff, R. L. Blake, C. Paden, and M. Beachler. 1997. "Modifying the Culture of Medical Education: The First Three Years of the RWJ General Physician Initiative." *Academic Medicine* 72: 745–53.

Congressional Budget Office. 1997. Trends in Health Care Spending by the Private Sector. Washington, D.C.: Congressional Budget Office.

Cornfield, D. B. 1986. "Declining Union Membership in the Post-War Era: The United Furniture Workers of America, 1939–1982." *American Journal of Sociology* 91: 1112–53.

Curran, B. A. 1986. "American Lawyers in the 1980's: A Profession in Transition." *Law and Society Review* 20: 19.

Daft, Richard L. 1988. *Organizational Theory and Design*, third edition. St. Paul, Minnesota: West Publishing.

D'Aunno, T. and H. Zuckerman. 1987. "The Emergence of Hospital Federations: An Integration of Perspectives from Organizational Theory." *Medical Care Review* 44: 323–44.

Derber, C. and W. A. Schwartz. 1991. "New Mandarins or New Proletariat?: Professional Power at Work." *Research In the Sociology of Organizations* 8: 71–96.

Derber, Charles, William A., Schwartz, and Yale Magrass. 1990. *Power in the Highest Degree*. New York: Oxford University Press.

Dill, A. 1995. "Case Management as a Cultural Practice." *Advances in Medical Sociology* 6: 81–117.

DiMaggio, P. J. and W. W. Powell. 1983. "The Iron Cage Revisited: Institutional Isomorphism and Collective Rationality in Organizational Fields." *American Sociological Review* 48: 147–60.

DiPrete, T. A. 1989. *The Bureaucratic Labor Market: The Case of the Federal Civil Service*. New York: Plenum.

DiPrete, T. A. and D. B. Grusky. 1990. "The Multilevel Analysis of Trends with Repeated Cross-sectional Data." *Sociological Methodology* 20: 337–68.

Domhoff, G. William 1986. *Who Rules America*. New York: Simon and Scheuster.

Donaldson, G. 1963. "Financial Goals: Management Versus Stockholders." *Harvard Business Review* May–June: 116–29.

Drucker, Peter F. 1986. *The Frontiers of Management*. New York: Truman Talley Books.

——. 1995. *Managing in a Time of Great Change*. New York: Truman Talley Books.

Dunkerly, Michael. 1996. *The Jobless Economy?* Cambridge: Polity Press.

Durkheim, E. 1933. *The Division of Labor in Society*. New York: Free Press.

Economist, The. 2000. "The Future of Work: Career Evolution." *The Economist*, January 29, 2000: 89–92.

Eder, K. 1993. *The New Politics of Class: Social Movements and Cultural Dynamics in Advanced Societies*. Newbury Park, CA: Sage.

Edwards, R. 1979. *Contested Terrain*. New York: Basic Books.

——. 1993. *Rights at Work: Employment Relations in a Post-Union Era*. Washington, D.C.: Brookings Institution.

Elder, Glenn. 1976. *Children of the Great Depression: Social Change and Life Experience*. Chicago, IL: University of Chicago Press.

Emerson, R. 1962. "Power-Dependence Relations." *American Sociological Review* 27: 31–40.

England, P. 1982. "The Failure of Human Capital Theory to Explain Occupational Sex Segregation." *Journal of Human Resources* 17: 358–70.

Epstein, Cynthia Fuchs. 1993. *Women in Law*. Urbana: University of Illinois Press.

Ernst, R. L. and D. E. Yett. 1985. *Physician Location and Specialty Choice.* Ann Arbor, MI: Health Administration Press.

Fama, E. F. 1980. "Agency Problems and the Theory of the Firm." *Journal of Political Economy*. 88: 288–307.

Feder, J., J. Hadley, and S. Zuckerman. 1987. "How Did Medicare's Prospective Payment System Affect Hospitals?" *New England Journal of Medicine* 317: 867–73.

Fennell, M. L. and J. A. Alexander. 1987. "Organizational Boundary Spanning in Institutionalized Environments." *Academy of Management Journal* 30: 456–76.

Fennell, M. L. and J. A. Alexander. 1989. "Governing Boards and Profound Organizational Change in Hospitals." *Medical Care Review* 46: 157–88.

——. 1993. "Perspectives on Organizational Change in the US Medical Care Sector." *Annual Review of Sociology* 19: 89–112.

Fennell, M. L. and K. T. Leicht. 1998. "The Changing Organizational Context of Professional Work: Implications for Gender Representation in Corporate Law." Presented at the 1998 meetings of the American Sociological Association, Toronto, Ontario, Canada and National Science Foundation SBR#9310557

Fincher, R. M. E., L. A. Lewis, and L. Q. Rogers. 1992. "Classification Model that Predicts Medical Students' Coices of Primary Care or Non-Primary Care Specialities." *Acad. Med.* 67: 324–27.

Finkelstein, S. and D. C. Hambrick. 1990. "Top-Management Team Structure and Organizational Outcomes: The Moderating Role of Managerial Discretion." *Administrative Science Quarterly* 35: 484–503.

Fischer, M. J. and M. W. Dirsmith. 1995. "Strategy, Technology and Social Processes within Professional Cultures: A Negotiated Order, Ethnographic Perspective." *Symbolic Interaction* 18: 381–421.

Flesher, Dale L. 1991. *The Third-Quarter Century of the American Accounting Association 1966–1991.* The American Accounting Association.

Fligstein, N. 1990. *The Transformation of Corporate Control.* Cambridge, MA: Harvard University Press.

Flood, A. B., W. R. Scott, and S. M. Shortell. 1994. "Organizational Performance: Managing for Efficiency and Effectiveness." Pps. 316–351 in *Health Care Management: A Text in Organizational Theory*, third edition, ed. S. M. Shortell and A. Kaluzny. Albany, New York: Delmar.

Flood, A. B. and M. L. Fennell. 1995. "Through the Lenses of Organizational Sociology: The Role of Organizational Theory and Research in Conceptualizing and Examining our Health Care System." *Journal of Health and Social Behavior* 36: 154–69.

Form. W. 1987. "On the Degradation of Skills." *Annual Review of Sociology* 13: 29–47.

Foucault, M. 1977. *Discipline and Punish: The Birth of a Prison.* London: Allen Lane.

Freeman, R. B. and J. L. Medoff. 1984. *What Do Unions Do?* New York: Basic Books.

Friedson, E. 1984. "The Changing Nature of Professional Control." *Annual Review of Sociology* 10: 1–20.

——. 1986. *Professional Powers: A Study of the Institutionalization of Formal Knowledge.* Chicago: University of Chicago Press.

——. 1994. *Professionalism Reborn: Theory, Prophecy and Policy.* Chicago: University of Chicago Press.

Giddens, A. 1994. *Beyond Left and Right: The Future of Radical Politics.* Stanford: Stanford University Press.

Gieryn, T. F. 1983. "Boundary-Work and the Demarcation of Science from Non-Science: Strains and Interests in Professional Ideologies of Scientists." *American Sociological Review* 48: 781–94.

Gilespie, R. 1991. *Manufacturing Knowledge: A History of the Hawthorne Experiments.* Cambridge: Cambridge University Press.

Goode, W. J. 1957. "Community Within a Community: The Professions: Psychology, Sociology and Medicine." *American Sociological Review* 25: 902–14.

Gordon, David M. 1996. *Fat and Mean.* New York: The Free Press.

Gordon, David M., Richard, Edwards, and Michael Reich. 1982. *Segmented Work, Divided Workers: The Historical Transformation of Labor in the United States.* New York: Cambridge University Press.

Hafferty, F. W. and D. W. Light. 1995. "Professional Dynamics and the Changing Nature of Medical Work." *Journal of Health and Social Behavior* 36: 132–53.

Hafferty, F. W. and J. B. McKinlay, eds. 1993. *The Changing Medical Profession: An International Perspective.* New York: Oxford University Press.

Hagan, J. 1990. "The Gender Stratification of Income Inequality Among Lawyers." *Social Forces* 68: 835–55.

Hagan, John and Kay Fiona. 1995. *Gender in Practice: A Study of Lawyers' Lives.* New York: Oxford University Press.

Halliday, T. C. 1987. *Beyond Monopoly: Lawyers, State Crises, and Professional Empowerment.* Chicago: University of Chicago Press.

Halliday, T. C., M. J. Powell, and M. W. Granfors. 1993. "After Minimalism: Transformations of State Bar Assiciations from Market Dependence to State Reliance, 1918–1950." *American Sociological Review* 58: 515–35.

Halpern, Sydney A. 1988. *Pediatrics: The Social Dynamics of Professionalism 1880–1980.* Berkley, CA: University of California Press.

Hamermesh, D. S. and A. Rees. 1988. *The Economics of Work and Pay, Fourth Edition.* New York: Harper and Row.

Handy, C. 1989. *The Age of Unreason.* Boston, MA: Harvard Business School Press.

Hannan, M. T. and J. Freeman. 1984. "Structural Inertia and Organizational Change." *American Sociological Review* 49: 149–64.

——. 1989. *Organizational Ecology.* Cambridge, MA: Harvard University Press.

Haveman, Heather A. and Lisa E. Cohen. 1994. "The Ecological Dynamics of Careers: The Impact of Organizational Founding, Dissolution, and Merger on Job Mobility." *American Journal of Sociology* 100: 104–52.

Heikes, E. J. 1991. "When Men are the Minority: The Case of Men in Nursing." *The Sociological Quarterly* 32: 389–401.

Hoff, T. J. 1997. "The New Breed." *Physician Executive* 23: 31–36.

Hoff, T. J. and D. P. McCaffrey. 1996. "Adapting, Resisting and Negotiation: How Physicians Cope with Organizational and Economic Change." *Work and Occupations* 23: 165–89.

Hughes, E. C. 1958. *Twenty Thousand Nurses Tell Their Story: A Report on Studies of Nursing Functions Sponsored by the American Nurses Association.* Philadelphia, PA: Lippincott.

Hurst, J. W. 1970. *The Legitimacy of the Business Corporation in the Law of the United States, 1780–1970.* Charlottesville: University Press.

Ibarra, H. 1995. "Race, Opportunity, and Diversity of Social Circles in Managerial Networks." *Academy of Management Journal* 38: 673–703.

Illich, Ivan. 1982. *Medical Nemesis: The Expropriation of Health.* New York: Pantheon Books.

Inglehart, R. 1990. *Cultural Shift in Advanced Industrial Society.* Princeton, NJ: Princeton University Press.

Jackall, Robert. 1988. *Moral Mazes: The World of Corporate Managers.* New York: Oxford University Press.

Jenkins, J. C. and K. T. Leicht. 1997. "Class Analysis and Social Movements: A Critique and Reformulation." Pp. 386–417 In J. R. Hall, ed., *Reworking Class.* Ithaca, NY: Cornell University.

Jensen, M. and W. Mackling. 1976. "Theory of the Firm: Managerial Behavior, Agency Costs, and Ownership Structure." *Journal of Financial Economics* 3: 305–60.

Jencks, C., L. Perman, and L. Rainwater. 1988. "What is a Good Job? A New Measure of Labor Market Success." *American Journal of Sociology* 93: 1322–57.

Joint Commission on Accreditation of Healthcare Organizations. 1992. *Cornerstones of Healthcare in the Nineties: Forging a Framework of Excellence.* Hot Springs, VA: Homestead.

Kagan, R. A. and R. L. Nelson. 1985. "On the Social Significance of Large Law Firm Practice." *Stanford Law Review* 37: 399–464.

Kalleberg, A. L. and I. Berg. 1987. *Work and Industry.* New York: Plenum Press.

Kalleberg, A. L., D. Knoke, P. V. Marsden, and J. L. Spaeth. 1996. *Organizations in America: Analyzing their Structures and Human Resource Practices.* Thousand Oaks, CA: Sage.

Kanter, R. M. 1977. *Men and Women of the Corporation.* New York: Basic Books.

Kasarda, John. 1989. "Urban Industrial Transition and the Underclass." *Annals, AAPSS* 501: 26–47.

Kassebaum, D. G., P. L. Szenas, A. L. Ruffin, and D. R. Masters. 1995. "The Research Career Interests of Graduating Medical Students." *Acad. Med.* 70: 848–52.

Kaufman, B. E. 1993. *The Origins and Evolution of the Field of Industrial Relations in the United States.* Ithaca, New York: The Guilford Press.

Kenney, Martin and Richard Florida. 1993. *Beyond Mass Production: The Japanese System and Its Transfer to the US.* New York: Oxford University Press.

Korman, A. K. and Associates. 1994. *Human Dilemmas in Work Organizations: Strategies for Resolution*. New York: Guilford Press.

Korten, R. 1995. *When Corporations Rule the World*. West Hartford, CT: Kumarian Press.

Korten, R. 1999. *The Post-Corporate World: Life After Capitalism*. West Hartford, CT: Kumarian Press.

Kramer, J. H. and J. T. Ulmer. 1996. "Sentencing Disparity and Departures from Guidelines." *Justice Quarterly* 13: 81–106.

Krasner, M. I. 1989. *The Nursing Shortage: New Approaches to an Old Problem*. New York: United Hospital Fund of New York.

Kronman, A. T. 1995. *The Lost Lawyer: Failing Ideals of the Legal Profession*. Cambridge, MA: Harvard University Press.

Kunda, G. 1992. *Engineering Culture: Control and Commitment in a High-Tech Corporation*. Philadelphia: Temple University Press.

Larsen, M. S. 1977. *The Rise of Professionalism: A Sociological Analysis*. Berkeley, CA: University of California Press.

Law and Business Directory of Corporate Counsel (1980, 1982, 1984, 1987, 1988, 1990, and 1995). Aspen, Colorado: Aspen Law and Business.

Leicht, K. T. and Mary L. Fennell. 1993. "Gender Stratification in Corporate Legal Departments: an Analysis of Organizational Structure and Individual Careers." National Science Foundation Grant, SES-9310557.

——. 1997. "The Changing Organizational Context of Professional Work." *Annual Review of Sociology* 23: 215–31.

——. 1996. "Gender Representation in Corporate Law: Normative and Coercive Effects on the Structure of Corporate Legal Departments." 91st Annual Meeting of the American Sociology Association, New York.

Leicht, K. T., M. L. Fennell, and K. M. Witkowski. 1995. "The Effects of Hospital Characteristics and Radical Organizational Change on the Relative Standing of Health Care Professions." *Journal of Health and Social Behavior* 36: 151–67.

Leicht, Kevin T. and J. Craig Jenkins. 1998. "Political Resources and Direct State Intervention: The Adoption of Public Venture Capital Programs in the American States, 1974–1990." *Social Forces* 76: 1323–45.

Light, D. 1993. "Countervailing Power: The Changing Character of the Medical Profession in the United States." Pp. 69–79 in *The Changing Medical Profession: An International Perspective*, ed. F. W. Hafferty and J. B. McKinlay. New York: Oxford University Press.

Light, D. 1995. "Countervailing Powers: A Framework for Professions in Transition." Pp. 25–41 in *Health Professions and the State in Europe*, ed. T. Johnson, G. Larkin, and M. Saks. New York: Routlege.

Littler, C. 1982. *The Development of the Labor Process in Capitalist Societies*. Exeter, NH: Heinemann Educational.

Logan, John R. and Harvey L. Molotch. 1987. *Urban Fortunes: The Political Economy of Place*. Berkeley, CA: University of California Press.

Long, J. S. 1992. "Measures of Sex Differences in Scientific Productivity." *Social Forces*. 71: 159–78.

Long, J. S., P. D. Allison, and R. McGinnis. 1993. "Rank Advancement in Academic Careers: Sex Differences and the Effects of Productivity." *American Sociological Review* 58: 703–22.

Manza, J. and C. Brooks. 1999. *Social Cleavage and Political Change: Voter Alignments and U.S. Party Coalitions.* New York: Oxford University Press.

Marglin, S. A. 1974. "What do Bosses do? The Origins and Functions of Hierarchy in Capitalist Production." *Review of Radical Political Economics* 6: 33–60.

Marx, K. 1889. *Capital.* New York: Appleton.

Massey, Douglas. 1996. "The Age of Extremes: Concentrated Affluence and Poverty in the Twenty-First Century." *Demography* 33: 395–412.

Mead, Lawrence. 1991. *The New Politics of Poverty.* New York: HarperPerennial.

Mechanic, D. 1994. "Managed Care: Rhetoric and Realities." *Inquiry* 31: 124–28.

Menkel-Meadow, C. 1989. "Feminization of the Legal Profession: The Comparative Sociology of Women Lawyers. Pp. 196–255 in *Lawyers in Society: Comparative Theories,* ed. Richard L. Abel and Philip S. C. Lewis. Berkeley: University of California Press, 1989.

Meyer, M. 1978. "Leadership and Organizational Structure." Pp. 220–32 in *Environments and Organizations,* ed. M. Meyer and Associates. San Francisco, CA: Jossey-Bass.

Meyer, J. W. and W. R. Scott. 1983. *Organizational Environments: Ritual and Rationality.* Beverly Hills, CA: Sage.

Mick, S. and Associates. 1990. *Innovations in Health Care Delivery.* San Fransisco: Jossey-Bass.

Mizruchi, M. 1982. *The American Corporate Network, 1904–1974.* Beverly Hills, CA: Sage.

Monsen, R. and A. Downs. 1965. "A Theory of Large Managerial Firms." *Journal of Political Economy.* June: 221–36.

Montgomery, D. 1979. *Workers' Control in America.* Cambridge: Cambridge University Press.

Montgomery, K. 1990. "A Prospective Look at the Specialty of Medical Management." *Work and Occupations* 17: 178–98.

Morello, K. B. 1986. *The Invisible Bar: The Woman Lawyer in America from 1638 to the Present.* New York: Random House.

Morrison, A. M. and M. Von Glinow. 1990. "Women and Minorities in Management." *American Psychologist* 45: 200–8.

Munzer, S. R. 1990. *A Theory of Property.* New York: Cambridge University Press.

Naisbitt, J. 1994. *Global Paradox: The Bigger the World's Economy, The More Powerful Its Smallest Players.* New York: W. Morrow.

Nelson, R. L. 1988. *Partners with Power: The Social Tranformation of the Large Law Firm.* Berkeley: University of California Press.

Nelson, R. L. and W. P. Bridges. 1999. *Legalizing Gender Inequality: Courts, Markets and Unequal Pay for Women in America.* Cambridge: Cambridge University Press.

Nelson, R. L., D. M. Trubeck, and R. L. Solomon. 1992. *Lawyers' Ideals/ Lawyers' Practices: Transformations of the American Legal Profession.* Ithaca, NY: Cornell University Press.

New York Times. 1996. *The Downsizing of America.* New York: Times Books.

O'Connor, J. 1973. *The Fiscal Crisis of the State.* New York: St. Martin's Press.

Oliver, C. 1991. "Strategic Responses to Institutional Processes." *Academy of Management Review* 16: 145–79.

Ospina, S. 1996. *Illusions of Opportunity: Employee Expectations and Workplace Inequality.* Ithaca, NY: Cornell University Press.

Parsons, T. 1937. *The Structure of Social Action.* New York: McGraw-Hill.

Perrucci, C. et al. 1988. *Plant Closings: International Contexts and Social Costs.* New York: De Gruyter.

Perrucci, R. 1971. "Engineers: Professional Servants of Power." *American Behavioral Scientist* 14: 492–506.

Pfeffer, J. 1972. "Size, Composition and Function of Hospital Boards of Directors: A Study of Organizational-Environment Linkage." *Administrative Science Quarterly* 18: 349–64.

Pfeffer, J. and G. Salancik. 1978. *The External Control of Organizations.* New York: Harper and Row.

Pfeffer, J. 1982. *Organizations and Organization Theory.* Boston, MA: Pittman.

Pfeffer, J. and Y. Cohen. 1984. "Determinants of Internal Labor Markets in Organizations." *Administrative Science Quarterly* 29: 550–72.

Phillips, K. 1990. *The Politics of Rich and Poor: Wealth and the American Electorate in the Reagan Aftermath.* New York: HarperPerennial.

Porter, M. E. 1998. *Competitive Advantage: Creating and Sustaining Superior Performance.* New York: Free Press.

Powell, M. J. 1985. "Developments in the Regulation of Lawyers: Competing Segments and Market, Client and Government Controls." *Social Forces* 64: 281–305.

Powell, W. 1990. "Niether Market Nor Hierarchy: Network Forms of Organization." *Research in the Sociology of Organizations* 12: 295–336.

Powell, W. W. and P. J. DiMaggio. 1991. *The New Institutionalism in Organizational Analysis.* Chicago: University of Chicago Press.

Prechel, H. and A. Gupman. 1995. "Changing Economic Conditions and Their Effects on Professional Autonomy: An Analysis of Family Practitioners and Oncologists." *Sociological Forum* 10: 245–71.

Ratcliff, J. L. 1996. "Descretion and Constraint in Faculty Decision-Making Regarding the Curriculum." 91st Annual Meeting of the American Sociology Association, New York.

Renshaw, L. J. Kimberly, and J. S. Schwartz. 1990. "Technology Diffusion and Ecological Analysis." Pp. 181–206 in *Innovation in Health Care Delivery*, ed. Steven Mick and Associates. San Francisco, CA: Jossey-Bass.

Reskin, Barbara F. and Patricia A. Roos. 1990. *Job Queues, Gender Queues.* Philadelphia: Temple University Press.

Riche, R. W., D. E. Hecker, and J. U. Burgan. 1983. "High Technology Today and Tomorrow." *Monthly Labor Review* 106: 50–8.

Rifkin, Jeremy. 1995. *The End of Work*. New York: Putnam.

Roach, S. L. 1990. "Men and Women Lawyers in In-House Legal Departments: Recruitment and Career Patterns." *Gender and Society* 4: 207–19.

Roos, Patricia A. 1985. *Gender & Work: A Comparative Analysis of Industrial Societies*. Albany: State University of New York Press.

Rosen, R. 1989. "The Inside Counsel Movement, Professional Judgment and Organizational Representation." *Indiana Law Journal* 64: 479–553.

Rosenbaum, J. E. 1979. "Organizational Career Mobility: Promotion Chances in a Corporation During Periods of Growth and Contraction." *American Journal of Sociology* 85: 21–48.

Rosenbaum, J. E. 1984. *Career Mobility in a Corporate Hierarchy*. Orlando: Academic Press.

Rosoff, S. M. and M. Leone. 1991. "The Public Prestige of Medical Specialties: Overviews and Undercurrents." *Social Science Medicine* 32: 321–6.

Roth, J. 1974. "Care of the Sick: Professionalism vs. Love." *Scientific Medical Management* 1: 173–80.

Rule, J. and P. Attewell. 1989. "What Do Computers Do?" *Social Problems* 36: 225–41.

Secretary's Commission on Nursing. 1988. *Final Report, Volume 1*. Washington, D.C.: Department of Health and Human Services.

Scott, W. R. 1992. *Organizations: rational, natural and open systems*. New York: Prentice-Hall.

——. 1995. *Institutions and Organizations*. Newbury Park, CA: Sage.

——. 1982. "Managing Professional Work: Three Models of Control for Health Organizations." *Health Services Research* 17: 213–40.

——. 1993. "The Organization of Medical Care Services: Towards an Integrated Theoretical Model." *Medical Care Review* 50: 271–302.

Sherman, A. W. and G. W. Bohlander. 1992. *Managing Human Resources*. Cincinnati, Ohio: South-Western Publishing Co.

Singh, J. V., J. House, and D. J. Tucker. 1986. "Organizational Change and Organizational Mortality." *Administrative Science Quarterly* 31: 587–611.

Skaggs, Bruce C. and Kevin T. Leicht. 1997. "Management Paradigm Change in the United States: A Professional Autonomy Perspective." Presented at the Academy of Management Meetings, August, 1997, Boston, Massachusetts.

Spangler, E. 1993. *Lawyers for Hire: Salaried Professionals at Work*. New Haven, CT: Yale University Press.

Spilerman, S. 1977. "Careers, Labor Market Structure, and Socioeconomic Acheivement." *American Journal of Sociology* 83: 551–93.

Standard and Poor's Corporation. 1980–1995. *Register of Corporations, Directors and Executives*. New York: Standard and Poor's Corporation.

Starr, P. 1982. *The Social Transformation of American Medicine*. New York: Basic Books.

Stevens, R. 1989. *In Sickness and in Wealth: American Hospitals in the Twentieth Century*. New York: Basic Books.

Stein, J. 1983. *Monetarist, Keynesian, and New Classical Economics*. Oxford, UK: Blackwell.

Stewman, S. and S. L. Konda. 1983. "Careers and Organizational Labor Markets: Demographic Models of Organizational Behavior." *American Journal of Sociology* 88: 637–85.

Stinchcombe, A. 1990. *Information and Organizations*. Berkeley, CA: University of California Press.

Stinchcombe, A. 1997. "In Praise of the Old Institutionalism." *Annual Review of Sociology*.

Stolzenberg, L. and S. J. D'Alessio. 1994. "Sentencing and Unwarranted Disparity: An Empirical Assessment of the Long Term Impact of Sentencing Guidelines in Minnesota." *Criminology* 32: 301–10.

Stone, K. 1974. "The Origins of Job Structures in the Steel Industry." *Review of Radical Political Economics* 6: 61–67.

Strang, D. 1995. "Health Maintenance Organizations." Pp. 163–82 in *Organizations in Industry: Strategy, Structure, and Selection*, ed. Glenn R. Carroll and Michael T. Hannan. New York: Oxford University Press.

Tang, Joyce and Earl Smith. 1996. *Women and Minorities in American Professions*. Albany: State University of New York Press.

Taylor, F. 1903. *Shop Management*. New York: Harper and Row.

——. 1911. *The Principles of Scientific Management*. New York: Harper and Row.

Thomas, R. 1995. *What Machines Can't Do*. Cambridge, MA: MIT Press.

Thompson, E. P. 1963. *The Making of the English Working Class*. New York: Pantheon Books.

Thompson, J. D. 1967. *Organizations in Action*. New York: McGraw-Hill.

Thurow, L. C. 1975. *Generating Inequality*. New York: Basic Books.

Toffler, Alvin. 1990. *Powershift: Knowledge, Wealth, and Violence in the 21st Century*. New York: Bantam.

Tolbert, P. S. and R. N. Stern. 1991. "Organizations of Professionals: Governance Structures in Large Law Firms." *Research in the Sociology of Organizations* 8: 97–117.

Tonry, M. ed. 1993. *Crime and Justice: A Review of Research*. Chicago: University of Chicago Press.

Torres, D. L. 1991. "What, If Anything, is Professionalism?: Institutions and the Problem of Change." *Research in the Sociology of Organizations* 8: 43–68.

U.S. Census Bureau. *Current Population Surveys*. Various years. Washington, D.C.: U.S. Bureau of the Census.

U.S. *Congressional Record* (1914, 1935).

U.S. Department of Labor, Bureau of Labor Statistics. 1992. *Outlook: 1990–2005*. Washington, D.C.: US Bureau of Labor Statistics. (May).

U.S. Department of Labor, Bureau of Labor Statistics. 1997. *Occupational Outlook Handbook*. Washington, D.C.: US Department of Labor.

Wallace, J. E. 1995. "Corporatist Control and Organizational Commitment Among Professionals: The Case of Lawyers Working in Law Firms." *Social Forces* 73: 811–40.

——. 1993. Professional and Organizational Commitment: Compatible or Incompatible? *Journal of Vocational Behavior* 42: 333–49.

Wallace, M. and A. L. Kalleberg. 1981. "Economic Organization of Firms and Labor Market Consequences." Pp. 7–117 in *Sociological Perspectives on Labor Markets*, ed. Ivar Berg. New York: Academic Press.

Wallace, M. and A. L. Kalleberg. 1982. "Industrial Transformation and the Decline of Craft: The Decomposition of Skill in the Printing Industry, 1931–1978." *American Sociological Review* 47: 307–24.

Wallerstein, I. 1975. *The Modern World System*. New York: Academic Press.

——. 1991. *Geopolitics and geoculture: Essays on the Changing World System*. Cambridge: Cambridge University Press.

Weber, M. 1947. *The Theory of Social and Economic Organization*. New York: Oxford University Press.

Whalley, P. 1986. *The Social Production of Technical Work*. Albany: State University of New York Press.

——. 1991. "Negotiating the Boundaries of Engineering: Professionals, Managers, and Manual Work." *Research in the Sociology of Organizations* 8: 191–215.

Wilensky, H. L. 1964. "The Professionalization of Everyone?" *American Journal of Sociology* 70: 137–58.

White, H. 1970. *Chains of Opportunity: System Models of Mobility in Organizations*. Cambridge, MA: Harvard University Press.

Williamson, O. 1975. *Markets and Hierarchies: Analysis and Antitrust Implications*. New York: Free Press.

——. 1985. *The Economic Institutions of Capitalism*. New York: Free Press.

Wilson, W. J. 1997. *When Work Disappears: The World of the Urban Poor*. New York: Alfred Knopf.

Wren, D. A. 1994. *The Evolution of Management Thought*, 4th edition. New York: Wiley and Sons.

Zajac, E. J. and S. M. Shortell. 1989. "Changing Generic Strategies: Likelihood, Direction, and Performance Implications." *Strategic Management Journal* 10: 413–30.

Zald, M. 1971. *Occupations and Organizations in American Society*. Chicago, IL: Markham.

Zuckerman, H., J. R. Cole, and J. T. Bruer, eds. 1991. *The Outer Circle: Women in the Scientific Community*. New York: Norton.

Zussman, Robert. 1985. *Mechanics of the Middle Class*. Berkeley: University of California Press.

Index